Organisatic

Organisations, Identities and the Self

Janette Webb

First published 2006 by
PALGRAVE MACMILLAN
Houndmills, Basingstoke, Hampshire RG21 6XS and
175 Fifth Avenue, New York, N.Y. 10010
Companies and representatives throughout the world

PALGRAVE MACMILLAN is the global academic imprint of the Palgrave
Macmillan division of St. Martin's Press, LLC and of Palgrave Macmillan Ltd.
Macmillan® is a registered trademark in the United States, United Kingdom
and other countries. Palgrave is a registered trademark in the European
Union and other countries.

ISBN–13: 978-0-333-80487-2   hardback
ISBN–10: 0-333-80487-2   hardback
ISBN–13: 978-0-333-80488-9   paperback
ISBN–10: 0-333-80488-0   paperback

This book is printed on paper suitable for recycling and made from fully
managed and sustained forest sources.

A catalog record for this book is available from the Library of Congress.

10   9   8   7   6   5   4   3   2   1
15   14   13   12   11   10   09   08   07   06
Printed in China

To Islay and Catherine

Contents

List of Figures   xi

List of Tables   xii

Acknowledgements   xiii

Introduction   1

A Sociological Perspective on Organisations   3
The Distinctiveness of Modern Organisations   4
Structure and Agency in the Context of Organisations   5
The Challenge of Postmodernism   7
An Analytic Distinction between Self and Identity   10
Interpretative Approaches to the Interconnections of
    Organisations, Identities and the Self   11
The Structure of the Book and Chapter Outline   12

**1 Understanding Organisations, Identities and the Self:
a Conceptual Framework**   15

The Sociological Perspective on the Self and Social Identities   15
The Postmodernist Treatment of Identity and Subjectivity   17
The Historical Development of the Self as Agent: from
    Ascribed to Achieved Identity   19
A Circumscribed and Instrumental Form of Agency? Weber's
    'Iron Cage' of Rationalisation   20
Self-determination and Agency Dissolved in a Postmodern
    'Invisible Cage' of Total Institutions   23
Do Organisations Determine Identities?   26
Sociological Evidence from Organisations: Agency Continues   26
A New Oversocialised Concept of Organisations as
    Determined by Cultural Identities   29
The Dialectical Relationship between Agency, Identity
    and Organisation   31
Conclusion   34

2 Globalising Economies and Organisations   36

The Globalist Model: the Inevitability of a Global Market?   37

The Traditionalist Critique of the Globalisation Perspective   38
Change *and* Continuity? The Transformationalist Perspective   39
Organising Deregulated Global Markets: the Role of the IMF,
    World Bank and WTO   40
Global Finance and the Strategies and Identities of Corporations   44
The Irrationalities of Rationalised Economies: Corporate
    Identity and the Enron Case   47
The Politics of Identity and its Connection to Globalised
    Financial Markets   50
Conclusion   51

3   **Organisations, Identities and Consumption**   **53**

Organisations and the Development of Consumer Markets   54
Why Globalising Markets Create the Need for
    Organisational Identities   57
Branding and Organisational Identity   59
An Industry in Organisational Identity?   60
Organisational Identity and 'Lifestyling'   62
Agency, Identity and Consumerism   64
Critique – the Indivisibility of Production and Consumption   68
Collective Consumer Identities and the Politics of Resistance   70
Conclusion   72

4   **Public Service Reorganisation, Work and Consumer**
    Citizenship   **74**

The Context: Social Democratic Welfare States and
    Social Identity   76
The Dual Crises of Welfare States: Neoliberalism and
    Identity Politics   77
The Reorganisation of Public Services: from Professional
    Bureaucracy to Management Tools and Markets   80
Public Management and a New Identity Project for
    Public Servants   84
Experiencing the Contradictions between Empowerment
    and Rationalisation   88
New Contracts for Public Service: Empowered Partners
    or Rationalised Labour?   89
The Identity of Consumer Citizenship   91
Conclusion   92

5   **Organisations and Global Divisions of Labour**   **95**

Theoretical Conjectures: the Restructuring of Work and
    Organisations?   96

Work and Occupational Change in Advanced Capitalist
    Countries: an Evaluation of Theoretical Assertions   97
The Globally Organised Interdependence of Labour   112
Conclusion   117
Appendix   119

6 Organisational Restructuring, Work and Social Divisions   126

Theoretical Conjectures about Employment and
    Occupational Change   128
Challenging the Myths of Mass Casualisation of Work,
    Short-termism in Employment and the End of Careers   129
The Power of Finance Capital and the Intensification of Work   133
Changing Class, Ethnic and Gender Divisions in Organisations?   133
Organisations and Restructured Gender Divisions   136
'Racialised' and Ethnic Divisions in Organisations   140
The Restructuring of Class Divisions in Organisations   143
Social Divisions and Processes of Cultural and Social
    Identity   144
Does Economic Individualisation Necessarily Produce
    Individualism?   147
Conclusion   148
Appendix   150

**7 'We Are the Company': Work, Control and Identity in the
Organisations of Advanced Capitalism   151**

Explaining the Organisational Emphasis on Managing
    Employee Identity   152
Organisational Control through Regulating Identity   154
The Organisational Colonisation of Identity?   160
Critique of the Effectiveness of Organisational Control
    through the Regulation of Identity   162
Organisational Power Relations, Social Divisions and
    the Meanings of Emotional Labour   165
Conclusion   172

**8 Organisations Are Us: Understanding Self-identity in
Organised Societies   174**

Globalising Markets, Organisations and Individualisation   175
The Organisation of a Productive Self: a Postmodernist
    Analysis   177
An Expertise of Self-improvement?   179
Is Work Treated as a Resource for Self-improvement?   180
Subversive Responses to the Enterprise of the Self   184

'Being Productive' in Work, Non-work and Leisure?   185
Evaluating the Concept of a Productive Subjectivity   187
Conclusion   191

Conclusion: Bringing Life Back to Organisations   **193**

A Summary of the Argument   193
Key Themes from Chapter 1   194
Key Themes from Chapter 2   196
Key Themes from Chapter 3   197
Key Themes from Chapter 4   198
Key Themes from Chapter 5   199
Key Themes from Chapter 6   200
Key Themes from Chapter 7   201
Key Themes from Chapter 8   202
In Conclusion   204

Bibliography   207

Index   225

List of Figures

5.1   UK: distribution of employment by industrial
      group, 1970–2004   99

5.2   USA: distribution of employment by industrial
      group, 1970–2004   100

5.3   Germany: distribution of employment by industrial
      group, 1970–2004   100

5.4   Japan: distribution of employment by industrial
      group, 1970–2004   101

5.5   UK: occupational groups, 1971–2004   104

5.6   USA: occupational groups, 1970–2002   104

5.7   Germany: occupational groups, 1976–2004   105

5.8   Japan: occupational groups, 1970–2004   105

5.9   Japan: employment by occupation, 1970–2004   107

5.10   USA: employment by occupation, 1970–2002   107

5.11   Germany: employment by occupation, 1976–2004   108

5.12   UK: employment by occupation, 1971–2004   108

5.13   Changes in part-time work, 1979–2004   115

5.14   Temporary employment as % of total employment
      in selected OECD countries   116

6.1   Women in part-time employment, 2004   132

6.2   Women's economic activity rates as % of
      female population, aged 15–64   138

List of Tables

5.1   UK: percentage distribution of employment by
      industrial sector, 1970–2004   119
5.2   USA: percentage distribution of employment by
      industrial sector, 1970–2004   120
5.3   Germany: percentage distribution of employment by
      industrial sector, 1970–2004   121
5.4   Japan: percentage distribution of employment by
      industrial sector, 1970–2004   122
5.5   UK: percentage distribution of employment by
      occupation, 1971–2004   122
5.6   USA: percentage distribution of employment by
      occupation, 1970–2002   123
5.7   Germany: percentage distribution of employment by
      occupation, 1976–2004   123
5.8   Japan: percentage distribution of employment by
      occupation, 1970–2004   124
5.9   All managerial, professional and technical
      occupations compared with all manual occupations
      as a percentage of total employment, 2004   124
5.10 Changes in part-time work, selected OECD
      countries, 1979–2004   124
5.11 Temporary employment as a percentage of total
      employment, in selected OECD countries, 1985–2000   125

6.1   Women's economic activity rates as a percentage
      of the female population, aged between
      15/16 and 64, 1970–2004   150
6.2   Changes in part-time work, selected OECD
      countries, 1979–2004   150

Acknowledgements

This book has been with me so long that I find it hard to remember how it started and to whom I owe thanks. Certainly when I scan my office bookshelves looking for reminders, I notice that, almost imperceptibly, the balance between books about organisations and books about society, social relations and sociology has shifted over the years towards the latter. It is this transition in my 'academic identity' that is tacitly traced in this book and where I begin my thanks.

Over a decade ago, I moved from a department of business studies to a department of sociology and discovered how little I really knew about sociology. I am still trying to catch up. The business and management studies' setting seemed to me to result in a narrower agenda for research and debate, which was often shorn of its wider social and disciplinary contexts. Reading sociological analyses of social change, the rise of individualism and the formation of modern societies gave me a richer understanding of organisations. Consequently, I felt there was some scope for a different kind of book about organisations, which would try to bring together the sociological interest in explaining modern societies, social divisions and identities with the organisational studies' interest in management, authority and the control and regulation of labour. I have struggled to write it, and this is the best I can do at present.

I have to thank therefore Malcolm Anderson, dean of social science at Edinburgh University when I moved into sociology, for enabling that institutional and personal 'reorganisation', which was the start of a process still carrying on. I also need to thank all my Edinburgh sociology colleagues in the department in the 1990s for accepting my application to join them. The first chair of sociology at Edinburgh was held by Tom Burns. He was an influential advocate for the sociology of organisations, and for a sociology that engaged the public in debate about its institutions: I hope I have contributed to that tradition.

Since joining sociology, I have been fortunate to receive two periods of sabbatical leave, which enabled me to make the most progress with drafting and subsequently revising the book. In the last ten years, the university has restructured itself a few times, so I also acknowledge the support of what is now the School of Social and Political Studies, particularly under its current head, Lorraine Waterhouse. Successive groups of students have been very helpful in responding to ideas tried out in lectures and seminar discussions. For their academic insights and friendship, I also wish to thank Esther Breitenbach, Alice Brown, Rosemary Crompton, Tricia Findlay, Cynthia Fuchs Epstein, Fiona Mackay and Adrian Sinfield.

At Palgrave Macmillan, I have received excellent feedback, constructive direction, prompt responses and help from anonymous reviewers, from editors Catherine Gray and Emily Salz, and from editorial assistant Sarah Lodge. Maggie Lythgoe was a helpful, efficient and accurate copy editor.

More widely, I'd like to thank all those who work for the organisations I have crossed paths with as a researcher and (more recently) as a non-executive member of the board of NHS Health Scotland. Paraphrasing Tom Burns on the management of innovation, I am impressed by the extraordinary gap between the knowledge, insight, perceptiveness and ingenuity of the people who work in organisations and the cumbersome, often counterproductive features of the structures of power and authority that constrain their efforts and their thinking. A revolution in priorities and values is needed to create the kinds of organisations that are fit for people.

At a personal level, the writing of this book has been with me through the sudden death of my husband Colin Bell. Consequently, the person who finished this book is a different one from the person who started it. I've learned a lot about love and mortality, and wish to thank friends, aside from those already named above, for their invaluable love and kindness: Rachel Bell, Luke Bell, Kevin and Linda Clarke, Anna and Mure Dickie, Judith Dyson, Heather and Jamie Fleck, Pam and Ross Flockhart, Bashabi Fraser, Christine Hallett, Alex Howson, Doris Littlejohn, Catherine Maclean, Lesley McMillan, Sue Renton and Alan Sutton. Above all I would not have been able to finish writing the book without the love, encouragement and academic insights of David McCrone, who gave me the space and the confidence to finish what my daughters, Islay and Catherine, came to refer to as 'that damn book'. Needless to say, the limitations of what emerged remain mine.

Every effort has been made to trace all the copyright holders but if any have been inadvertently overlooked the publishers will be pleased to make the necessary arrangements at the first opportunity.

Introduction

Even before I left the house this morning, I had used the products and services of a large number of complex organisations: clean water, electricity, gas, media, telecommunications, food, clothing and domestic goods producers all informed the ordinary activities of getting up. Most people in affluent societies take the infrastructure of organisations for granted, although we know relatively little about their finances, expertise or employment practices. Governments, public services, utilities, banking, global media and telecommunications and manufacturing all rely on feats of organisation, risk management and technical expertise, unthinkable two to three hundred years ago. In this period, and particularly during the last hundred years, the economic power of large-scale business organisations has become enormously concentrated: the US Institute for Policy Studies (IPS) estimates that the top 200 corporations control over a quarter of the world's economic activity, although they employ less than a third of 1% of the world's population (Anderson and Cavanagh, 2000). When corporate revenues are compared with the GDP of nation states, 52 of the 100 largest 'economies' turn out to be corporations: Wal-Mart is bigger than Sweden or Austria, while General Motors is bigger than Turkey. Even using a more cautious value-added calculation, the UNCTAD *World Investment Report* (UNCTAD, 2002) includes 29 multinational corporations (MNCs) in its table of the 100 largest 'economies'.

Ordinary people, politicians and business representatives often express ambivalent attitudes towards large organisations, criticising them for wasting resources, being unresponsive, inflexible or unproductive, yet relying on them for work, leisure, welfare and a degree of participation in civil society and government. In their review of the organisational studies' literature, Thompson and McHugh (2002) note that such ambivalence is often reproduced in academic analysis. Hence some theorists adopt a functionalist model of the trajectories of organisations, and argue that their power and scale is a logical result of technological progress and market efficiency. The rationality of economic growth and organisation development is taken for granted, and predicted to result in the convergence of industrial societies around the principles of a rationalised science of economic and technological decision-making, steered by a professional and managerial elite (Bell, 1960, 1976; Kerr et al., 1960). Critical analyses have often gone to the other extreme, suggesting instead that organisations are a means of domination by

1

a power elite, which result in money-making and calculative attitudes to life becoming ends in themselves (Perrow, 1979; Weber, 1968). The problem with each of these approaches is that they tend to obscure, or marginalise, questions about how such organisations were brought about, how they are changed and their continuing diversity, depending on their goals, their economic and cultural contexts, political priorities and processes of coalition-building and negotiation between conflicting interest groups (Clegg, 1990; Thompson and McHugh, 2002). Studies of political, legal and economic decision-making in fact show that there is nothing inevitable about the shape or scale of organisations that we have (Thelen, 2004), or the associated concentration of power and wealth (Perrow, 2002). While a 'non-organisational society' is almost unimaginable, this does not mean that there are no choices to be made about the use and control of the vast resources and scientific and technological knowledge produced. In fact, Castells (2000) concludes, from his encyclopedic study of the social, economic and cultural transformations from an industrial into an informational era, that we have 'reached the level of knowledge and social organisation that will allow us to live in a predominantly social world' (p. 509). If his conclusions are even approximately correct, then the need for purposive, informed action to create more tolerant, secure and less unequal societies is more critical than ever. Public debate about the accountability and activities of big public and private sector organisations is an essential component of this.

There are many ways in which sociology can contribute to this debate, but one of them is to cast light on the connections between organisations and people's sense of themselves. This book argues that our sense of self and social identities are significantly shaped by our experiences of organisations, our dependence on them for political, economic and cultural infrastructure, and our development of new organisational expertise that reshapes societies. The rise of organisations has often been associated with the loss of meaningful selfhood, but this neglects the evidence of continuing agency, organised resistance and challenge to the dominant directions and values of neoliberal market capitalism. Such agency is expressed, for example, in organised consumer resistance to certain corporate products, in continuing conflict and tension about the exploitation of labour, and in public critique of the impact of neoliberal economics on well-being. We live in an era where organisations are the key means of coordinating social life across space and time, but this does not wipe out agency; instead it is remade in the context of changed opportunity structures.

This book consequently faces in two directions. It seeks to demonstrate the value of sociological insights to debate the control and public accountability of complex organisations. It also aims to rescue the analysis of organisations for sociology, in the light of contemporary debate about personal and social identity. The middle-range analysis of organisations provides a valuable means of making connections between personal biography and private troubles and the public issues of the day. It is a means of grounding sociological debates in the diverse and messy realities of practice.

A Sociological Perspective on Organisations

To the sociologist, management and business texts present a *normative* account of organisations, rather than a critical analysis: they aim to provide prescriptive guides to how management and business practice *should* be done in order to maximise economic productivity and profitability. The latter are treated as amenable to technical solutions, which tends to exclude questions of politics, power and conflict, or critical discussion of organisational goals. Questions about the experiences of people who make up organisations, their attitudes to managerial strategies, problems of the legitimacy of those in authority, and the power struggles and tensions that result, are also obscured.

This book is in the tradition of critical analysis. It juxtaposes normative identities, shaped by organisational processes, with evidence about people's experiences, actions and forms of compliance, consent and resistance. These forms of agency need to be seen in the context of the agency exercised by those in positions of power. Heads of government, business leaders, venture capitalists, media owners and so on comprise the social elites who are typically least accessible to critical social science, and yet exercise enormous influence materially and culturally. This book aims to reveal some of the ways in which the agency of powerful elites is itself expressed in organisational goals and priorities. Its aim is to show that the dominant trajectories of organisations, and the associated identities of advanced capitalist societies, are not the inevitable unfolding of immutable laws, but are the intended, as well as unintended, results of orchestrated social action.

Much of the recent empirical work informed by a sociological perspective on organisations has originated in business and management schools. Marxist theories, radical interpretations of Weber's work and latterly Foucault's writings on power have been deployed in the analysis of organisations as workplaces (see for example Clegg and Dunkerley, 1980; Parker, 2000; Reed, 1985; Thompson and McHugh, 2002). The result is a body of work focusing on the 'dialectic of control' between management and labour, and the analysis of the ongoing evolution of labour control strategies (Reed, 1992). The emphasis on the sphere of production derives at least partly from a functional separation in business and management schools between 'organisational behaviour' and 'human resource management' on the one hand, and 'marketing' and 'consumer behaviour' on the other, resulting in a tacit intellectual divorce between analyses of production and analyses of consumption. This paints a partial picture of the interrelations of organisations, identities and the self: organisations are not solely workplaces, but are also sites of social and economic policy-making, consumption, education, social welfare and citizenship. Organisations influence normative identities in all these spheres, but they also encounter resistance, whether from consumers, voters or civil society. From a wider sociological perspective, it is important to break with a view of organisations as first and foremost sites of work and production, in order also to see their significance as sites of consumption, and of the governance of society.

The core questions of sociology have been concerned with the emergence and development of distinctively modern societies, social divisions, power and individualisation. The historical dimension lent by such questions enables us to see that current forms of organisation are not inevitable, but are the intended and unintended consequences of past actions (Hall and Gieben, 1992; Kumar, 1988a; Perrow, 2002; Streeck, 2001). The sociological imagination strives to understand the ways in which apparently individual, or private, troubles are structured by public issues (Mills, 2000 [1959]). In other words, if people are anxious or depressed, the sociological imagination looks for the source not in individual psychology, but in the institutional and structural order of society. Mills' ambitions were for a sociology that engaged with major public issues, and that explained how big institutions affected ordinary life. Individual biography, he argued, could not be understood without situating it in the context of social structures, political power and historical change. Sociology seeks to illuminate the interconnections between these spheres, in order to enable people to see that there are alternative ways of organising society, and to reason out the choices available to them. Writing in the 1950s, Mills was critical of what he regarded as the emerging bureaucratic mass society of the USA, where consumerism gave the illusion of freedom and happiness, but left people apathetic or uneasy and unable to influence government decisions. His argument remains relevant today, where corporations are increasingly organised on a global scale through the operations of global financial markets, and are, if anything, less accessible and less accountable to civil society than they were fifty years ago (Castells, 2000; Perrow, 2002).

The Distinctiveness of Modern Organisations

> Who says modernity says not just organisations but organisation – the regularised control of social relations across indefinite time-space distances. (Giddens, 1993: 289)

It is hard, from the perspective of the present, to grasp the scale of the social changes wrought by the emergence of modern organisations. From the sixteenth century onwards, industrialisation and modern capitalism developed in western societies, disrupting traditional social relations based on status, kinship and patriarchal and religious authority, and stimulating societies structured around social class, individualism, rationalised decision-making and scientific and technological knowledge (Hall and Gieben, 1992; Kumar, 1988a). The emergence of a distinct organisational form, characterised by Max Weber as 'rational-legal bureaucracy', was crucial to this process, and it was Weber who, of all the classical theorists, 'recognised both the historical singularity of modern organisations and their material and cultural potency' (Ackroyd, 2000: 90). Bureaucracy was distinct from traditional forms of organisation oriented to kinship and ritual. It was governed by general rules and regulations, which were formally impersonal, impartial and independent of personal favouritism. Bureaucracy enabled the development of calculative action and the instrumental pursuit of goals, through a specialist division of labour: it 'expressed the triumph of the scientific method and scientific expertise in social life' (Kumar, 1988a: 22) and thus constituted 'the organisational weapon of the modern project' (Albrow, 1997: 164).

Organisations enable the generation, differentiation and coordination of knowledge, expertise and resources across time and space in endlessly varied ways, continuously reorganising social life in the process. Such processes have been depicted as universally corrosive of social solidarity (Ackroyd, 2000), but this seems too simple: there are ways in which the universalising principles of organisation have proved empowering in relation to new kinds of collective identity formation and solidarity. The results have often been unpredictable, but wide access to cultural resources and education have enabled forms of social solidarity based on associations of choice, giving new impetus to social movements, notably of late those concerned with a politics of identity (Castells, 2000; Lash and Urry, 1994).

Structure and Agency in the Context of Organisations

The power of large organisations poses problems for any attempt to understand selfhood and the exercise of agency. The active, meaningful engagement of people is critical to organisational functioning, yet the classical theories of Marx and Weber and the contemporary writings of Foucault on power and the regulation of subjectivity, when applied to organisations, have often been used to draw pessimistic conclusions that rationalisation, alienation and regulation have overwhelmed independent thought and critical analysis.

While drawing on work in each of these traditions, this book argues that agency and meaningful selfhood are not eliminated through organisations, but are progressively reconstituted in terms of different priorities and values, notably those of individualism, choice and voluntarism, but also those of personal accountability and responsibility. Agency is exercised not just in the capacity of organisational employee, but also in people's interaction with organisations as consumers, or clients, and as members of civil society. In each capacity, social interaction entails a degree of spontaneity and unpredictability (Goffman, 1983). The paradox is that the agency and creativity of social interaction is generally experienced as perpetuating and reproducing organisational structures, even in the face of an active critique of, and resistance to, their priorities or values. This 'problem' of accounting for both structure *and* agency, continuity *and* social change is at the heart of sociology and organisation studies.

C. Wright Mills' work was an early attempt to overcome a simple dichotomy between agency and structure, by linking these with historical and political processes and arguing for their simultaneous, ongoing interconnections: individual lives cannot be understood without reference to the social and political institutions and historical forces that frame them, but equally societies cannot be understood without recourse to the historical and contemporary biographies of the people who comprise them (Brewer, 2003). By extension, organisations cannot be understood either solely as structures inhabited by passive and entirely interchangeable people, or solely as the sum of their constituent actors.

This book treats organisations as constituted through social practice, and it eschews rigid conceptual distinctions between action and structure. In order to account for their capacity to structure and reproduce social order, and to tolerate and absorb dissent, modern organisations are treated both as the embodiments of analytic and technical expertise, and as a providing a legitimate basis to question their priorities and practices. Forms of specialist and technical expertise inform instrumental and calculative action, which reproduces social order (Flyvbjerg, 2001). Yet the capacity to challenge that reproduction is also constituted through the organisational, rational-legal framework of individual responsibility and accountability. Organisational employees, even in relatively routinised jobs, are expected to exercise judgement and to be accountable for their actions. The exercise of such autonomy is not simple and is heavily constrained by circumstances, but a sense of personal accountability for our actions produces a continuing irreducible basis for practical reflection about, and evaluation and critique of, organisations and their goals.

This approach requires a model of power that allows for indeterminacy in the trajectories of organisations, deriving from the irreducible spontaneity of social interaction (Goffman, 1983) and the modern attribution of responsibility and accountability for our actions. This book argues that organisational trajectories are emergent rather than planned, and rationalised rather than rational. The historical trace of political-economic power shapes organisations. However, changes in the ways that people interpret their own biographical experiences of organisations have the potential to reshape history, politics and economic relations. Organisational elites may set out to prescribe legitimate identities and to shape common beliefs and desires, but history shows that consent to such prescriptions remains partial and prone to reversal (Lukes, 2005).

The Challenge of Postmodernism

The rise of modern industrial societies during the eighteenth and nineteenth centuries was associated with a narrative of progress, which placed the ideal of a rational-economic, self-interested agent at the centre of human history, and regarded organisations as the instrument of domination over nature. Increasing awareness of the environmental risks and social ills created by the imperatives of economic growth and mass consumption has stimulated numerous critiques of this self-aggrandising model of Man, and its privileging of imperialist and patriarchal perspectives on society.

One strand of critique has centred on the postmodern deconstruction of the modern idea of the self-determining, rational-economic 'agent'. Foucault's writing, for example, deconstructs the nineteenth-century concept of the individual, treating it as an invention of power (Foucault, 1970, 1980, 1982). He argues that the individualising discourse operates as an all-pervasive form of discipline, imposing the requirement of autonomy, separating people from each other, making them calculating and calculable, and making them responsible for themselves. Dependence is rendered illegitimate. The historical imposition of individuality should, he argued, be revealed and resisted (Foucault, 1982, 1986). The idea of a self with autonomous powers is treated as a linguistic fallacy, constructed by discourses of power and knowledge, exemplified in texts and language (Gergen, 1991; Hall, 1996). From this perspective, the individual is an illusory construct arising out of the current 'regime of truth'.

In organisational studies, Foucault's work on power and the regulation of subjectivity has been a stimulant to some insightful analyses of organisational attempts at shaping identities, but this has paradoxically tended to produce its own deterministic orthodoxy that sees little if any scope for resistance or social change (Ackroyd and Thompson, 1999; Knights, 2004). Some postmodernist analysis concludes, for example, that recent developments in management practices, particularly those oriented to aligning personal identity with organisational 'brand' identity, have more or less eradicated employee resistance (see for example Casey, 1995; Ray, 1986; Sewell and Wilkinson, 1992). Applications of Foucault's theories to organisations have also tended to lose sight of the particular material conditions and experiences of work and consumption, such that organisations are indistinguishable from each other and from other institutional settings. The result is paradoxically a reinforced sense that the individual, locked in an existential 'struggle for identity', is all there is to life.

The postmodern perspective has also generated some heated debate about the nature of knowledge of society and organisations, stimulating a divide between 'postmodernists' and 'realists'. Postmodernists have charged 'modern' social science with the claim that it relies on a positivist, one-dimensional view of reality as objectively knowable and calculable (Parker, 1998). By implication, all the work that draws on modern theory and concepts of agency is seen as contributing to the 'tools of domination', which postmodernism seeks to dismantle through its interpretive deconstruction of the discourses of power and knowledge. Defenders of a 'modern' materialist perspective, on the other hand, have responded that this is itself a simplistic polarising of the field, which ignores all critical organisational studies. The latter tradition, drawing on Marx and Weber, connects the social structures of capitalist political economy and organisational regulation with the meanings that actors give to their situations (Ackroyd and Fleetwood, 2000). Such studies have challenged, rather than promoted, rational-economic doctrines, and have examined the alternative perspectives held by different interest groups on the 'reality' of organisations. The continuing resilience of labour in contesting and responding to new forms of managerial control has been highlighted.

Defenders of the value of classical social theory for understanding contemporary organisational change have argued for a 'critical realist' perspective, which connects political economy and social divisions with organisational strategy and social action: without this, it is argued, social science cannot cast light on the workings of advanced capitalism and its implications for social life (Ackroyd and Fleetwood, 2000; Kumar, 1995). Critics have also charged postmodernist writers with promoting a damaging relativism and nihilism, where any account of organisations is as good as any other: 'These anti-realist doctrines undermine confidence in the value of disinterested efforts to determine what is true and what is false' (Frankfurt, 2004: 65). In the social sciences, extreme relativism results in a self-defeating dead end: attempts to bring reasoned argument and evidence to bear, for example, on questions of who gains and who loses in a neoliberal market economy become untenable, as do judgements about the value of alternative ways of organising society. The tendency for sociology to turn inwards on itself and become preoccupied with epistemology, rather than, for example, investigating the problems of organisational society, is not new (see for example Bell and Newby, 1981 for a critique of narcissism in sociology). The danger is that sociology itself, instead of investigating and elucidating the forms of organisation that lead people to believe in, and identify with, the idea of an individualised 'authentic self', contributes to perpetuating the power of that individualising discourse.

In his later work, as Archer (2000) and Lukes (2005) point out, Foucault (1982) retreated from the radical position that there is no subject outside the regime of power, to readmit a knowing form of agency and resistance. The postmodern turn to culture and discourse highlights the cultural and performative dimensions of identities, and their treatment as symbolic resources in a sign- and image-oriented consumer capitalism. However, the material and practical dimensions of such identities are intimately inter-connected to the cultural, and cannot be unravelled merely through parody and the play on meaning: some people have far more capacity to remake their identity, because they are wealthier and more powerful.

Without some concept of agency, which is fallible and constrained by history and circumstance, but which has some potential for self-evaluation, independent thought and action, there is little chance of understanding the development and directions of organisations. Archer (2000) argues that social theory, both modern and postmodern, has progressively dimin-ished human properties and lost sight of human powers. She argues for prioritising the study of practical commitments and activities over linguistic forms and discourses of social order:

> there is nothing in the world which dictates how we list our priorities, although there are plenty of forces inducing us this way or that ... Instead, through external information and internal deliberation, all who achieve personal iden-tity work out their own distinctive constellation of values. It is then through dedicating ourselves to the subjects and objects of our caring that we make our mark upon reality – natural, practical and social. (p. 319)

Overall it seems to me mistaken to put rigid boundaries between different approaches that share some common aims of social critique and insight into the contradictory and contested workings of power and identities. In this book I have tried to resist being drawn heavily into epistemological debate, instead forefronting organisations and our experiences of them. I am critical of a modernist model of rational, instrumental Man, who is enabled by science and expertise to gain progressive mastery and control of nature. I am also unsympathetic to the radical postmodern position, which argues for the death of the subject, and its dissolution into discur-sive, disembodied structures, or the play of identities. The 'puppet'-like status of such a being would mean that social organisation could not be

elucidated by social analysis in any form, because its 'authors' are themselves products of the same regime of truth that they claim to reveal. So
I prioritise organisations and social life over and above an academic preoccupation with epistemology, the object being to enhance understanding
of the interconnections of organisations, identities and the self.

An Analytic Distinction between Self and Identity

In the mainstream tradition of sociology, I draw a pragmatic distinction
between 'self' and 'identity'. I treat a sense of self as our personal awareness of a continuity of being, which is unique, physically embodied and,
in common with others, shares a capacity for agency (Archer, 2000; Berger
and Luckmann, 1966; Jenkins, 1996). The biography of a self is shaped
through interaction and experience, and by the experience of being held
accountable by others for our actions. Selfhood is not solely a result of conscious thought or reflection: practical experience, tacit understandings and
feelings shape selfhood in ways which cannot be easily articulated.

The sense of a particularity of self is in contrast with the experience we
have of multiple and fluid social identities, which are differentially important in different situations, life stages and historical periods. Social and
personal identities are publicly problematised in contemporary societies
through debates about everything from 'Britishness', in the wake of ter-
rorist attacks on London by British citizens, to the popular interest in 'self-
improvement', reflected in the proliferation of self-help books and TV
programmes. It is impossible to give a categorical answer to questions
such as 'what is identity?' because there is (fortunately) no ultimate authority that can decree a definitive use of the term. Identity and selfhood are not
objects, but processes invested with varied, contested, negotiated and
unstable meanings, in everyday life as well as in academic debate. Used in
this way, identity focuses on processes of categorising people or allocating
them to groups, such as 'European', 'chief executive', 'working class',
'Muslim' or 'unemployed'. Such identity categories are countless and the
processes of their construction and negotiation are open-ended and
diverse (Brubaker and Cooper, 2000; Jenkins, 1996; Williams, 2000).

The concept of identity provides a means of connecting the self as agent
to social structure: a capacity for agency means that what *particular* people
make of constructed identities is always to some degree indeterminate
and open-ended. For the purposes of this book, I focus on those identities concerned with production and consumption, which are commonly
associated with organisations. Large-scale organisations, from health services to theme parks, are instrumental in processes of identity formation
and negotiation, both as places of work and as providers of goods and

services that influence social values and self-esteem. Corporations and public service bodies are themselves increasingly investing large sums of money in the creation of a corporate 'identity', as they aim to win the hearts and minds of customers, clients and employees (Hatch and Schultz, 2004). Conversely, businesses may expect people to treat themselves as commodities with a marketable identity: 'Today more than ever human beings are brands' (Ridderstråle and Nordström, 2004: 13). The capacity to invent yourself as a 'brand' in a labour market concerned with individual distinction appears to promise enhanced choice and self-determination, but for most people the day-to-day experience of organisationally conferred identities is likely to be characterised by constraint: we may want to be the next Richard Branson or Bill Gates, but we find ourselves constrained by a lack of access to training, financial support or the right social networks. In this sense, modern organisations are significant sources of individual opportunities, but they are also important arenas for the exercise of power. Those who control resources, whether financial, material or knowledge-based, are able to channel and structure opportunities, enabling certain identities and constraining others. The negotiation and evolution of organisational identities therefore offer valuable insights into the workings of power relations.

Interpretative Approaches to the Interconnections of Organisations, Identities and the Self

A sociology of organisations and identities is necessarily interpretative and reflexive in approach, because its theories and descriptions are simultaneously component parts of a situation and may contribute an apparent objectivity to the practices they describe (Albrow, 1997). Giddens (1996) describes this as a double hermeneutic, where 'the concepts and theories . . . apply to a world constituted of the activities of conceptualizing and theorizing individuals' (p. 76). People interpret their own and others' lives, and their conduct is mediated by the meanings derived from social interaction, both informally with friends and intimates, and in the structured and formal encounters of citizenship, work, welfare and market exchange. Interaction does not have to be experienced directly: much of our knowledge is derived from mass media interpretations of events, which are themselves produced by large-scale organisations. Social science concepts are themselves deployed by organisations in their attempts to influence employees and public opinion, with far-reaching significance for social life: the theories advanced by social science are part of the materials that create and articulate the character of modern organisations, identities and selves.

The Structure of the Book and Chapter Outline

The book is structured around an exposition of the interconnected changes in political economy, organisations and people's lives as consumers, workers and citizens. Agency is centre stage of the analysis, and structures are presented as both constraining and enabling. Unlike many recent books in the field, the chapters cover debates from different angles. I adopt a broad-based view of relevant conceptual and empirical literature, drawing on materialist and postmodern perspectives where appropriate, but also using some non-academic sources when these provide new and apt illustrations of emerging social trends. In particular I try to give plenty of examples that show how agency works to challenge dominant neoliberal economic agendas and to criticise the social consequences of laissez-faire markets. The book is international in scope and comparison, although drawing on literature mainly of Northern European and North American origin. It distinguishes between capitalism and organisations in different societal contexts, notably in relation to globalisation (Chapter 2) and the work and occupational structures of advanced capitalist societies (Chapter 5). It examines both private and public sector organisations, and appraises the role of transnational organisations, such as the International Monetary Fund, World Bank and World Trade Organization, in structuring the core social identities of laissez-faire market capitalism. Its structure moves from an analysis of the globally organised directions of consumer capitalism to an increasing focus on people's experience, social identities and agency.

Chapter 1 develops and exemplifies the conceptual framework briefly introduced so far. In particular it reviews debates about the nature of selfhood, agency and social identities and situates these in the context of the distinctive qualities of contemporary organisations, which drive differentiation, specialisation and individualisation. It reviews the tensions between modernist, or materialist, and postmodernist perspectives and argues against overly determinist models of organisations and identity.

Chapter 2 shows how the organisational structures and processes of globalising economies are shaped by the actions of political-economic elites, and questions the apparent inevitability of current neoliberal economic trajectories. It assesses the impact of deregulatory economic strategies on the restructuring of businesses, and on the identities and priorities of corporations and their senior managers and officials.

Chapter 3 turns from the organisational relations of production to those of consumption and examines the organisation of consumer identities, paying attention to their historical emergence, and the phenomenon of *organisational* identity-making through marketing, advertising and branding. It examines claims that organisations increasingly dominate and 'dupe' consumers, and questions assertions that marketing and advertising strategies are 'overwhelming agency'. It does this through an examination of the phenomena of social movements and the 'collective consumer'. Such groups campaign for public accountability and democratic control of corporations and states. Raised awareness of global environmental risks and social injustices creates renewed demands on organisations to practise fair employment and fair trade, to improve the quality of goods and services and to establish their 'green credentials'.

Having established the macro-social parameters of contemporary organisational change, subsequent chapters focus particularly on the interconnections of structural change and the material and cultural dimensions of social and personal identities. Chapter 4 takes the theme of consumer markets and identities into the sphere of welfare organisation and citizenship. It reviews the experience of new, managerial identities for public servants, and analyses the identity of the 'consumer-citizen' and its social consequences.

Chapter 5 examines the global restructuring of work and occupational categories over the past twenty to thirty years, using international comparisons between Germany, Japan, the UK and the USA. It offers an appraisal of changing divisions of labour, and the relative growth of white-collar professional, managerial and technical jobs in affluent economies, alongside the reassertion of material inequalities in both advanced and developing countries.

Chapter 6 explores the implications of occupational restructuring for employment and the intersecting social divisions of class, gender and ethnicity. It treats organisations as instrumental in the structuring of social strata and explores the paradox that organisations both constrain opportunities for marginalised or disadvantaged groups, and yet are also implicated in enabling significant social change, notably in the experience of women.

Chapter 7 looks at the consequences of macro-structural changes for the experience of work in advanced consumer capitalism, where most people work with symbols, rather than producing manufactured goods, and employers are increasingly reliant on the willing engagement of labour in enacting high-quality service. It focuses particularly on attempts by organisations to capture the hearts and minds of employees by aligning employee identity with the organisational 'brand'. It compares and contrasts research which suggests that people's capacity for resistance to employer-defined identities is eroded by new means of cultural control, with research which concludes that employees deploy a range of creative, innovative, knowledgeable and socially skilful responses to such control strategies.

Chapter 8 explores how the rationalities of global finance and the drive to extend markets, discussed in Chapters 2 and 3, are resulting in the erosion of boundaries between 'production' and 'consumption', and the intensification of work and leisure. The chapter examines the interrelations between competitive markets and processes of individualisation through aspirations to continuous 'self-improvement'. It explores the varied responses that people make in partially resisting, complying with and consenting to a 'productive subjectivity'. Social and collective identities, crafted out of the experiences of work and consumption, ensure that subjectivity remains indeterminate and contested, as people struggle to understand their circumstances and act in the light of that understanding.

The Conclusion summarises the main themes of the chapters and comments on the need for a reinvigorated public sphere, free of commercial pressures, where the accountability of organisations and the conduct and better regulation of markets can be openly debated.

This book is centrally concerned with a renewed sociological perspective on the interconnections between personal biographies, social identities and organisations, in this particular period of history and political economy. In a nutshell, it argues that large-scale organisations have been instrumental in facilitating a historical shift in processes of identity formation, such that we are increasingly expected, and expect, to have choice over how we identify ourselves and how we act in the light of such negotiated and malleable identities. Instead of experiencing identity as something that is ascribed through birth, we experience it as something that has to be achieved, through circumscribed choices and forms of market competition structured by class, gender and ethnic divisions. Organisations provide significant resources and opportunities for such identity formation through wealth creation, social mobility and freedom of association. They also promote particular normative identities. Notably, the emerging forms of global capitalism, oriented to the extension and intensification of markets, rely on individualised self-identities oriented to continuous, competitive self-growth and productivity through harder work and higher levels of consumption. Identities are not, however, determined by the imperatives of advanced capitalist organisations: this kind of argument confuses organisational prescription with the diversity of practical experiences, which involve people in trying to make sense of the contradictions, complexities and ironies of lives framed by organisational rationalities. An orientation to practice shows the innovative and creative purposes that people pursue, drawing on organisational resources, but making new political and pragmatic adjustments to circumstances, which drive significant social and organisational changes.

In the next chapter, I take the conceptual framework introduced here and elaborate this as a foundation for the sociological perspective at the heart of the book.

1

Understanding Organisations, Identities and the Self: a Conceptual Framework

Each of the three key terms, organisations, identities and the self, are subject to a wide range of uses, and none are uncontentious in the analysis of social relations. In steering a course through the controversies discussed here, I suggest that the organisational sphere provides an important middle-range conceptual link between political economy on the one hand, and personal and social identities on the other. It is through interactions with organisations that people experience the political and economic forces that structure daily life and shape understandings of themselves and others.

The Sociological Perspective on the Self and Social Identities

Within sociology and social theory, the examination of self and identity has a long history and has generated an extensive literature concerned with questions about the extent to which people choose their own actions, on the one hand, or are the products of social and institutional structures on the other (see for example reviews by Jenkins, 1996; Williams, 2000). Modernist European and North American social science has typically drawn a contrast between the sense of continuity of a *unique* self, and the constitution of multiple intersecting and often contradictory *social* identities. The latter entails socially constructed, multiple differences and inequalities between groups and categories who may never interact with each other, but have characteristics imputed to them by virtue of education, occupation, generation, religion, sex, nationality, ethnicity and so on.

The concept of the 'self' recognises the experience of a singular, embodied and mortal being, with the creative capacities to act reflexively and purposively in relation to themselves and others, to consider alternative courses

15

of action, and exercise some control over actions, and to strive deliberately to change circumstances. Sociology's account of selfhood has been influenced by George Herbert Mead's (1934) treatment of self-consciousness as a social process dependent on language. Language is the basis of reflection on our own thoughts and actions, producing awareness of a self as both subject and object of our own and others' attention. Mead described these aspects of subjective processes as the 'I' and the 'me'. The 'I' is the source of creativity and agency, while the 'me' is an intrinsically social identity derived from internalising the attitude of the 'generalised other', resulting in an ongoing dialogue between what we want and what we imagine others might think of us. The particular meanings of selfhood are collectively accomplished through interaction, which forms the material for reflection on social identity. Our personal biography, formed through the accretions of past memories and future anticipations, habits, feelings, forms of knowledge and expectations, gives us a sense of uniqueness and, simultaneously, connects us to all others (Jamieson, 2004). In short, 'society is a conversation between people; the mind is an internalisation of that conversation; the self lies within and between the two' (Jenkins, 1996: 43).

This implies that selfhood is a process rooted in history and is not pre-social or autonomous. Much of selfhood is tacit, learned by practice, is emotionally charged, perhaps taken for granted, and not readily available to conscious thought. Most people, for instance, have limited awareness of the influences of early childhood relationships over their gestures, habits or preoccupations. The idea of 'being gendered', which is encountered in practical experiences from birth onwards, is often used as an example of the early emotional, and largely unconscious, shaping of a sense of self, through the differential treatment of the sexes (Connell, 1987, 2002; Jackson, 1999). Habit, emotional and unconscious sources of selfhood may nevertheless become amenable to reflection at different life stages, and may in theory be treated as material for both social and personal change, as evidenced by the power of the women's movement in defining the 'personal as political' and raising awareness of gendered power relations.

The concept of 'social identity' has proved attractive because it appears to provide a bridge between 'structure' and 'agency', or society and self (Williams, 2000). In any given day, social interaction entails negotiating multiple coexisting, and often contradictory, 'identities' that have both personal and public meanings: from parent, to worker, to man or woman, young or old, white or black, patient, consumer, entrepreneur, politician – the list is endless. Social identities are neither solely cultural and discursive, nor material: for example, the category 'British' has material dimensions, in conferring benefits of citizenship and welfare, but its cultural meanings are diverse, and subject to change and renegotiation through both formal and informal means. The tensions between the normative expectation that

'I' am the agent of my own destiny and the experience of a multiplicity of sources of identity, some more negative and constraining than others, lends ambiguity and anxiety to self-presentation. Different identity categories are also differentially salient: some are highly consequential, because they mark people out for differential treatment, whether in terms of material benefits, or discrimination and harassment; these are likely to have enduring personal significance. Other identity categories may become prominent only in certain contexts, or at different stages of life, and yet others may be proactively used as resources for political mobilisation and resistance.

As a concept, social identity has provided a means of connecting personal biography to historical processes of social categorisation and identification, such as the constitution of social classes, genders and racialised groups. Such categorising typically works to legitimate and rationalise differential treatment and is often associated with the unequal distribution of life chances and material resources, with consequential effects on dignity and self-worth. Reviewing the disparate analytical uses of the term, Brubaker and Cooper (2000) argue that it has become a way of relabelling and redescribing diverse social processes, instead of a means of disaggregating and clarifying them. MacInnes (2004) also concludes that social identity is an overused concept, reflecting the analytical weakness of contemporary sociology, which has been swept along with forces of social change, instead of providing some critical purchase on them. In both cases, the authors suggest that the fashion for postmodernist deconstruction of a structural analysis of society and the aim of collapsing analytic distinctions between subject and object, or structure and action, power and subjectivity have resulted in weaker, rather than more powerful, conceptualisations. There are, however, important recurring themes reflected in both modernist and postmodernist thinking, in particular a concern with the workings of power and resistance, as processes inscribed on social identities. There are also some shared weaknesses in conceptualisation, reflected in a tendency to alternate between treating identity either as entirely determined by social forces or as entirely individual and self-willed.

The Postmodernist Treatment of Identity and Subjectivity

Postmodern epistemology charges conventional modernist thought with constructing false dualisms between 'self and society' or agency and structure. In the attempt to dissolve such analytic divisions and break with any assumptions about agency and rationality as guiding social relations, postmodernist writers have made subjectivity and identities the key to the practices of power and the means of its operation. This has stimulated accounts of identity as an assembly of fragmented and perpetually shifting discursive positions and performative effects. 'Identities' become the unstable, fluid and hybrid compiling of subject positions, perpetually reassembled around new, discontinuous narratives, rather than having a 'core' of continuity through selfhood or agency (Butler, 1991; Collinson, 2003; Henriques et al., 1998; Linstead, 2004).

The emphasis on the inseparability of power, cultural discourse and identity has, however, been used in quite different ways. On the one hand, concepts such as 'multiplicity', 'fluidity' and 'hybridity' have been used to forefront the active remaking and reclaiming of marginalised identities, as a political process and as an act of resistance to powerful elites. Stuart Hall's work (1996, 1997) is a prominent example of this. He rejects the idea of a core self-identity, but his work makes an analytic distinction between ascribed and adopted identities and depicts a conflict-ridden struggle for agency through social movements. The Black Power and black consciousness movements, for example, challenged white imperialist and colonial racialised definitions of people, remaking black as a political identity (Lewis and Phoenix, 2004).

In the hands of other writers, postmodern perspectives have been used to draw an extremely voluntarist picture of identity as entailing a kind of individualised 'pick'n'mix' choice, where people may play identity games and reinvent themselves perpetually, in line with a shifting, expanding and incoherent network of relationships (Gergen, 1991). Such free-flowing individualism and flux is in contrast with the use of a postmodernist perspective in other cases to conclude that identities are governed by forms of regulatory power, which exclude the possibility of authentic choice and agency. In organisational analyses, for example, identities have been treated as constituted through discursive 'regimes of truth', with subjects becoming passive carriers of power/knowledge discourse, leaving little scope for knowing forms of agency and resistance (see for example Sewell and Wilkinson, 1992; Webster and Robbins, 1993).

The attempt to collapse distinctions between agency and structure, or self and society, does not therefore overcome the problems of modernist perspectives, since postmodernist accounts have shared the same tendency to swing between oversocialised and undersocialised models (Wrong, 1961), treating identity either as the fluid epiphenomena of determining social forces, or as the project of a resourceful and autonomous being that gives direction to history. Whatever the tools of analysis, it seems that the same contradictions are reproduced. In postmodernism, agency has been variously depicted as erased by internalised disciplinary powers, or glorified in the idea of identity as a post-materialist, empowering play of performative effects. Equally, modernist theories have treated agency both as erased by determining economic structures, and as the determining force of history in the form of a reasoning, calculating individual. Indeed, Williams (2000) structures his combined discussion of modern and postmodern theoretical accounts of identity around the distinction between those whose work has focused on 'identity without agency' and those whose work focuses on identity as an individual accomplishment.

Neither position is satisfactory: the oversocialised view of self-identity denies the possibility of creative thought and improvised interaction, while the undersocialised view suggests a self that is without social and cultural knowledge and understanding. Neither of these beings could communicate, recognise injustice, run a railroad, criticise corporate power or love their children. Yet history clearly indicates that people do all of these and far more. It is important therefore to use concepts that allow for a continuing dialectic of 'structure' and 'agency' and to accept that attempts to collapse these distinctions into each other result in excluding significant phenomena from discussion: 'each refers to real and different aspects of the world and we have to take account of all of them' (Craib, 1997: 7). Insights into identity and the interaction of the social and the personal depend on making some analytic distinctions between 'the properties and powers of the practitioner [and] the properties and powers of the environment in which practices are conducted' (Archer, 2000: 6).

The Historical Development of the Self as Agent: from Ascribed to Achieved Identity

A central contention of sociology is that understandings of self and identity are linked to the social and cultural formations characterising particular historical periods. The normative idea that people are agents in control of their own destiny is contingent on the circumstances of modern society, in particular the growth of instrumental reason (discussed in the next section) and liberal Enlightenment ideals of individual freedom and equality. The sense of an individualised identity, based around chosen routes through life, is in marked contrast with traditional societies, where identity was ascribed by birth and legitimised by religious institutions and family status, in a feudal and patriarchal system. Where traditional societies were marked by belief in a God-given natural order, modern societies are marked by the belief that people are responsible for acting on the world to create their own meanings and direction through life (Taylor, 1989).

Industrialisation, the extension and deepening of market-based exchange, the development of scientific thought, secularisation, the growth

of democratised nation states and the notion of individual rights, each contributed to the particular conditions of self-conscious individualism (Kumar,
1988a). Differentiated, specialised political and economic infrastructures of
states, finance, product and labour markets resulted in increasing individualisation of education, work and consumption. Identity was no longer
ascribed by birth, but became something to be achieved in a market for
labour and commodified goods. Traditionally, people had subsisted in a
household economy, working irregularly at a variety of tasks, according to
the rhythms of the seasons. The notion of an achievement-oriented or aspirational attitude to life, through striving to attain a higher material standard
of living, was largely absent. Factory owners, aiming to increase productivity and profitability, wanted a disciplined, controllable workforce, but
waged labour was not looked on favourably by most. In a process taking
some two hundred years, people were forced to become more dependent
on wage labour by land enclosures, which withdrew other means of sub-
sistence, and by factory-based production, with its new time and work
organisation disciplines (Thompson, 1967).

Early recognition that labour productivity depended not just on the
'sticks' of authority and discipline, but also on persuading people that such
effort was in their *own* interest, added an aspirational, consumer counterpart to the model of the disciplined, productive self. Kumar (1988b) credits
Bishop Berkeley in 1755 with recognising the potential boost to productivity to be gained from stimulating the creation of wants or needs. More
famously, Adam Smith argued that higher wages were an incentive to
harder work, because they brought higher standards of living within sight
of larger numbers of people and therefore encouraged greater effort.

Dramatic social changes over the past two hundred years or so created
new conditions for identity, individualising experience through differenti-
ations between work, non-work and leisure. Dependence on waged work,
in a competitive market for labour, and the social value placed on material
wealth and consumer artefacts stimulated a more instrumental and calculative orientation to life. Rather than being ascribed, identity became something that must be achieved, as people were effectively constrained to
choose routes through education, work and consumption and 'make up'
their own biographies (Giddens, 1991; Rose, 1999).

A Circumscribed and Instrumental Form of Agency? Weber's 'Iron Cage' of Rationalisation

The nineteenth-century theorists of modernisation, Marx, Weber and
Durkheim, held in common the view that traditional societies and social
identities would be transformed by emerging forms of individualism,

knowledge, technology and markets (Giddens, 1971). Each treated modernisation processes as universalising and governed by one particular causal dynamic. For both Marx and Durkheim, organisations were implicit, rather than explicit, mechanisms of social change. Durkheim (1984) saw the division of labour in society as the key to modernisation, which he predicted would result in the proliferation of available social identities, damaging social cohesion. Marx's principal argument was that the mode of production determined the dynamics of society. Economic relations and the dynamics of class thus governed identity: under capitalism, he predicted that society would comprise two structurally antagonistic classes, the small elite comprising the owners of the means of production, and the mass of wage labourers who must sell their labour power to live. He believed that the contradictions of capitalist production, resulting in the need for an increasingly intense exploitation of labour, would eventually unite the working class and lead to the overthrow of capitalism, enabling the utopian re-establishment of 'authentic' identities, emanating from communal ownership and control of production.

It was the writings of Weber, however, which placed organisations at the centre of modern processes of agency and identity. He recognised the centrality of capitalism in revolutionising the social order and concentrating power in the hands of the economically powerful, but regarded the invasion of instrumental reason into all spheres, through bureaucratic organisations, as more significant. For Weber, it was this process of rationalisation which provided the unifying principle of modernisation, and it was this process which informed his ambivalence towards modernity. Released from the belief that society had a sacred structure reflecting the will of God, social arrangements could be remade according to the goals specified by society, but this new awareness of the potential for self-determination poses terrible anxieties and difficulties as well as promising great opportunities: what goals should inform the social order; who should specify them, and even assuming that such goals can be specified, what arrangements will work to ensure they are achieved?

For Weber, it was instrumental reason which would provide the means of managing the freedom, complexity and uncertainties of modern society, and enable purposeful action and organisation. The powers of instrumental reason would produce rationalisation, or the progressive disenchantment of the world, as superstition, tradition and faith in unseen forces were challenged by scientific and critical analyses of events. Weber (1947) distinguished two forms of rationality: formal (or instrumental) and substantive. Substantive rationality entails the absolute values that inform goals and the ethical, political, utilitarian or other bases of judgement. Formal or instrumental rationality entails the calculation of the most expedient means to achieve predefined goals. The goals themselves are taken as given, and may be economic, as in the pursuit of profit, social, as in the fair distribution of benefits, or concerned with the achievement of political domination by one nation over another. Differentiated and specialised institutions, with formalised knowledge and expertise embodied in the organisations of the state, the market, technology and law, rely on the progressive development of techniques of instrumental or formal rationality to control actions, making them calculable, predictable and reliable (Weber, 1968).

Weber understood the liberating force of rationalisation, but feared that its instrumentalism would inevitably become the dominant feature of social life: substantive rationality would become subordinated to the power of technical reason and systems of monetary calculation. He predicted that all decisions would come to be based on some form of 'cost–benefit analysis', such that other values would be overridden by concerns with instrumental efficiency and demands to maximise output (Taylor, 1992). Instrumental reason would come to be valued as an end in itself, dominating all forms of organisation, and resulting in a new sort of identity: that of the expert without spirit, psychically imprisoned by techniques of rational calculation.

The means of such bondage would, Weber argued, be the public and private sector bureaucratic organisations necessitated by the technical and economic bases of modernisation and the resulting need for calculability:

> Bureaucracy is superior to any other form in precision, in stability, in the stringency of its discipline and in its reliability. It thus makes possible a particularly high degree of calculability of results for the head of the organisation and those acting in relation to it. (Weber, 1968: 223)

He exemplified the principles of bureaucracy according to an 'ideal type', briefly outlined below, and consisting of an abstract description of its essential features under the rule of laws whose legitimacy was derived from the framework of a modern rational-legal system.

He was well aware that bureaucracy would never exist in its idealised form, but its depiction in these terms served Weber's purpose of establishing its stark contrast with traditional status-based systems. In principle, bureaucracy produced more systematic, speedy and reliable decisions based on impersonal rules, rather than arbitrary personal preferences, political patronage or favouritism. In this sense, Weber depicted bureaucracy as a moral project and a means to establishing ideals of fair treatment and principled decision-making. At the same time he suspected that its rule-governed conduct, hierarchy of authority and delimited spheres of competence would become ends in themselves and undermine the wider capacities for substantively rational organisation.

It was certainly not Weber's intention to promote instrumental reason as a means to 'efficiency' of the type associated with classical economics and

Weber's 'ideal type'

1. A continuous organisation of official functions bound by rules (a predictable pattern to functions, not subject to arbitrary change)

2. Officers have a specified sphere of competence (rule-governed and delimited spheres of authority, in a systematic division of labour)

3. A hierarchy of authority (a chain of command between superior and subordinate from top to bottom makes coordinated action possible)

4. Codified rules govern conduct

5. Administrative acts, decisions and rules are recorded

6. Office holders appointed according to merit and expertise, salaried and having tenure of office, with potential career advancement

7. The office is typically the primary or sole occupation (unlike patrimonial authority)

8. Office holders do not own their tools and resources (there is separation of 'office' and 'personal' spheres)

9. Nor do they 'own their position' (officers cannot decide who will take their place or sell their position to another)

10. Impersonality (business is conducted without regard to personal preference or favouritism, and decisions are based on general rules, not personal desires or interests)

management theory, whose work paradoxically set out to further the project of rationalisation, by devising its tools. Weber was clear that the growth of bureaucratic organisations was not due to their efficiency, but derived from the cultural value placed on rationalisation itself (Albrow, 1970; Clegg, 1990). In Weber's pessimistic world-view, modern freedom from superstition, tradition and the authority of God and King would be lost through the marriage of identity to organisational and instrumental imperatives. The anxieties provoked by the newly recognised responsibility for autonomous choice of ends and means would thus be contained by reducing them to a bounded, 'manageable' alignment of identity with organisational goals.

Self-determination and Agency Dissolved in a Postmodern 'Invisible Cage' of Total Institutions

Such grand narratives (Lyotard, 1984) of a singular unifying account of modernisation with a determined end point have been the stimulus to self-consciously postmodernist critiques. At its widest, postmodernist thought set out to criticise and dismantle what were taken to be overly rational theories of society. Such theories, it was argued, served the colonial and patriarchal projects of a powerful European male governing class. Lyotard argued that the twentieth-century horrors of genocide at Auschwitz and the Soviet experience of Stalinism discredited both Marxist historical material-ism and European Enlightenment visions of progress through rationality.

In the context of organisations, it is the postmodern theories of Michel Foucault that have had the most significant impact. There are however some surprising parallels between the conclusions of Weber and those of Foucault: in both cases agency and identity are treated as subordinate to the increasing power of organisations, represented by Weber in the metaphor of the 'iron cage' of rationalisation and by Foucault (1972, 1977, 1984) in the imagery of the panopticon and the development of self-surveillance, disciplinary power and biopower. The panopticon is derived from Bentham's design principle for a circular building with a central observa-tion tower, which facilitated a unidirectional gaze, subjecting the observed to continuous surveillance but hiding the observers.

Foucault (1979, 1980, 1982) developed his work in opposition to mod-ern individualism through his argument that the idea of the rational agent is an effect of cultural domination, which deludes people into believing that they 'possess' a unique personal identity that has to be 'discovered' (Jameson, 1988). This existential 'search' is however self-defeating and therefore disempowering: it makes people believe that they are individu-ally responsible for their own fate, and hence works through an intern-alised disciplinary gaze, without the need for external coercion:

> Foucault's anti-humanism led him to believe that the most subtle form of dis-cipline was indeed the demand that humanism places on us all to be self-referential, a target of each other's judgements and responsible for our own subjective well-being. (Knights, 2004: 25)

Foucault's ideas proved attractive to critics of managerialist prescriptions for organisational efficiency, because his model of power and its mech-anisms seemed to reveal the managerial apparatus of disciplinary control over labour, and the means of inducing an internalised, self-disciplining docility (Reed, 2000). In opposition to what Foucault characterised as a modernist 'sovereign' view of power as a resource possessed by agents, or controlled by states, corporations or elites, he argued that power should be understood without reference to agency: power is treated as productive as well as repressive, structuring 'the possible field of actions of others' (Foucault, 1980: 221). Through its embodiment in heterogeneous micro-practices, it produces knowledge, which in turn shapes and governs conduct through discursive characterisations of reality and identity. Power thus operates by producing identities appropriate to the rationalities created (Rose, 1999). It is intimately linked to subjectivity, producing its 'subjects' through its diffusion in language, texts, cultural signifiers and discourses, which dissolve the internal/external language of agency/structure into 'practices that systematically form the objects of which they speak' (Foucault, 1972: 49).

Foucault's depiction of power is derived from a historical account of its distinctive modern development out of the practices of religious institutions, asylums, prisons and workhouses. Modern disciplinary techniques and knowledge, taken up by factories and state bureaucracies, were in these terms based on refinements of carceral power and detailed practices of surveillance concerned with categorising, assessing and administering populations. Using the idea of biopower to account for the administration of populations and the establishing of 'normal' conduct, Foucault (1982) also depicted modern power as focused on the body. In its recent forms, medicine and psychiatry are seen as the power/knowledge discourses, which elaborate and refine the normal, and discipline and punish deviation from its standards. Resistance is part of the relational quality of power, and enables the further refinement of disciplinary practices; in this sense, attempts to contest the 'rationalities of rule' are tantamount to seduction into its terms. The alignment of rationalities of rule with technologies of the self produce the means of 'governing through freedom' (Foucault, 1987). The result of such disciplinary power is a normalised, docile and disciplined self, with a malleable identity: the humanist Enlightenment idea of a rational, autonomous moral agent becomes an invention of power rather than an achievement of modernity (Foucault, 1977, 1979).

In organisational analyses, Foucault's account of disciplinary power, and its production of willing self-confinement and subjugation, has frequently resulted in a vision of power as monolithic, leaving no spaces outside its networks from which to criticise its workings (Lukes, 2005). Deetz (1992), for example, analyses disciplinary power in the modern corporation, arguing that management monopolises power, creating 'discursive closure' that marginalises other identities, and producing a colonised, obedient subject who wants what the corporation wants. Such accounts lead to the conclusion that, although we may not live in total institutions, 'the institutional organisation of our lives is total' (Burrell, 1988: 232). Weber's vision of pervasive rationalisation has it seems been outflanked by an iron cage reinforced by the surveillance and disciplinary power/knowledge discourses of government and corporate organisations, which are invisible and totalising because they are in the soul of their subjects (Dandeker, 1990; Rose, 1999).

Do Organisations Determine Identities?

Both modernist and postmodernist analysts of identity and organisations have therefore reproduced a deterministic account of identity. Whether informed by the classical theories of Weber or Marx, or the postmodern perspective of Foucault, organisations are seen as colonising the self. The modern perspective sees available identities as determined by the rationalising imperatives of profit and economic growth; the postmodern perspective sees subjectivities as governed through disciplinary power/knowledge discourses. Recent studies are also drawn to similar conclusions: using postmodern concepts, for example, Ezzy (2001) describes the 'self-gratificatory narcissistic individualism' encouraged by living life as a 'consumer of organisationally produced meanings', while Sennett (1998) adopts a modernist framework to describe the 'corrosion of character' resulting from contemporary flexible forms of capital accumulation.

It is clear that contemporary public life is experienced through numerous complex organisations, but does it follow from this that identity and selfhood are colonised by them? The argument here is that such theories are inadequate, because they do not account for the empirical reality of organisational diversity, or the varied and organised articulation of conflicting political positions and continuing debate over the substantive rationality of organisational goals. Both modernist and postmodernist perspectives have in this sense tended to result in a reductionist account of social organisation and identity. Yet when confronted with social practice, what has typically been observed is the distinctiveness of, for example, French bread or Asian enterprise (Clegg, 1990), or the variety of forms of resistance and recalcitrance in the face of new managerial controls or organisational discipline (Ackroyd and Thompson, 1999).

Sociological Evidence from Organisations: Agency Continues

Much of Weber's cultural pessimism about the inevitability of rationalisation and the iron cage of bureaucracy was shown, by early empirical studies of organisations, to be misplaced. Such studies demonstrated the inevitably imperfect workings of rationalised authority, and the capacity of people to resist, to exercise discretion and to make their own meanings out of any framework of rules and regulations. Detailed reviews of these studies can be found in Clegg and Dunkerley (1980) and Thompson and McHugh (2002), but the main points of relevance are summarised below.

Early studies building on Weber's analysis of bureaucracy as an ideal type demonstrated first that formal rationality produces its own substantive irrationalities (Merton, 1940), and second that formal organisations rely on the informal, innovative and creative activities of their members in order to function. Agency is exercised both in terms of the active, knowing engagement with goals, and in continuing resistance to exploitative or abusive forms of power and authority. Merton's work made it clear that organisations are never solely functional, disembodied machines: officers and managers are also people with values, loyalties, fears, prejudices and ambitions. In interpreting the framework of rules and regulations, they affect its enactment.

Later work developed Merton's analysis into an account of the dynamics of authority relations and resistance to rationalisation. Alvin Gouldner's (1955) *Patterns of Industrial Bureaucracy* showed that the same rules could be given quite different meanings, and had different consequences, depending on their context. Focusing on questions about whose values are embodied in organisational rules, and whose values are violated, he distinguished three 'patterns of bureaucracy'. Where formal rules and hierarchical authority are imposed by an external party, Gouldner considered this to be a 'mock bureaucracy'. Where all parties accept the legitimacy of the rules, this constituted a 'representative bureaucracy', but the same rules could have quite the opposite effect in a 'punishment-centred' bureaucracy, where one party sought to enforce the rules on another, generating considerable conflict in the process. In a later study, Gouldner (1957) considered the ways that different groups in organisations may have different interpretations of the same rules. Contrasting 'cosmopolitans' with 'locals', he suggested that the former groups, made up of professionals, have cross-cutting affiliations to a professional community, while the latter are tied to progression within the bureaucracy, resulting in different actions and different orientations to the same rules. Blau's (1963) study of US government agencies also examined actors' orientations to the framework of rules, and found that enforcing laws or applying regulations depended on officers actively making sense of and working round them, in order to achieve formal goals. Formal goals were met by disregarding, subverting or bending the rules rather than by following them.

Weber tended to assume an unquestioning obedience to authority in a rational-legal system, and hence did not give a central place to questions about compliance. Etzioni (1961) recognised however that people might bring different motives to their organisational participation, and hence might comply with the rules out of love, fear or the need for money, terming these respectively 'normative', 'coercive' and 'remunerative' bases of organisational power. Matching these with types of involvement in organisations, he distinguished between 'alienative', 'calculative' and 'moral' forms. Alienative involvement characterises those who are forced into the organisation, such as prisoners; calculative involvement characterises wage earners, and moral involvement might describe those who work as volunteers in campaigning organisations or charities. Among other things, Etzioni's typology serves as a reminder that substantive, or value-based rationality is not inevitably destroyed by rationalisation, since different organisational forms and associated orientations continue to be purposefully devised.

These examples of early organisation studies building on Weberian theory show that rationalisation is not inevitable, but depends (as Weber recognised in his wider analyses of the cultural constitution of economic life) on political decisions, and the social context of values and norms. Weber's bureaucratic ideal type can therefore be better understood, and is more valuable, as an expression of tendencies variably enacted in different social and economic circumstances (Clegg, 1990). The imperative command envisaged as a central feature of ideal typical bureaucracy is inevitably only partially attained, because of the inherently relational and emotional character of authority (Sennett, 1980). Obedience is not automatic, as shown by the demise of the planned economies of Eastern Europe and the Soviet Union: centralised bureaucratic control and surveillance did not prevent social movements demanding transformation (Eldridge, 1994). This is not to deny the power of rationalised organisation in public and private sectors in regulating activity and shaping political agendas, and indeed in recuperating power despite resistance, but agency and self-determination are not inevitably overwhelmed.

The nihilism of Weber's model of modern identity as subordinated to the machine-like qualities of organisation was reprised in Braverman's (1974) Marxist-informed thesis that the progressive degradation of all labour was inevitable under monopoly capitalism. Again research showed that the iron cage of capitalist organisations continued to be characterised by resistance to deskilling, intensification and direct control (for reviews of relevant work see for example Knights and Willmott, 1990; Thompson and Warhurst, 1998). In crediting management with autonomy and instrumental rationality, but not labour, Braverman's analysis simultaneously underestimated the active will of the workforce, and overestimated the rationality of managers and employers. Attempts to assert direct control over employees are less effective, and less universal, than Braverman argues: employers differentiate between sections of the workforce, giving a high degree of autonomy to those in professional, executive and technical occupations, and using direct supervision of less skilled labour (Friedman, 1977). Even in apparently deskilled jobs, people exercise considerable tacit knowledge about how to work round the process, control bottlenecks, avoid system failures and so on. Although certain types of skilled work, notably manual craft work in large firms, have been steadily eroded, new skills are created, as technologies and work organisation change, and through the expansion of services reliant on communication and problem-solving skills (Gallie et al., 1998). Organisations therefore continue to rely on the active consent and willing engagement of labour, and this is never automatic.

Similar criticisms can be made of the radical Foucauldian assertion that organisations have now perfected the practices of power, such that subjectivities are constituted by it, cannot see 'outside it' and are thus rendered 'docile'. This conclusion reflects the overprivileging of text and discourse, to the neglect of political economy, material conditions and the empirical analysis of whether modern forms of power do, or do not, produce compliant subjects. The variety of organisational practices is lost sight of, as is the difference between organisational activity and its representation in language. It has long been observed that what is *said* or written about how organisations work is not the same as what is *done* in and through organisations (Thompson, 2003).

Empirical studies of power and identity informed by Foucault's thinking have explored the subtleties of power, and deconstructed what Munro (1997) refers to as 'the disciplining powers of our current truth regime' (p. 21), but have not supported the radical model of power as eradicating agency (Lukes, 2005). Those whose empirical work has been inspired by Foucault have returned to the conundrum of how exactly compliance to an 'organisational order' is secured through the internalisation of norms and self-surveillance (see for example Flyvbjerg, 1998; McKinley and Starkey, 1998). In his work on 'governmentality', Foucault (1987) is regarded as having stepped back from his radical view to acknowledge agency and resistance (Lukes, 2005). Indeed Foucault acknowledged the value of the Enlightenment, not in its guise as doctrine or theory, but as an attitude that prioritises independent thought and critical analysis of the limits imposed on us by social arrangements (Foucault, 1984). The radical model of disciplinary and biopower is again better understood as an expression of tendencies variably enacted in different social and economic circumstances, where power and its norms are susceptible to unstable and contradictory effects.

A New Oversocialised Concept of Organisations as Determined by Cultural Identities

Among some theorists, the recognition that organisational rationalities have not, in any simple or absolute sense, 'colonised' identities has produced a different, but equally unviable, reverse form of reductionism. Instead of economic rationalisation or disciplinary power determining identities, a new cultural analysis has suggested that 'identity' determines organisation. The stimulus for such ideas was the emerging economic power of East Asian enterprise, which some writers in the 1970s and 1980s attributed predominantly to 'post-Confucian' values rooted in the identity of organisation members, and stressing familial duty, respect and obedience (Hofstede, 1980).

A re-emphasis on cultural identities and values has been taken up enthusiastically across North America and Europe, although with varying connotations and motives. In its conservative form, culture and values have been 'sold' as the cure for ailing businesses and public organisations through management consultancy texts such as Peters and Waterman's (1982) *In Search of Excellence*. This, and subsequent texts taking up the theme of cultural identity, initiated massive corporate interest in the development of distinctive *organisational* identities as a means to greater profitability (Hatch and Schultz, 2004) and in aligning employee identity with organisational goals, through 'designer work cultures' (Casey, 1996) and 'brand' identities, which would persuade employees and clients alike to 'love the organisation' (Alvesson and Willmott, 2004; Thompson and Warhurst, 1998). Renewed interest in identity is also exemplified in attempts by public and commercial organisations to map and measure 'identity' and subjective states as a potential 'value-added' resource to be drawn on by employers, governments and corporations alike (Lyon, 2001), perversely reinforcing Foucault's fears about the refinement of the technologies of governing through freedom. With a subversive postmodern twist, the 'turn to culture' has also entailed the celebration of fragmentation, ambiguity and illusion, in a politics of identity opposed to the concentration of corporate power and economic rationalisation (Beck, 1992; Fraser, 1995; Jameson, 1990). The interest in developing a distinctive, culturally informed organisational identity, and harnessing the cultural resources of employees, is considered in Chapters 3 and 7 for the light cast on the experience of work and consumption.

To suggest that organisational identities are culturally determined is to offer an equally reductionist account to that which suggests that identity and organisation are defined by economic rationalisation. Clegg's (1990) examination of the organisational arrangements of East Asian enterprise makes clear that culture is important, but not in a deterministic sense; its significance is filtered and contextualised by the institutional frameworks of political and economic rationales for action:

> In organisational terms, culture works through framing the assumptions that agents are able to operate with . . . The crucial factor is not that a manager or an organisation is Japanese rather than American or Australian. It is what being Japanese makes available in terms of normal ways of accounting for action, of calculating strategy, of constituting rationalities . . . which is important. (p. 150)

The Dialectical Relationship between Agency, Identity and Organisation

An adequate explanation of the interrelations between organisations, identities and the self needs to allow scope both for the structural power of instrumental and rationalising logics of action, which are universalising in their effects, and for personal, social and cultural meanings, which encode rules of economic action, and articulate its logics, through diverse political and cultural relations (Callon 1998; Granovetter, 1985). Simply expressed, the organisation of economic life is constituted by and embedded in social relations. Organisations are reliant on the sense-making activities of their workforces and clients, who continually renegotiate the meanings of organisational processes and goals through practical actions, but the historical development and institutionalising of the rationalising logics of economic expertise, markets and calculative exchange also continually disembed identity and action from its specific and local contexts.

Organisations are simultaneously the means of regulated, standardised exchange, and are embedded in particular, personal and social relationships, institutions of civil society and cultural norms. The distinctive feature of modern, bureaucratic, rational-legal forms of organisation, as Weber recognised, is the separation of the 'office' or organisational role from the person. This means that employment in organisations is non-inclusive, which in turn constitutes agency and identity as divisible. 'Work identity' is formally separable from other identities derived from family, community and public life: bureaucracy 'refrains from determining other aspects of people's lives that remain unrelated to organisational role performance' (Kallinikos, 2003: 606). The modern person is in this sense highly accomplished, moving between, and drawing on, differentiated and multiple sources of identity and making sufficient sense of the demands of all these as a participant in social relations. In organisations, we may both 'suspend judgement' in order to comply with the calculative requirements of work tasks, and draw on alternative sources of identity in order to achieve, or subvert, organisational goals.

Culturally distinct institutions, from labour markets to welfare regimes to households, inflect the universalising logics of organised market transactions with different meanings and expression: Japanese employment relations are different from those prevailing in Scotland, which differ again from those in India, the USA or Germany (Castells, 2000; Clegg, 1990; Kondo, 1990; Lash and Urry, 1994). Within any country, social identities, related to class, gender and ethnicity, are articulated beyond workplaces, through social movements, political parties, civil organisations and states. The economic conditions of different social groups are worked out not just at the level of the organisation, but also through alliances of corporate and state power and through civil campaigns for stronger forms of citizenship, and greater democratic control (Giddens, 1982). Within what might seem to be the same culture, subject to the same political-economic pressures, there is considerable variation in organisational ethos: food producers differ from banks, or IT firms; hospitals differ from social services and so on:

> What is additional is not simply specifiable in terms of a common set of organisational properties . . . but is dependent on the practical exigencies of agency and situated action. (Clegg, 1990: 8)

People interpret their situation and decide how to act, in the light of their circumstances. Situating actions in their social context provides a non-conspiratorial understanding of the relations between self, identities and organisations. It acts as a counter to both overly socialised conceptions of identity as purely cultural, and overly reductionist accounts of identity as determined by market economics and rationalisation. Identity cannot be read off from either 'culture', society or economic forces. The 'embedded' account of organisation recognises that there are multiple sources of identity in any situation, but the ways that these are drawn on and articulated will depend on the complex contingencies of economic, political and social variation. Agency is 'situated' in all of these; it both derives its logics of action from them and has contradictory and uncertain effects on them, as different interests are shaped and struggle for expression.

An adequate account of the interrelations of self, identity and organisations therefore entails recognising the powers of agency and its distinction from social structures, even as these continuously interact: structure constrains and conditions agency, but agency in turn elaborates and redefines structures (Archer, 2000). At an organisational level, agency is shaped by the historical trajectories and powers of complex organisations, but also makes and remakes organisations through ongoing political negotiation. The regulatory, spatial, temporal and economic properties of organisations form a structured context for action: to take an example close to home, the structures of a university have causal powers for the award of degrees, the pursuit of knowledge and education, the employment of staff and so on. Such structures embody the wider political and cultural economy of higher education and its funding regimes and performance assessments, which in turn inform the rationalities and motivations of different categories of staff and students. Through their control over cultural as well as material resources, and the powers invested in them by the rational-legal frameworks of modern states, private and public organisations are constitutive of major social strata and identities, privileging some groups and marginalising others. Positional hierarchies of class, gender and ethnicity take on meaning as actors struggle to make sense of their circumstances and exert influence over them. The biography of any particular person in an organisation is thus made under circumstances that they did not choose, but people may make very different biographies out of those circumstances. The capacity of people to reflect on and evaluate their situation means that they develop a subjective sense of who they are, the constraints and opportunities available to them, and indeed the contradictions of those.

Spontaneity and improvisation are always potentially present in interaction, even when it is routinised through constant repetition and structured by formal regulatory powers: the 'loose coupling' in contemporary liberal democratic societies between interactional practices and structures (Goffman, 1983) means that sources of identity that are formally 'external' will be drawn on and their relevance tacitly negotiated. Organisations are inherently vulnerable to 'the interaction order':

> in so far as agents of social organisations of any scale, from states to households, can be persuaded, cajoled, flattered, intimidated or otherwise influenced by effects only achievable in face to face dealings, then . . . the interaction order bluntly impinges on macroscopic entities. (Goffman, 1983: 8)

Depending on the power afforded to actors by that combination of circumstances and the human capacity for improvised action, they may (intentionally or otherwise) rewrite the rules of financial markets, as prominent speculators did in the 2000 boom and bust of dot.com shares, or challenge the rules of social segregation as black people and women did in the USA campaigns for civil rights in the 1960s.

Organisations have not colonised and undermined selfhood, agency and identity, but they have contributed to remaking these in ways that have opened up both personal freedoms and responsibilities, and anxieties about who we are and what values dominate such societies. In creating mass markets, corporations have been charged with seducing people into unnecessary spending and irresponsible consumerism, but such markets have also widened access to cultural media, the arts and travel, which continue to provide sources of opposition to the materialistic, instrumental priorities of modern societies (Lash and Urry, 1994). New social movements, concerned with ecology, feminism, peace and community, juxtapose expressive values against organisational expertise and scientific and rationalist solutions to social problems. Such an identity politics is itself distinctively modern by virtue of its reflexivity: that is, those who espouse an alternative politics are actively mobilising and redefining negatively tagged identities by creating positive associations for women, ethnic minorities, gay and lesbian sexuality, disabled groups and so on. 'Life politics' puts questions of how we live and substantive values, repressed by an emphasis on productivity and economic growth, back on the mainstream political agenda (Giddens, 1991).

Conclusion

The rise of large-scale organisations, which drive processes of differentiation, standardisation and individualisation, has been instrumental in the
development of modern understandings of the self as an agent responsible for our own lives. It is this condition, where identity is achieved
rather than ascribed, that is at the heart of current concerns with questions
about 'who we are', and it is the perpetual change inherent in the dynamics of capitalist markets that renders answers to such questions temporary
and unstable.

The role of organisations has been alternately celebrated and condemned,
and it has often been assumed that there is an inevitability about their
operations, which are seen as governed by immutable laws of calculative
economics and capitalist accounting. The sociological perspective argues
that this 'taken for granted' belief in the inevitability of rationalised organisation, and consent to its values, is socially produced. Consent to its values and priorities remains a matter of negotiation and such consent can be
withdrawn (Lukes, 2005). Organisations are the *products* of social and
political decisions, and consequently they embody the cultural value placed
on money-making and economic growth as ends in themselves. It is
important to recognise that the predominance of these values has not
eradicated alternative sources of identification, and that rationalisation
remains contested. Public service and non-profit organisations with alternative goals continue to foster public debate about substantive values and
social priorities, and the regulation of private profit through forms of public accountability continues to be a major concern, as reflected in the current interest in corporate social responsibility. Corporations themselves
are not characterised by uniformity of values, but have considerable
capacity to tolerate and reincorporate dissent (Ackroyd, 2000). There is
nothing inevitable therefore about organisational logics of efficiency or
rationalisation, and organisations do not determine identities. Personal
and social identities cannot be read off from organisational prescriptions
but are crafted through practice.

Complex organisations have however enabled the 'disembedding' of
organisations and identities from local contexts and meanings. Modern
principles of organisation initiated a formalised separation of 'office', or
occupation, from the person, stimulating greater individualisation. This
has resulted in a capacity to constitute agency and identity in more segmented and piecemeal ways, according to the demands of distinct institutional realms (Kallinikos, 2003). Identities are constituted and constrained
by the contingencies of political-economic power and welfare regimes as
well as being socially and culturally varied, and are expressive of the
resulting conflicting and contradictory demands. Agency derives its logics

of action from these circumstances and is always to some degree improvisatory. Selfhood is founded both in biographical experience and in social relations, and alternative sources of values to those of organised production and consumption continue to be guides to action.

In the next chapter I examine the structural contingencies of political-economic power, by discussing its embodiment in some of the transnational organisations that are shaping and governing the processes of globalisation. The aim here is to exemplify the kinds of human agency exercised in constituting global financial markets. I argue that the current trajectories of global finance are not inevitable, but are the products of organised social action. Once set in motion, however, the logic of deregulated financial markets also reshapes the identities of powerful corporations and their employees.

2

Globalising Economies and Organisations

The emergence of a global market is often presented as the inevitable out-come of the laws of advanced capitalism, in a new 'information economy'. Using concepts and evidence from economic sociology, I will argue instead that there is never a simple 'efficiency rule', or economic law, determining the course of events. Forms of human agency, expressed through the power of organised interest groups, influence and shape such transformations in economic life (Fligstein, 2001, 2005; Thelen, 2004). Current globalisation trends are informed by a distinct neoliberal political-economic project, which has facilitated the deregulation of financial markets and growth in world trade, as well as increasing inequalities in income and wealth. This project constitutes a significant constraining and enabling framework for action by organisational elites, who construct strategies, priorities and rationales according to its opportunity structures. The implications for the identities of organisations and the dynamics of resistance identities are considered.

The chapter begins at the macro-level of analysis and introduces the argument that transnational organisations govern the norms of global political-economic activity and control significant cultural and economic resources. There are increasing numbers of such institutions, but I focus here on the International Monetary Fund (IMF), and to a lesser extent the World Bank and the World Trade Organization (WTO), as the significant foundations of the contemporary economic order. They were set in motion by the 1944 international conference in Bretton Woods, New Hampshire, and they continue to play a central part in establishing the key parameters of global economic relations (Held et al., 1999). The chapter then moves to the meso-level, with a focus on firms and inter-firm networks, and considers the implications of globalising markets for corporate strategies and identities. These top-down perspectives are counterbalanced by a brief account of the grass roots level, where an identity politics is evident in resistance to globalisation by social movements, which are themselves increasingly adopting transnational forms of organisation.

Current economic relations emerged out of the regionalised, nationally regulated Cold War environment, prevailing in the middle part of the twentieth century, where industrial production, postcolonial hierarchies and the political stand-off between capitalist and communist states dominated monetary exchange and trade arrangements. Post-war economic expansion in the affluent North American and European economies was halted in the 1970s by recession, rising debt, consequent on steeply increasing oil prices, and competition from newly industrialising Pacific rim economies, notably Japan, South Korea, Hong Kong, Taiwan and Singapore. This stimulated a profound restructuring of capitalist activity, state intervention to deregulate financial markets, and extensive debate in advanced capitalist societies about the affordability of public provision for social welfare.

Based on an empirically substantive study of social and economic transformations in the latter part of the twentieth century, Castells (2000) concluded that we are experiencing the emergence of a new information age, characterised by 'global networks of capital, management and information, whose access to technological know-how is at the roots of productivity and competitiveness' (p. 502). Although the dynamism and power of information and communication technologies (ICTs) are fundamental to the claimed historically unique qualities of the period, it is clear that current forms of capitalism are also distinctive. For the first time in history, capitalism has not only become global in its reach, but the means of profit-making have changed. In particular, finance and foreign exchange markets have been deregulated and are linked through electronic networks of continuously updated information and knowledge:

> Capital accumulation proceeds, and its value-making is generated, increasingly, in the global financial markets enacted by information networks in the timeless space of financial flows. (Castells, 2000: 503)

Money is made, and lost, through investments in all forms of activity, including manufacturing and services, but finance capital and speculative transactions have become dominant.

The Globalist Model: the Inevitability of a Global Market?

The political ideology associated with the global reach of an information- and knowledge-based finance capitalism asserts that globalisation is an economic process with a predetermined end point of a global, self-regulating market, emanating from a rationalised, uniform capitalism based on the Anglo-American model (see for example Mulgan, 1998; Reinicke, 1998). Accounts written from a globalist perspective assert that the globalising economy renders nation states increasingly powerless; the role of the 'hollowed out' state is to create the enabling conditions for the race to attract mobile finance capital in a fiercely competitive market. Transnational corporations (TNCs) are expected to become more signifi-cant, even in social and environmental governance, taking the lead in pro-viding social welfare, as well as consumer and commercial goods. TNCs are thought of as having no national identity, but an increasingly cosmopolitan ethos, management style and organisational form. The global reach of the TNC is seen as enabling it to draw people into a common 'global village' of communications technologies, entertainment and consumer goods. Kenichi Ohmae (1995), for example, writes about the decline of nation states and the 'glue' provided instead by global brands such as Levi, Coca-Cola and Nike. Identities culturally converge in a global consumer marketplace for fast food, soft drinks, popular music, TV and fashion (Herman and McChesney, 1997; Mackay, 2000). Cultural resources themselves become commodities: commercial music, household furnishings and entertainment all mine local cultural artefacts for new ideas marketed for their 'ethnic appeal'. This global market is expected to stimulate economic growth, drawing local cul-tures, economies and politics into universalising global networks of trade, information and the flow of people, resources and knowledge.

Sociological analyses of global economic relations, however, show that the globalist scenario is an ideologically driven rationalisation of capitalist interests rather than an analysis of social relations. It is far from inevitable:

> No one except a few utopians in the business community expects the world to become a true single market . . . Such an expectation is a chimera of the corpor-ate imagination. Its role is to support the illusion of inevitability. (Gray, 1998: 64)

Economic life is characterised by continuing diversity of organisational arrangements and varieties of capitalism (Smelser and Swedberg, 2005): in other words, the same rationalising logics of financial markets continue to be articulated through different cultural frameworks and institutions, with different results.

The Traditionalist Critique of the Globalisation Perspective

The globalist ideology derives force from the assertion that we are experi-encing an unprecedented expansion in global trade, but traditionalist con-tributors to the debate have argued that this expansion is an illusion based on misinterpreting statistics on the apparent growth of foreign direct investment (FDI). These are frequently cited as key indicators of a unique globalised market: FDI was, for example, less than $50 billion per year in 1980, growing to around $750 billion in 2001 (UNCTAD, 2002). When FDI is expressed as a ratio of GDP, however, although international investment has been growing since the 1960s, current levels remain proportionately less than they were during the gold standard period (from about 1870 to the beginning of the First World War in 1913) (Hirst and Thompson, 1999; Thompson, 2000). Post-war trade liberalisation policies have produced renewed growth in FDI, but the majority of such investment continues to result from cross-border mergers and acquisitions between the economically powerful nations of the-then G7 (USA, Japan, Germany, France, UK, Italy and Canada) (Thompson, 2000).

The traditionalist perspective concludes that the financial system is far from a global free market, resulting from immutable, autonomous laws of capitalism, and is more accurately characterised as internationally and regionally interconnected, as a direct result of deliberate trade policies pursued by powerful states.

Change *and* Continuity? The Transformationalist Perspective

A third position in debates about globalisation also takes issue with globalist ideology, but suggests that the traditionalist focus on the economics of trade is too narrow to capture the real transformations taking place. It draws different conclusions from history to argue that the end of the Cold War, the increasing economic power of East Asian countries, and the speed of change facilitated by ICTs are combining to create a unique social formation, characterised by both qualitative and quantitative change (Gereffi, 2005; Held et al., 1999). The nineteenth-century flows of finance, goods and people had technological foundations in the invention of the telegraph and the development of shipping. World prices were established for many commodities and international operation of the gold standard set fixed exchange rates between currencies (Gray, 1998).

What is different now is not so much the monetary value of economic interaction, but its volatility and its extensive and intensive character: the speed and extent of interconnections and the density of information exchange, enabled by the revolution in ICTs and the internet, are without precedent (Castells, 2000; Held et al., 1999). Moreover, the gold standard era was one of predictable trading relationships hierarchically structured by colonialism. Since the 1980s, political-economic decisions have created a deregulated market in finance capital, enabling increasing and relatively autonomous movements of money around the globe via banks, institutional investors and stock exchanges. Deregulation of the financial industry enabled the development of new financial products in the 1980s and 1990s, including international bonds and equities and derivatives trading in the form of 'futures', 'options' and 'swaps', which encouraged rapid growth in speculative investments (Held et al., 1999). The scale of the resulting global market in credit has stimulated a form of privatisation of the global economy, where 95% of transactions are speculative and the daily volume of transactions is greater than the total foreign currency reserves of the world's central banks (Gray, 1998). What emerges is a global monetary system with many of the characteristics of the casino, where trading is increasingly about money, credit and debt, relatively detached from the processes of material production (Castells, 2000; Frank, 2001; Harvey, 1989; Lash and Urry, 1994; Wheen, 2004).

The rules of political-economic relations and capital accumulation have changed fundamentally. The combination of deregulated finance capital and shifting political and military power since 1945 is creating a distinctive social formation, with unpredictable consequences. Global capital mobility and financial speculation have subordinated the interests of stakeholders to those of shareholders, and governments are orienting their economic policies to the resulting flow of global capital, scientific and technological knowledge, and commodities.

Organising Deregulated Global Markets: the Role of the IMF, World Bank and WTO

Free markets, far from emerging spontaneously, have been achieved only through the organised efforts of powerful states (Frank, 2001; Gray, 1998; Wheen, 2004). The deregulated financial market is no exception and has been moulded by political ideologies and decisions, the mixed motives and self-interests of powerful nation states and corporations, and the unpredictable consequences of political conflict.

Neoliberal ideology is derived from monetarist economic theory, which is critical of regulation on the grounds that it creates inefficiencies, such as restraints on trade, increased costs and manipulation by powerful players (Hayek, 1967). The opposing argument, derived from political-economic and sociological perspectives, is that markets are always socially enacted, whatever their form, and that they work through specific cultural values embodied in institutional frameworks (Fligstein, 2005; Granovetter, 1985; Swedberg, 2005). In the case of neoliberal economics, the dominant value informing political judgements is that of formal, calculative rationality in a money economy. In the terms expressed by Weber in *Economy and Society* (1968), formal mechanisms of capital accounting, and the technical rationalities of profit and loss calculations, are treated as the true measure of value, and tend to become ends in themselves.

Since the 1980s, neoliberal political economy has gained precedence in the USA and Britain, with an ideological commitment to a laissez-faire market capitalism. Post-war expansionary economic policies, based on increasing state expenditure to stimulate demand, have been replaced with a set of prescriptions commonly known as 'the Washington Consensus', whose espoused tenets are budget discipline, deregulation of financial markets and liberalisation of trade (Stiglitz, 2002). From a sociological perspective, such prescriptions are social constructions emerging out of the complex, and partially contradictory and uncertain, interests and identities of states, which contend with labour and civil society as well as business interests (Fligstein, 2001, 2005). Attempts at global coordination of neoliberal economic measures, through organisations such as the IMF, the World Bank and the WTO, illustrate this process. The Washington Consensus could be said to emanate from the imposing modern marble and glass buildings of the IMF and World Bank, which face each other across the street in Washington DC. These organisations were set up by the Bretton Woods Conference in 1944 to finance European recovery and to prevent future global economic depression of the kind experienced in Europe and North America in the 1930s. The founding principles of the IMF were based on John Maynard Keynes' economic theory, which argued that markets needed to be managed through public spending to stimulate demand, thus avoiding massive unemployment and political instability. This was to be accomplished by providing loans, financed out of public taxes, to countries unable to spend to stimulate demand internally.

Joseph Stiglitz, Nobel prizewinner and chief economist at the World Bank until 2000, makes the claim that, instead of mitigating the economic crises of the last twenty years, the operations of the IMF and the World Bank have in fact contributed to them. In his book *Globalization and its Discontents* (2002), he argues that the substantive goals of furthering economic stability and welfare have gradually and tacitly been displaced by the more parochial interests of the finance industry, particularly Wall Street bankers. The division of labour between the World Bank and the IMF, where the IMF focused on macroeconomics (inflation and debt for example), while the World Bank dealt with structural issues (spending on new development), became blurred (Gore, 2000). The two organisations increasingly worked in concert, so that the World Bank made development loans contingent on IMF approval and conditions. In Weberian terms, the instrumental rationality of a money economy has overridden the value-rational goals of stability and social welfare.

Economic prescriptions based on neoliberalism were originally devised by a 'new school' of IMF economists, with backgrounds in investment and commercial banking, who argued that markets needed to be freed from the interventions and regulations of the state (Fligstein, 2005; Stiglitz, 2002). The measures were intended to address the problems of budget deficits and loss-making state-owned enterprises in the inflation-ridden economies of Latin American countries in the 1980s. They centred on the liberalisation of capital, finance and product markets, the creation of an independent central bank focusing solely on controlling inflation, and the privatisation of state enterprises. Loans were made conditional on the implementation of cuts in government spending, which typically resulted in cuts in education, health and social care, and raised interest rates, causing bankruptcies to rise as the costs of credit increased. History has shown, however, that the deflationary, market-oriented reforms have neither lessened poverty, nor produced sustainable economies. In the case of the 2001 Argentinian crisis, for example, deregulation in financial services resulted in a domestic banking industry dominated by large, foreign-owned banks, which were unwilling to lend to smaller, local enterprises. Lack of growth produced mounting deficits, which meant further cuts in government spending and increased taxes. Altogether this was a recipe for economic decline and social upheaval, rather than sustainable recovery. Measured in terms of per capita income and debt, Argentina's relative economic status has declined in the past twenty years: Guillen's (2001) comparative analysis of globalised markets and business groups in Argentina, Spain and South Korea shows that Argentina has moved from being the richest of the three to the poorest.

Designed as a supposedly technically rational means to an end, the prescriptions became ends in themselves, used formulaically in Eastern Europe, and African, Asian and Latin American countries. As Stiglitz makes clear, each measure may be instrumentally rational in certain contexts, but applied as a universal package, which had to be implemented more or less simultaneously in the poorest countries, they were substantively irrational, acting as the means of further instability and deprivation for most. In a process of goal displacement, the emphasis came to be on opening up new financial markets for foreign investors and then ensuring that foreign creditors were repaid, rather than on measures to support a local economic infrastructure suitable to sustaining enterprise and lessening poverty (Weisbrot et al., 2005).

As an organisation pursuing a neoliberal ideology of laissez-faire markets, the IMF, Stiglitz argues, came to believe in its own infallibility, which meant it could not admit to mistakes, or analyse the limitations or incoherence of its policies. An opaque bureaucracy evolved, characterised by rigid thinking, and enforced boundaries both internally and externally: information coming out was strictly controlled, while alternative perspectives from outside were unable to penetrate, and authority relations meant that the top of the bureaucracy remained oblivious to intelligence from lower levels about the impact of its policies. In turn, it was unable to learn from the past and adopted an arrogant and patronising stance towards its critics.

The WTO was charged with supporting global wealth creation by overcoming trade restrictions, whereby one country imposed tariffs on imported goods in order to protect the domestic economy, but protested when others did the same to them. The need for such a body, and resistance to its creation, particularly from a USA concerned about economic sovereignty, again makes clear that 'free markets' are neither 'natural elements' of activity, nor spontaneously self-organising. Nevertheless, during the era of the narrower General Agreement on Tariffs and Trade (GATT), tariffs on manufactured goods fell from around 40% to an average of 5%. A WTO was finally agreed at the 1986 Uruguay negotiations, which brought 96 countries together to discuss cuts in industrial tariffs, reductions in agricultural subsidies, intellectual property rights (IPR) and liberalisation of finance and services. Set up in 1995, it now has 146 member governments, and provides a negotiating forum for agreements, which it has formal power to enforce. Based in an unremarkable building on the outskirts of Geneva, it is a highly bureaucratic organisation staffed by experts in the technicalities of trade agreements, tariff measures, the laws of patenting and IPR.

In theory, the WTO was intended to provide a degree of shelter for developing industries in poorer countries, while facilitating their access to more affluent export markets. Stiglitz (2002) again argues that its goals have been subverted by the unequal economic power and vested interests of its members. Whereas finance ministers and heads of financial institutions represent their countries at the IMF, it is trade ministers who dominate the WTO. Their perspective is derived from the business sector, which negotiates for favourable access to foreign markets, but protectionism and subsidies at home. The more powerful countries have pursued the liberalisation of product and financial markets in developing countries, while resisting the ending of agricultural, textile and steel subsidies at home (Watkins, 2002).

The coordinated actions of the IMF and World Bank, combined with the WTO as a bargaining forum, have enabled the USA, alongside the EU and Japan, to exercise enormous power over the trajectories of globalisation, with many of the benefits accruing to the wealthy in powerful states (Atkinson, 2002; Deacon et al., 1997; Gordon, 2002; Kolko, 1999; Townsend, 2002). The acceptance of the legitimacy of a world trade organisation does however enable less powerful states to build alliances to contest dominant economic rationales. In Cancun in 2003, a coalition of developing countries, the G21, led by China, India and Brazil, opposed the EU and US agenda for further financial deregulation, and demanded cuts in farm subsidies in the EU, Japan and the US, and better access to western markets for their own goods, but negotiations failed to reach agreement. Subsequent negotiations in Hong Kong in 2005 ended acrimoniously, and further talks in 2006 failed to gain agreement from EU members and the US to reductions in their use of agricultural and industrial subsidies.

Global Finance and the Strategies and Identities of Corporations

Deregulated financial markets, mobile capital and speculative trading have proved powerful drivers of change in the structuring of large-scale corporations. One way of characterising the logic of the process is in terms of a Weberian account of rationalisation, this time taking place at the level of entire industries and supply chains (Ritzer, 1996; Smart, 1999). The deregulated financial market is an expression of instrumental, or formal, rationality in a money economy, which promises a single means of orienting enterprises. The apparent technical precision of capital accounting, through continuously updated electronic databases, enables formal calculations of profit and loss, which are treated as a universal standard of value. At an organisational level, the result is a sharper managerial focus on financial performance, which entails a shift from controlling and planning inputs, to an emphasis on output and performance indicators; for companies quoted on the stock exchange, this is expressed as share price. Corporations have generally adopted two strategies, identified by Gereffi (2005) and Thompson (2003). The first relies on moves to extract higher returns on investment from the entire supply chain through active management of assets and suppliers. In the case of producers, this includes forms of disaggregation, as well as mergers and acquisitions. In the case of buyers, such as retailers, this is also likely to entail intensive cost-cutting rationalisation through the supply chain. The second relies on the application of a related logic to labour, through attempts to extract better value either by deskilling and reducing labour costs, or by drawing more on the capacity of labour for creativity, commitment and higher productivity. The implications for labour are addressed in Chapters 4–8. Here the emphasis is on the former strategies, concerned with the rationalisation of corporate structures.

Whereas vertically integrated production arrangements provided profitable economies of scale for US corporations in the mid-twentieth century (Aglietta, 1980), recent attempts to gain competitive advantage have used more diverse forms of organisation. While ownership and control of corporations has become more concentrated through mergers and acquisitions, innovations in supply chain relationships and forms of outsourcing have also increased (Gereffi, 2005; Thompson and Warhurst, 1998). Castells (2000) argues that a new paradigm is in evidence, creating a network, rather than a hierarchical, identity for the ideal-typical organisation. The metaphor of the dynamically configured, expandable network is one that in theory enables continuous adaptation to uncertain financial markets. While some analysts have focused on the emergence of globally coordinated *production* networks, driven by large firms such as car manufacturers, others have studied the development of *commodity* chains, driven by global buyers such as food and clothing retailers (Gereffi, 2001, 2005). In both cases, producers in different countries, with different ownership forms, have constructed supply networks, serviced by transport, insurance, telecommunications and other business logistic enterprises, to coordinate goods and services from computer production to the retail supply of cut flowers (Hughes, 2004).

This has furthered a global division of labour, where companies outsource 'non-core' manufacturing and service activities to local and remote providers, depending on labour costs and skills and the investment incentives provided by states (UNCTAD, 2002). In China, for example, government tax incentives have encouraged FDI, and the increasingly skilled labour is paid between five and twenty times less than in the UK. Much of the outsourcing of manufacturing has gone to the Pearl River delta of Guangdong province, to the extent that China dominates global production in many goods in daily use. We may not have heard of Zhuji, but most of us have probably worn its socks, since it produces 8 billion pairs each year. In nearby Taiwan, a single shoe factory has 279 production lines and is estimated to make one in every seven shoes. It has supply contracts with Dr Martens, Reebok, Adidas, Nike, Timberland, Puma and Hush Puppy (*Guardian*, 19.11.03).

UNCTAD (2002) estimates that some 65,000 large-scale corporations are working with 850,000 foreign affiliates, indicating a proliferation of supply chain linkages, entailing franchising, licensing, subcontracting and long-term, trust-based relationships. Joint ventures and strategic alliances between competitors, with links to research laboratories and science parks, are also increasingly used to share the costs of new ventures and R&D (Held et al., 1999). Small and medium-sized enterprises (SMEs) gain access to global networks of production, through subcontracting relationships with larger businesses, and Castells (2000) argues that SMEs have a degree of market autonomy, despite their small size, by virtue of continuing change in niche markets. Larger firms, however, are able to use such links to enhance their own flexibility by passing costs and risks onto subcontractors.

The logic of this process has entailed the hollowing out of many well-known corporations: direct manufacturing is reduced or contracted out completely, and the core business becomes that of coordinating the expertise, the R&D, the materials, the labour and the marketing and distribution of finished products, on the 'make nothing, command everything principle' (Molotch, 2003). Such corporations function as 'asset-light' entities at the centre of evolving networks of suppliers. They typically invest heavily in branding and corporate identity-building, and the resulting brand identity carries a significant stock market value. (This phenomenon is discussed in the next chapter.)

Forms of vertical integration have re-emerged in the newly industrialising economies, with firms offering to manage the uncertainties and risks of supply chains on behalf of well-known 'big brand' companies. Flextronics (www.flextronics.com), for example, is an electronics manufacturer, with a head office in Singapore, a presence in 29 countries and 45,000 employees in the Asia Pacific region (China, Japan, Taiwan, India, Thailand, Malaysia and Singapore) alone. It markets itself as offering a 'total supply chain solution' for companies needing product design, manufacturing, distribution and maintenance and repair services.

Unlike the globalists' predictions, the articulation of global production and commodity networks has not been synonymous with the emergence of genuinely transnational forms of organisation, devoid of local culture and institutional specificity. There are a few prominent exceptions, notably the politically and culturally influential media, leisure and entertainment corporation News International, which is closely identified with its Australian head, Rupert Murdoch, whose family controls 30% of stock. Among other assets, the firm controls 132 newspapers, Twentieth Century Fox, 22 US TV stations, and cable and satellite networks around the world. It operates in nine different media on six continents, making most of its money in the US, and has further plans for global expansion (Herman and McChesney, 1997). Its communications infrastructure enables it to bypass nation states, creating the potential for enormous power over access to information and the shaping of public opinions (Mackay, 2000).

It remains more common for global production and commodity chains to be combined with nationally based corporate ownership and centralised control of assets, board membership, management styles, organisation strategy, ethos and R&D (Held et al., 1999; Held, 2000; Thompson, 2000; UNCTAD, 2002). The Honda Motor Corporation of Japan is, for example, one of the largest international companies. It has an extensive production network, linking subsidiaries in Europe with manufacturing in Japan, the USA and Brazil, but two-thirds of its assets and sales are located in Japan (Thompson, 2000). It is also evident that rationalised financial markets do not create homogeneity of globalised organisations. Recent research tracing the impact of globalised markets on the evolution of organisations producing goods and services, from finance to railroads to computer technologies, repeatedly finds diversity and idiosyncrasy in organisations and practices, which remain rooted in specific cultures and institutions (Donaghy and Clarke, 2003; Ferner et al., 2004; Guillen, 2001; Harzing and Sorge, 2003). West's (2002) comparison of US and Japanese-owned semiconductor businesses found that the organisational strategies of leading firms grew increasingly differentiated, rather than more homogeneous, as markets globalised.

The continuity of multinational, as opposed to genuinely transnational, forms of organisation also indicates that the architecture of the network does not equate to the end of hierarchical control of business activity. Instead, the capacity of ICTs to routinise data collection and reporting has enabled more adaptable forms of centralisation of strategic control, focused on a national corporate headquarters, with operations decentralised across the globe (Harrison, 1994; Thompson and Warhurst, 1998). Mergers and acquisitions continue to form the largest proportion of FDI, with larger firms gaining competitive advantage as much by shaping and organising markets, as by production arrangements (Held et al., 1999):

> global markets . . . increasingly involve competition between entire production systems, orchestrated by corporations, rather than between individual factories or firms. (UNCTAD, 2002: 16)

The global span of corporations, their control of world trade (Watkins, 2002) and the concentration of corporate power, particularly in the USA (Hutton, 2002), in the last quarter of the twentieth century, is unprecedented. Vertical integration and hierarchy as principles of control are far from dead, but are being reconfigured as corporations seek to maximise profits in the context of deregulated and speculative markets.

The Irrationalities of Rationalised Economies: Corporate Identity and the Enron Case

Weber's study of *Economy and Society* (1968 edition) gives an account of the conditions where instrumental rationality in a money economy is likely to produce forms of substantive irrationality. One of those conditions concerns the circumstances where an organisation is subject to the calculations of outside interests, in the form of financial institutions and predators, who acquire share capital in another organisation for the purposes of short-term speculative profit. Deregulation of the finance industry created an opportunity structure that enabled this particular form of irrationality to thrive in the 1990s, as corporations focused on financial trading and share prices as the key source of profit.

The irrationalities are amply illustrated by the Enron case, which was a pioneer of energy privatisation and deregulation. Enron was created in the mid-1980s from the merger of two medium-sized firms operating natural gas pipelines, transporting or selling 17.5% of US gas, in a government-regulated, profitable bureaucracy. Privatisation enabled it to acquire utility companies around the world, and deregulation enabled it to use its assets to centre activities on speculative trading, with little public scrutiny. The 1999 development of Enron Online turned the business into the biggest e-commerce operation in the world and enabled Enron to become effectively a derivatives trader. As a key financial 'product' of the 1990s, derivatives gain their value from betting on the likely future prices of assets. Its rapid expansion and transformation into a speculative trader was applauded by governments and the media: it was rated by *Fortune* magazine for five years, from 1996 on, as a star performer in the new economy and received awards from the *Financial Times* in 2000 for its successful investment decisions.

By November 2001, Enron had filed for bankruptcy, declaring that it had overstated its earnings by $600 million. Behind the image of successful money-making was an illusion created by clever branding, promotional activity, creative finance and the quasi-religious rhetoric of its chairman and chief executive (Bryce, 2002; Wheen, 2004). In March 2003, the court-appointed examiner published a 2000-page report detailing the measures taken by Enron to conceal its true financial position. Numerous banks were implicated and its own bankers, Merrill Lynch, were charged with criminal conspiracy. Enron executives have been charged with fraud and money laundering and have been investigated for, among other things, bribery, tax evasion and the declaration of non-existent earnings. A small number of senior managers made personal fortunes from its activities; its collapse deprived most of its employees not only of incomes, but also their investments in pensions; it destroyed its auditors Arthur Andersen; and revealed the enormous, and inappropriate, influence it had over governments in America, Europe and Asia.

Enron's growth contributed to the 'irrational exuberance' of financial markets in the 1990s (Shiller, 2000). Governments, investment brokers and merchant bankers alike were caught up in the belief that a new paradigm had been created by virtue of financial instruments such as hedge funds, which supposedly protected share values from the speculative instability of deregulated markets. Writers such as Charles Leadbetter, in his book *Living on Thin Air*, produced accounts of the new economy where corporate identity in the form of branding, marketing and promotional activity *was* the new means of wealth creation. Enron's Chairman Kenneth Lay,

Chief Executive Jeff Skilling and Finance Director Andrew Fastow proved adept at building the image of fast-paced, seductive dot.com capitalism that the markets celebrated. The trading culture of risk-taking, high living and deal-making, combined with the recruitment of people who believed themselves to be 'the best and the brightest', encouraged a belief in the invincibility of the organisation. Grey (2003) suggests that similar processes were at work in the auditors, Andersen, which had reorganised to create a highly individualised, aggressive competition for career success, and a similar culture of self-aggrandisement. This meant that criticism of the accounting practices of a client such as Enron was tantamount to career suicide: 'In both organisations, a heady brew of macho competitiveness and insecurity bred a form of precarious heroism' (p. 574), undermining the traditional requirement of professional distance between auditor and client, and allowing everyone to assume that new norms of wealth creation were operating.

Enron is not in any way a special case, but is symptomatic of the enabling logic of financial deregulation, online trading and the resultant singular focus on share value to the exclusion of all else. To make a profit, Enron trading relied on betting on whether the price of a commodity would go up or down at some fixed future point. Such was the scale of its business, however, that

> it didn't just own the casino. On any given deal Enron could be the house, the dealer, the odds-maker and the guy across the table you're trying to beat in diesel-fuel futures, gas futures, or the California electricity market. (Bryce, 2002: 3)

The cash flow required to sustain such activities was reliant on increasing levels of debt. In order to increase borrowing without affecting its credit rating, financial 'special purpose entities' were invented to keep much of the debt off the balance sheet (Deakin and Konzelmann, 2003). Innovation in forms of speculative finance and deal-making enabled firms such as Enron to manipulate earnings, inflate profits and hide from investors the levels of risk entailed. This allowed corrupt, self-interested corporate conduct to appear entirely legitimate to many, and sufficiently normative to prevent middle-level managers from challenging what they observed (Werther, 2003).

The high-profile bankruptcy of Enron was not an isolated event, further emphasising that its trajectory was not about the personalities of senior executives, but stemmed from the prevailing opportunity structures, which resulted in the elevation of money-making into an end in itself. Five of the ten largest ever US bankruptcies occurred in 2001–02: Enron, WorldCom, Global Crossing, United Airlines and Conseco. These contributed to the downturn in financial markets and further eroded public trust in the honesty and integrity of capitalist businesses. When trust in the trading networks of Enron and similar corporations began to evaporate, the virtual edifice of corporate identities disintegrated, and the literal 'hollowness' of corporate performance, measured only in terms of earnings per share, became evident. Public trust in the integrity and honesty of businesses has, not surprisingly, declined: 57% of Americans do not trust corporate executives and financial advisers, and in Britain the ratio of those saying they trust corporations has switched from two to one in favour to two to one against in the past thirty years (Zuboff and Maxim, 2003).

The scandals and financial losses surrounding large-scale corporations at the start of the twenty-first century have further challenged the globalists' claim that economic activity will necessarily converge around the Anglo-American model of laissez-faire market capitalism (Marens, 2003). Large corporations, far from governing where states fail, have shown themselves susceptible to the corruption and fraud that legal-rational forms of governance were intended to eliminate. The inadequacies of existing forms of corporate accountability were forcibly demonstrated, stimulating renewed demands for greater accountability to 'stakeholders' and social responsibility by corporations, but it has been suggested that reforms currently in place in the USA are cosmetic rather than substantive (Conrad, 2003).

The Politics of Identity and its Connection to Globalised Financial Markets

Deregulated global financial markets and restructured corporations have not produced personal and social identities that are simplistically 'aligned' with corporate goals. On the contrary, economic globalisation has been met with new forms of resistance identities, evident in the social movement organisations centred on feminism, anti-war campaigns and environmentalism (Castells, 1997). Since its meeting in Seattle in 1999, the WTO has been a focus of global protest by non-governmental organisations (NGOs) and social movement organisations, arguing for trade justice and action on poverty. Networked organisations, through campaigns such as Make Poverty History, have articulated the connections between global laissez-faire economic policies and social troubles.

The universal benefits claimed by states and corporations for neoliberal economic policies have proved elusive. Economists at the Washington DC Centre for Economic Performance have used the IMF and the World Bank's own data on economic growth and social welfare to show that neoliberal economic measures in use since 1980 have been associated with slower growth and reduced social progress in the majority of low- and middle-income countries, when compared to the previous twenty years (Weisbrot et al., 2005). The average rise in incomes of 2.4% annually over the past forty years disguises widening inequality within and between regions and locales: the income gap between the richest and the poorest fifth has increased from a ratio of thirty to one in the 1970s to a ratio of seventy-four to one now. Fifty-four countries are poorer than they were ten years ago and almost half the world's population live on less than $2 a day, with the numbers increasing by close to 100 million over the past decade (UN, 2005). Such evidence, together with the increasingly evident social breakdown resulting from rapid, enforced deregulation in poorer countries and the impact of economic instability on the wealthier states, has produced global protest by social movement organisations, NGOs and the UN.

Such resistance identities challenge the instrumental rationality of a money economy, by counterposing its values against those of social democracy and welfare, equality, justice and sustainability. These are social goals that are themselves globally articulated, and would require global forms of civil and democratic institutions capable of regulating the enormous power of corporations. Some incremental changes have taken place, such as those embodied in the fair trade movement, and in voluntary governance schemes to improve employment standards or cut pollution (Gereffi, 2005). Policy in the World Bank, IMF and WTO has also been affected (Jenkins, R., 2003; World Development Movement, 2002). Notably, poverty has been put back on the agenda, with political agreement to work for the UN goals of halving the number of people living in poverty, cutting infant mortality by two-thirds and ensuring that all children receive basic education. Progress remains slow however (see for example reports at www.guardian.co.uk/wto).

Conclusion

The term 'globalisation' is often treated as synonymous with the inevitability of global deregulated markets. This loses sight of the combined role of social and political agency and indeterminacy, assuming instead that the apparent 'laws of advanced capitalism' operate independently of social action. The organisation of economic life is not subject to immutable laws, unless we act to make it so. A focus on the organisational sphere in the operation of markets makes it evident that apparently abstract laws of capital and economic exchange are brought about through institutions of economic governance, which have complex and sometimes contradictory and shifting motivations.

Laissez-faire market capitalism is not a 'natural outcome' of modern-isation, but is the dominant political project of particular organised inter-ests of advanced capitalist states and associated financial and trade bodies. As in any period of history, such projects are contested, dynamic and indeterminate. Large-scale private and public organisations provide the infrastructure that mediates globalisation; their complexity and their com-peting and cross-cutting agendas alone produce a high level of uncer-tainty. The logic of global trade and investment through the US dollar underwrites the hegemonic power of the USA and the Anglo-American laissez-faire model of capitalism, but it would be a mistake to assume that its tenets represent the end point in the evolution of capitalism. The last third of the twentieth century produced considerable realignment in the distribution of capital, technology and manufacturing capacity towards the Asia Pacific region. The growing economic power of China and India in particular indicates that there is nothing fixed or universal about forms of capitalism (Atkinson, 2002; Gray, 1998; Watkins, 2002).

In short, globalisation is not a one-dimensional, linear process with a fixed content or pre-given end. It comprises multifaceted, interconnected processes, shaped by economic, political and civil organisations, which are not driven by a single agenda or common goals. The unintended con-sequences of deregulated markets include corporate scandals, corruption and fraud, as illustrated here by the example of Enron. Such unintended consequences and growing evidence of the highly unequal distribution of wealth from deregulated finance provide a source of challenge to the neoliberal 'globalist' agenda. Organised resistance identities contest the rationalising logics of monetarist economics, through the articulation of substantive goals of social cohesion, toleration, well-being and justice. Global media, rapid flows of information and mass travel enable not just power elites but also ordinary people to gain an understanding of the interconnections between global economic activities and local quality of life, selfhood and social identities. Such reflexivity is not necessarily prod-uctive of cohesive relationships or cultural homogeneity, but entails conflicting, varied and unpredictable agendas for the future. The uneven trajectories of global trade, and negotiations over the application of sup-posedly universal principles of deregulated product and commodity markets, show that the directions of global social relations are indetermi-nate and subject to the discretion and agency of the different institutions at local, regional and global levels. Its trajectories depend critically on the struggle between governments, corporations and civil society organisations.

The next chapter focuses these arguments on the organisational relations of consumption, and examines in more depth the organisation of consumer identities, and the phenomenon of organisational identity-making through marketing, advertising and branding.

3

Organisations, Identities and Consumption

In late 2005, the Apple Corporation saw its share price fall, despite a significant rise in sales and profits. The market was disappointed because actual
sales were lower than those forecast. It is not surprising then that organisations pay close attention to the minutiae of consumer behaviour, constructing differentiated consumer identities and investing heavily in branding,
marketing and advertising designed to maximise the loyalty of customers
and employees and to persuade people to buy more of their products.

Much of the debate about the social implications of contemporary consumerism has been characterised by polarised views. Advocates defend the
rights of a sovereign consumer to improved choice, at less cost, or discuss
the identity-creating pleasures of consumption practices, while critics see the
manipulation of people into false needs and their entrapment in a web of debt
and excess. Where consumption has been related to production, a Marxist-
informed economic reductionism has often prevailed, such that the capitalist
processes of rationalisation and commodification are seen as dominating
cultural values and social practices of consumption, leaving little scope for
agency. Although cultural studies has treated consumption as identity-
creating, with writers such as de Certeau (1984) and Du Gay (1996) emphasising the inventiveness of consumption practices and the scope for
agency, other postmodern writers have treated such agency as illusory, on
the grounds that it is captive to a false idea of freedom as constituted by
the obligation to make choices defined by a market in both products and
self-identities (Rose, 1999).

The complexity and variety of actual consumption practices are often neglected in the arguments about the pros and cons of consumerism (Fine and
Leopold, 1993). People's responses to organisational constructions of consumer identities are far from passive: organisational meanings are variously
adapted to, resisted, creatively consumed and challenged, through personal
biography and the counter-organisation of collective consumer identities.
Consumption has long been politicised through consumer movements

(Cohen, 2003), exemplified in the contemporary articulation of anti-consumerist identities, through campaigns for fair trade and environmental sustainability. In the mainstream, in relation to the links between food and health, for example, there is concern about the marketing of processed foods to children, food safety and animal welfare (Lang, 2003). Neoliberal ideologies claim that people have the right and the responsibility to choose for themselves, according to publicly available information, but the concentration of ownership in the food supply chain, large advertising and marketing budgets, and industry lobbying of governments pose challenges to informed choice (Blythman, 2004; Lawrence, 2004; Lawrence and Evans, 2004; Schlosser, 2001).

This chapter situates current patterns of consumption in a social and economic context, through a brief examination of the organisational development of mass markets, and consideration of the phenomena of organisational branding and identity. Current social science debate on 'organisational identity' has become preoccupied with the question of whether it is meaningful to attribute a social capacity for 'identity' to an objectified organisation, and with exploring organisational attempts to define such an identity (for an overview of the field see readings in Hatch and Schultz, 2004). Little attention is paid in this literature to the context of neoliberal economics and globalising markets, which create the *need* for an organisational identity. When many goods and services themselves are generic and functionally interchangeable, corporations have to invest increasing effort in developing the symbolic meanings of their products in order to distinguish them from the competition. Share values thus fluctuate according to estimates of 'brand values', and advertising and promotional campaigns promote the brand, while seeking to persuade potential buyers that *their* brand will deliver personal style and distinction, or entertainment and escapism and so on. Through organisational marketing, modernity's ideal of an individualised self-identity is connected to choices between branded and symbolically loaded artefacts and services – clothes, cars, furniture, travel, entertainment and so on – in multiple and differentiated markets. The complexity of consumption practices and their politicisation, however, means that any single theory of an essential 'consumer identity' is unlikely to be adequate. Instead there is a need to highlight the interdependence of the processes of production and consumption in the context of globalising markets and the forms of agency exercised by organised, 'collective consumers'. These are issues that have been relatively neglected by the conventional agendas of both sociology and organisational studies.

Organisations and the Development of Consumer Markets

Although there is division of opinion about when and where modern consumerism emerged, it is generally agreed that there is nothing natural or inevitable about the existence of mass consumer markets. Forms of consumption organised by the relations of monetary exchange, for anything from tinned beans to new houses, entail the application of the same principles of rationalisation and commodification as applied to the sphere of production (Ritzer, 1996). By the eighteenth century, the processes of industrialisation had established economies of scale that resulted in production capacity outstripping sales. Customers, as well as products, needed to be manufactured, and entrepreneurs and the new breed of managers had to invent some organisational solutions to a new set of problems concerned with selling, rather than making, commodities. Those solutions relied in large part on creating the kinds of social and economic infrastructures that would enable, and encourage, growing numbers of people to conceive of themselves as consumers with needs for an increasing variety of products.

The growth of consumerism was, for example, responsible for changes in the organisation and expression of pleasure, extending it beyond traditional forms of hedonism connected with activities such as eating and drinking, to encompass imagination and the emotions. Campbell (1989) argues that Weber gave insufficient emphasis to the emergence of the Romantic ethic during the late eighteenth and early nineteenth centuries, which facilitated a more open, pleasure-oriented attitude to consumption. The Romantic ethic linked the hope for salvation to a form of goodness evidenced through feelings of sympathy with others and the aesthetic appreciation of beauty, demonstrated through displays of good taste. The ability to imagine pleasure as potentially connected to an infinite range of objects and activities is an important adjunct to modern consumerism because it enables producers to move beyond informing people about the availability of commodities and their functions, to suggesting through images that products represent the fulfilment of desires, social distinction, escapism and so on.

The entrepreneurialism of manufacturers such as Josiah Wedgewood contributed to a shift in social attitudes and expectations away from restraint towards extravagance and display (Uglow, 2002). An emerging middle class was ready to emulate the lifestyles of the rich, and Wedgewood not only developed the means of making affordable copies of expensive porcelain, but also recognised the importance of promoting desire for the goods, by displaying them in showcases and illustrated mail order catalogues (McKendrick et al., 1982). By the early part of the twentieth century, assembly line production had radically reduced the cost of cars manufactured at the Ford Highland Park car works in Michigan. Henry Ford understood that the car had to become a mass market good rather than a luxury item, and that it was the task of the Ford company to engineer such a market. Car purchase was promoted initially through savings schemes, but in 1919 General Motors saw the potential market growth, and profit, to be made from a new type of financial product – consumer credit (Peterson, 1987).

The invention of expertise in marketing, product design, advertising and promotion contributed to structuring critical dimensions of the experience of being modern. Ford, General Motors and so on have long since ceased to be simply car manufacturers. They have also turned their attention, through marketing, advertising and promotional expertise, to organising social dependence on the ownership of a car, and to creating the perception that car ownership symbolises status, independence, mobility and opportunity. Similarly, the travel industry has been instrumental in the creation of the idea that, in consuming travel and tourism, we are both entertained and made into better people. Lash and Urry (1994) suggest that Thomas Cook and Son, which emerged in the nineteenth century, was at least as important in the generation of organised capitalism as Ford. In the 1840s, Thomas Cook saw the potential in rail travel for a new form of freedom, providing recreational, educative and social benefits to a significant proportion of the population, but interest in, and desire for, travel had to be popularised. Cook recognised the value of imagination and played on the popularity of nostalgic and literary images of place, such as those of Scotland promoted through the novels and poems of Sir Walter Scott.

To make this idea of a market a reality, and to convince people of the safety and reliability of rail travel, also required an organisational infrastructure that could coordinate journeys and produce unified, affordable tickets. Timetabling, journey planning, ticketing and reservation systems made travel an affordable, rationalised, predictable activity, but the firm also deliberately cultivated the role of the expert, promoting claims to specialist knowledge to encourage people to trust in the service being sold. During the early twentieth century, a new expertise of marketing and advertising facilitated the development of a shared understanding among people of new experiences and ways of being. In a study of the history of American advertising, Ewen (1976) suggests that early campaigns were powerful because they presented people with apparent solutions to the anxieties created by urbanisation, the breaking down of traditional ways of life and familiar patterns of work and community. This contributed to the move away from a selfhood framed by ethical values and stable character towards a self-identity defined by presentation, style and personality. Previously unstructured experiences and unidentified 'needs' thus became packaged into new ways of understanding personal and social identity.

It was not, however, until after the Second World War that governments made consumerism a key instrument of economic policy, linking it with rising prosperity and economic growth. In post-war America, Cohen (2003) argues, a new consensus emerged, associating private consumption with the public interest. A focus on 'the consumer' was presented as socially progressive, distracting attention from more contentious political demands for the redistribution of wealth. In the context of Cold War politics, the concept of a 'consumers' republic' provided the United States with a means of claiming superiority over the Soviet Union, and products such as Coca-Cola became icons of American values (Miller, 1987). The 'vices' of hedonism and self-indulgence became virtues, and the values of thrift and self-denial were displaced by an aspirational, self-improving orientation to life (Featherstone, 1991). A tolerance of debt also had to be engineered, such that buying on credit was not only socially acceptable, but made virtually an obligation of modern citizenship (Ritzer, 1995). Marketing sought to persuade people to develop a critical attitude to their life and self-image, and depicted products as the means to a better, more fulfilled life (Fjellman, 1992). The expansion of markets was not simply a matter of selling more goods, but of associating consumerist values and attitudes with self-esteem and a sense of citizenship.

Why Globalising Markets Create the Need for Organisational Identities

Consumerism was a key facet of the expansion and profitability of North American and European corporations until the 1970s, when rising oil prices exacerbated pre-existing problems of inflation. At the same time, the industrialising economies of the Pacific rim began to compete on price and quality of goods in western markets (Castells, 2000). As discussed in the previous chapter, the development of neoliberal economic instruments, led by the USA under Ronald Reagan's Republican presidency and emulated by the Conservative government of Margaret Thatcher in the UK, resulted in the deregulation of financial markets, the dismantling of regulations designed to limit the concentration of ownership of businesses and the weakening of employment protections. The new 'rules' of capital accumulation incentivised measures to increase the productivity of both capital and labour, through globalised markets and production arrangements. In the USA, deregulation fuelled mergers and acquisitions 'and the creation of huge conglomerates that are more or less beyond the law' (Ritzer, 2002: 8).

Such capitalist expansion through the logic of globalising markets, in an informational economy, drives the preoccupations of organisations with image, identity and brand values (Clegg, 2005; Gabriel, 2005; Ritzer, 2002). Consumer markets are increasingly characterised by competition between producers of essentially generic, interchangeable artefacts and services, making sales dependent on the ability to convince potential buyers of the distinctive qualities of *this* credit card, holiday, mobile phone or car, rather than any other. The growth of services and informational products also places emphasis on intangible, often fleeting impressions of organisations: a number of global airlines, for example, have invested heavily in a 'brand identity' designed to distinguish their service from others. Standardised products, with similar features and price, lack particularistic relations to time and place, and potential purchasers generally lack awareness of their producers or the conditions of their production. Ritzer (2003, 2004) argues that this constitutes the marketing of 'nothing' rather than 'something', as many products and services lose their locally specific and substantive meanings. The firms selling such products have to inject them with symbolic meanings and qualities, making investment in advertising, marketing and branding a crucial feature of corporate strategy. Increasing numbers of very similar products have diverted advertising from a concern with product functions and features (Lury, 1996) into a means of infusing aesthetics into consumption, educating 'tastes' and introducing the idea of 'lifestyling' (Jameson, 1991).

In many cases the material qualities of a product are displaced by ideas about it, with carefully created imagery and symbolism becoming central to the construction of perceived need, and symbols are in turn consumed to satisfy such needs. The result, Clegg (2005) argues, is a pronounced shift in the direction of a 'positional economy' of goods whose value depends less on their material functionality than on a social estimate of their desirability as a sign of personal distinction. How else can people be persuaded to replace last year's clothing, car, mobile phone or kitchen, when 'last year's model' is perfectly functional? The same argument applies to the relative anonymity of the vast organisations created through mergers and acquisitions. Employees may have little or no direct knowledge of senior management and directors, yet their dealings with customers may be critical to profitability. Constructed organisational identities are designed to convey positive messages and favourable impressions to employees through promotional videos, websites, 'founder stories' and corporate entertainment (Alvesson, 2004).

The need to show perpetually increasing profits, in financial markets prioritising short-term return on investments, drives producers to increase the pace of product development and obsolescence, through stylistic and aesthetic, as well as technical changes, and through associating their 'new range' of goods with new, desirable forms of distinction. Exclusivity is elusive and ephemeral in an era of mass affordable and generic goods, drawing corporations into continual, reflexive engagement with target groups, in the attempt to second-guess and define what products will constitute 'cool', must-have artefacts for successive groups of young people (Klein, 2000). Although the social dynamic of 'cool' is indeterminate and not controlled directly by business, producers have proved adept at associating stylistic changes with subcultural identities and at appealing to personal concerns with identity formation and self-improvement, by extending the range of experiential products such as therapies, dietary regimes and health and beauty treatments.

Mass media commentary on organisation performance adds to the reflexivity of the process, requiring a favourable image to be projected, monitored and adapted to subtle changes in public mood (Gioia et al., 2004). The expansion and density of professionalised communications mean that organisations compete for the attention of targeted groups. Some advertisers have deployed increasingly extreme, negative images in their attempts to engage the attention of an overstimulated audience. Benetton's use of disturbing images of catastrophes, Falk (1997) suggests, is part of a struggle to gain the attention of an instrumental knowing audience, routinely exposed to a plethora of images. The effect of attempts to design organisational identity is not easily predictable, however, because such symbolic products are amenable to contest and challenge. Royal Dutch Shell, one of the largest corporations, experienced this in 1995, when its government-approved decision to scrap the Brent Spar oil platform in the North Sea produced enormous public criticism and a boycott by organisations and consumers. Shell eventually agreed to tow the platform to a Norwegian fjord in preparation for scrapping it on land instead, but, as Cheney and Christensen (2004) point out, the environmental issues of safe disposal were actually pushed aside by the politics of identity. In this case, the environmentalist organisation Greenpeace occupied the platform and 'won' the PR campaign, even though some of the claims against Shell were later found to be erroneous. For Shell, an already controversial company, identity is a volatile political issue, and public criticism and investigations into its activities in Nigeria and Turkey are continuing. Control over organisational identity is therefore likely to be perceived as essential, but remains elusive, as commercial and non-profit organisations use the same tools and techniques, emulate each other's strategies and contest each other's claims (Alvesson, 2004).

Branding and Organisational Identity

In 1988, the Philip Morris corporation bought Kraft for something like six times its paper asset value, because of the perceived power of its name. Klein (2000) identifies this moment with the start of a trend that gave brand names themselves a monetary value, resulting in rising investments in organisational identity. Spending on advertising in the USA rose from around $50 billion dollars a year in the early 1980s to close to $150 billion by 2005 (World Advertising Research Centre, www.warc.com). Even during the recession of the early 1990s, large corporations such as Nike and Disney sharply increased their advertising budgets. In Britain, despite a 3% decline due to recession in 2001, statistics (based on constant prices) showed spending rose from £9.54 billion in 1992 to £17.46 billion in 2004 (Advertising Association, www.adassoc.org.uk).

In some cases, brand identity has become the 'real' (and profitable) product of many prominent companies, from Microsoft to Nike, while manufacturing is coordinated through global supply networks (Molotch, 2003). Used to delineate a distinct corporate culture and identity, brands have also been systematically built into an association with lifestyle, a sense of community and a set of values. The Nike corporation, for example, presents itself as 'enhancing people's lives through sports and fitness', while Polaroid is no longer a camera but a 'social lubricant' (cited in Klein, 2000: 23). Brands have been a key vehicle for the idea that when people buy clothes or cars or food they are choosing a lifestyle, which encompasses attitudes, values and a way of seeing the world (Lury, 2004). The 'brand image' may be attached to virtually anything. The Virgin Group, for example, has used the perceived reputational qualities of the name to sell airline and rail travel as well as cola and financial services. Tesco supermarket supplies mobile phone services, credit cards, savings, legal services and e-diets as well as groceries. In recognition of the centrality of organisational image, business information firm Forbes (www.forbes.com) now publishes surveys of brand values and their rise and fall. For 2005, for instance, a commissioned survey by the marketing consultancy Vivaldi Partners cites Apple as 'the fastest growing brand in the world', adding 38% to its value in four years, while the value of the Coca-Cola brand was calculated to have declined by 4% annually. Annual sales of the latter's carbonated drinks, however, far outstrip those of Apple products, and other 'brand companies' listed. Nevertheless, awareness of the connection between such publicity and volatile share values no doubt caused celebrations in Apple corporate offices and anxiety among Coca-Cola executives.

An Industry in Organisational Identity?

The phenomena of organisational identity, branding and image-making are presented as deeply concerned with the rediscovery of vision, imagination and creativity in rationalised organisations, but in practice they rely on extending rationalised control into the sphere of identity construction: 'In a rationalised age, visions can no longer be left to authentic individual insight, but are designed, created and crafted by vision consultants' (Clegg, 2005: 536), and used as instruments of business strategy. The marketing orientation has become ubiquitous in every sector, stimulating an industry in the 'organisational professions' of marketing, PR and advertising (Cheney and Christensen, 2004; Sulkunen et al., 1997). Although these originated as distinct specialisms, divisions between them have become blurred, as every organisation strives to represent itself as customer-focused and consumer-friendly (Cheney and Christensen, 2004; Du Gay and Salaman, 1992). From a sociological perspective, such specialists operate in an organisational 'knowledge market', where they compete alongside others to cultivate, control and sell technical solutions to the problems of managing uncertainty in global markets (Armstrong, 1984, 1986).

Advertising agencies have positioned themselves as critical to the nurturing of the brand, promising to identify the values of a corporation and package these as the means of articulating identity and 'vision' (Cheney and Christensen, 2004; Olins, 1989, 1995). Saatchi and Saatchi, for example, which has 138 offices in 82 countries and annual turnover of $7 billion, describes itself as aiming 'to be revered as the hothouse for world changing, creative ideas that transform our clients' businesses, brands and reputations' (www.saatchi.com). There is surprisingly little dispassionate research, however, either about the structures and processes of the advertising industry, or the range of attitudes towards branding and advertising. The industry conducts its own evaluative research, oriented to commercial concerns, but issues of commercial confidentiality hamper academic researchers. Such research as exists conveys an impression of an unstable industry, locked into continuous restructuring, driven by periodic recessions and re-evaluations by clients of the need for their services. Mattelart's (1991) study of the international operations of the industry, for example, finds considerable internal conflict and doubt about the effectiveness of advertising campaigns. It is difficult to show any correlation between sales and the amount spent on advertising and there is open acknowledgement that advertising is more about corporate image promotion and brand awareness than it is about directly measurable increases in sales (Nava, 1997). The fragmented nature of the industry, and the use of small production companies staffed by would-be film makers, means that the creative side of advertising production is increasingly indistinguishable from other cultural media (Nava, 1997). This results in an industry prioritising peer recognition of its products, rather than consumer manipulation. Attempts to evaluate the effect of advertising on sales have largely been displaced by a concern with competing for high-profile industry prizes awarded for originality, style, humour and so on. Hence the values are those of the creative industries more generally, and the ambition of producers may be more directly concerned with winning accolades for a clever ad than with increasing sales.

Marketing originated as an organisational response to post-war consumer rights campaigns, in order to create a strategic perspective on consumption, and to engage consumers in a debate about the merits of negatively perceived industries such as tobacco, oil and chemicals (Kotler, 1991). As one of the organisational professions, marketing tries to claim exclusive knowledge about the control of market uncertainties (Webb and Cleary, 1994), but in practice it has been only partially successful in such an interprofessional competition for monopoly over tools and techniques, and its status has fluctuated according to the state of the economy (Edwards, 2000). In the attempt to gain authority, marketing specialists have created increasingly diverse techniques for researching and predicting consumer behaviour, by adapting quantitative and qualitative social science methods to business purposes.

The combined impact of market liberalisation and ICTs has enabled a huge expansion of such data-gathering. Techniques of market segmentation have moved into the realms of the psychographic and psychoanalytic (Bowlby, 1993) as a means of devising lifestyle categories such as the 'Avant Guardians', the 'Self Admirers' and the 'Pontificators' (Edwards, 2000), or the 'Affluent Greys' vs the 'Council Estate Residents' (Lang, 2004).

As the boundaries between public and private sectors have become less distinct, and the potential for data storage increases, so commercial organisations have gained access to government data on citizens, as well as developing detailed records of people's consumption patterns, creating a market in personal information itself (Lace, 2005). Governments use the same techniques to assess the subjective states of the population and to respond to these through promotional activities. Personal data is increasingly used not just to document, categorise and monitor people's activities, but also to simulate and predict future behaviour (Lyon, 2001). Such market research has often been regarded as the arch tool of manipulation, but there is evidence that insiders regard such techniques as ritualistic legitimation of marketing (Lury and Warde, 1997; Nava, 1997). Bodies such as the UK National Consumer Council are also active in facilitating public debate about issues of privacy, confidentiality and civil liberties (Lace, 2005).

Whether or not people are persuaded by marketing and promotional activities to identify with particular brands is an open question. There is a sense, however, in which organisational concerns with identity and image may become ends in themselves, in a familiar process of goal displacement. The industry of advertising, PR and marketing needs to make itself indispensable, facilitating a self-referential world of symbols, where designed and packaged organisational identities float free of substantive points of reference to the particular organisation, in a process akin to Baudrillard's concept of the simulacrum, a copy that has no reference to an original.

Organisational Identity and 'Lifestyling'

The intensive investment in branding, organisational identity and 'vision' has been geared to an image of the consumer as an active, enterprising and knowing subject, whose attention and imagination have to be repeatedly sought after and engaged:

> consumers are constituted as autonomous, self-regulating and self-actualising individual actors seeking to . . . optimise the worth of their existence to themselves by assembling a lifestyle, or lifestyles, through personalised acts of choice in the marketplace. (Du Gay, 1996: 77)

Earlier ideas of a homogeneous 'consumer' oriented to quantity and cost have been displaced by ideas about how to maximise profits through the techniques of segmentation and differentiation. Prior to the 1980s, much of the competition for consumer markets centred on sales volume and price through mass marketing. The 1970s' combination of inflation, aggressive price competition and concentration of ownership, on the one hand, with more knowing and more affluent groups of consumers, on the other, stimulated greater differentiation in strategy.

Pressure to improve profitability through increased productivity of capital and labour required innovations in the practices of distributing, promoting and selling goods and services, and much of this centred on the marketing concept of 'lifestyling' (Du Gay, 1996). Lifestyling combined design and visual imagery with techniques of market segmentation that do not map straightforwardly onto social class categories, although competition for lucrative sales to high income groups was a powerful motivator. 'Value for money' or 'budget' products have themselves been reconstructed as 'branded lifestyle options', rather than as a social status related to income, and as one of numerous alternative choices open to consumers, in the construction of a 'pick and mix' identity. Marketing tools have been used to differentiate target populations according to socioeconomic status, demographic categories and psychological/attitudinal factors. Electronic point of sale (EPOS) technology allows retailers to monitor and analyse consumer choices minutely, in order to customise stocking and reordering, in turn lowering costs. The resulting 'market segments' have then been used as the basis for mapping 'desire' (Du Gay, 1996), contributing to the development of a positional economy of goods.

The construction of lifestyle categories enabled the marketing of aspirational identities, targeting imagination and aiming to capture people's desire, not for artefacts per se, but to be a distinctive sort of person, able to capitalise on market opportunities. Expressive appeals to personal relations, fantasy, escapism, pleasure and hedonism are combined with calculative appeals to investment in self-improvement and a 'marketable self-identity'. Tourism, for example, has restructured its products to respond to the falling demand for cheap, standardised package deals. Market segmentation is exemplified first in responses to the eco-critique of mass tourism as degrading the very sights and experiences it was designed to sell. This has resulted in more customised travel and 'green tourism', marketed as ecologically sensitive to the impacts of mass travel, and often as educational and self-fulfilling. At the other extreme, products are designed to play to the idea that consumers are perpetually looking for novelty or spectacle, by providing an array of niche products for different incomes, cultural categories and tastes (Lash and Urry, 1994).

Emphasis on the symbolic value of goods has resulted in significant investment in the staging and visual design of settings of consumption, in the attempt to capture the imagination of a public sceptical of the discourses and strategies of marketing. Visual spectacle and themed entertainment, Ritzer (1999) argues, aim to 're-enchant consumption' through new means, which he describes as 'cathedrals', oriented to novelty and pleasure, in a risk-free, stylised and predictable escape from routine life. Efforts to differentiate products from those of competitors have paradoxically led to declining differentiation between commercial spheres: shopping centres increasingly emulate leisure and theme parks, by including cinemas, food courts, bowling alleys, performers and amusement rides; theme parks have shopping malls, theatres, cinemas and restaurants; restaurants emulate theme parks, and so on.

The ubiquity of 'shopping', advertising and consumer credit leads Ritzer (1999) to argue that, in the USA at least, the new means of consumption make it increasingly difficult to avoid the risks of hyperconsumption. The Walt Disney Corporation theme parks, for example, are precisely simulated settings of a 'perfected' reality, such that distinctions between the real and the simulated are blurred and simulations themselves become the 'real' (Baudrillard, 1983; Fjellman, 1992). In Disney World Florida, water parks provide sanitised beaches and waves timed to arrive at perfectly regular intervals. The 500-acre Animal Kingdom has an elaborate artificial tree (paradoxically called the Tree of Life) at its centre, decorated with hundreds of animal shapes, and disguising a multimedia theatre. A simulated Africa, cleaned up and without a hint of famine or civil wars, includes a safari ride without the threat of real gunmen, and with animals controlled by hidden barriers. Interaction with 'cast member' employees is scripted, and visual spectacle acts as a commercial for Disney clothing, toys, memorabilia and food. In themed restaurants, such as the Hard Rock Café chain, Planet Hollywood or the Rainforest Café, standardised food is secondary to the visual consumption of cultural references to film, sport, fashion, music or nature (Beardsworth and Bryman, 1999). This transformation to a symbolic and image-oriented consumption produces artefacts designed to act as indicators of a ready-made 'individuality', in a market economy where the meanings of goods are interpreted by a target population who are likely to be well versed in the cultural references represented by the products on offer (Amin and Thrift, 2004; Du Gay, 1996).

Agency, Identity and Consumerism

Classical Accounts of Consumers as Manipulated by Capital

Organisational claims that business serves the interests of a sovereign consumer have been treated with scepticism in most social analysis. Classical Marxist theory regards consumer identity as determined by the logic of capital accumulation, which relies on the creation of endless 'wants and needs' and denies the possibility of 'authentic satisfaction'. Identity is reduced to the assembly of a restyled, but essentially superficial, fragile personality, in a market where business manipulates passive consumers. This reductionist analysis is rooted in an emphasis on work, not consumption, as the key to an authentic selfhood. In capitalist societies, work loses its inherent meanings and consumption becomes the domain of an illusory, and ultimately unsatisfactory, recompense for the lack of self-fulfilment in work. Advertising and marketing reduce personal meanings to those dictated by corporations', and the consumer is fully controlled by the dictates of capital (Lee, 1993).

Critical theory, espoused by the Frankfurt School writers, Adorno, Horkheimer and Marcuse, takes Marxist argument one step further to assert that mass consumption and popular culture are the key means of ideological control in capitalist societies. Consumers become 'cultural dopes', suffering 'false consciousness'. More recent social comment from writers such as Christopher Lasch (1980) attributes a degree of agency to consumers, but treats this as overwhelmed by the power of markets, resulting in a defensive retreat into a search for a coherent sense of self and personal meaning. According to Lasch (1980), this produces a narcissistic pathology, entailing a preoccupation with personal identity and the perpetual search for short-term gratifications through consumerism, which promises to solve personal insecurity with false promises that we can buy 'attractiveness and popularity'. Fjellman (1992) attributes the same state of mind to the growing crisis of legitimation of politics and state in the USA, resulting in retreat into a world of privatised self-interest, manifested through increasing consumption and debt.

Postmodern Accounts of Consumerism: Precarious Agency

Postmodern writing has criticised a view of consumers as totally determined by capital, and created more scope for the analysis of consumption practices as active and meaningful. Nevertheless, equally reductionist conclusions have sometimes been drawn. Baudrillard (1981), for example, criticised the Marxist assertion that preindustrial production-for-use had a straightforward, rational relationship to human needs. He argues that all needs and goods have some socially defined meanings, and inevitably have a 'sign value' concerned with their desirability. In consumer capitalism, however, Baudrillard asserts, sign values dominate use values. The media are particularly implicated in the increasing stylisation of consumption, via advertising and promotional techniques, and the production of a condition of hyper- or simulated reality, which cannot be 'known' outside its own terms. The result is a self-limiting preoccupation with 'lifestyle options', materialistic values and the fetish of an inherently unattainable, perfected self. Bauman (1987) is equally pessimistic in concluding that culture is subordinated to the logic of the market, which relies on stimulating dissatisfaction, and anxieties about self-worth, as a means of inducing people to more consumption, in a futile attempt to satisfy desires. Gergen's (1991) analysis of *The Saturated Self* suggests that the obligation to choose produces a crisis of the self, resulting from access to more information than we can assimilate, our awareness of multiple perspectives on every issue, and the multiplication of relationships through work and consumption:

> We realise increasingly that who and what we are is not so much the result of our 'personal essence' (real feelings, deep beliefs and the like), but of how we are constructed in various social groups. (p. 170)

Rose (1999) uses Foucault's theory of power as operating through the constitution of subjectivity in an account of modern selfhood as the obligation to choose, which acts as 'a message to ourselves and others as to the sort of person we are, each [choice] casts a glow back, illuminating the self of he or she who consumes' (Rose, 1999: 227). Calculative principles of efficiency and profitability have stimulated the invention of an expertise of subjectivity, concerned with measuring and categorising the dimensions of consumer attitudes and opinions and developing the capacities of the self. Widespread knowledge of the narratives and expertise of subjectivity in turn encourages people to apply such techniques to themselves, in the pursuit of self-improvement or self-actualisation. It is not so much that there is a conspiracy of the powerful to subjugate identity to the market, but that people

> have become attached to the project of freedom . . . [and] come to live it in terms of identity and to search for the means to enhance that autonomy through the application of expertise. (Rose, 1999: 258)

While Rose's analysis offers a subtler account of the workings of power through forms of subjectivity, his conclusion leaves no standpoint from which to criticise it. As argued in Chapter 1, this neglects the irreducible capacity of people to evaluate their situation and make changes in it.

Cultural studies have taken the interpretative and meaning-making activities of consumption seriously in developing a critique of the Marxist model of mass consumption as manipulation. Writers such as Paul Willis (1978) and Dick Hebdige (1981) argued that the meanings written into goods by their producers are not slavishly adhered to in practices of consumption. The uses of goods for self-defined ends, and the articulation of their meanings through social relations, create significant indeterminacy in practice, which is one of the reasons why producers invest heavily in market research. Willis (1978), for instance, showed the reappropriation of particular commodities by male working-class youths in the construction of oppositional identities. Subsequent work has argued that consumer culture provides a knowing critique of conventional depictions of manipulative consumerism: 'Increasingly consumers are represented as "cultural experts" or *bricoleurs*, assembling their own distinctive combinations of style – lifestyles – from a wealth of available signifiers' (Du Gay, 1996: 87). Cultural analyses of advertising have demonstrated that adverts themselves are actively consumed, but there is significant indeterminacy about their meanings and uses (Nava, 1992; O'Donohoe, 1997). The 'market in identity' becomes a resource rather than a cost, as people use the plethora of internet and media information to construct their own expertise of consumption, which may remain limited and fragmented, but provides the basis for deconstructing producers' claims.

Practices of Consuming: the Knowing, Expressive Consumer

Much of sociology and anthropology, with their concern for the ethnography of practice, have also treated consumption as an expressive sphere of social relations. Rather than being trapped by the calculative sphere of production, the emphasis is on the active, meaningful qualities of consumption and the indeterminacy of transactions. The ethnography of shopping, carried out by Miller (1998), for instance, concludes that most routine shopping is an expression of love and obligation to family and kin, and is enacted in acute awareness of the needs and desires of others. Shopping as an expression of individualised 'identity projects' was mainly limited to young people without domestic responsibilities. In relation to the experience of themed and simulated worlds, writers such as Beardsworth and Bryman (1999), Fjellman (1992) and Ritzer (1999) argue that people are not gullible, but knowing participants, looking for 'enchantment' in the novelty, spectacle and technical accomplishment of simulated realities. Consumers know that the production of illusion relies on highly rationalised foundations, standardised, controlled and predictable routines, safety and hygiene measures and so on. Indeed there are independent guides designed to work out the most efficient ways of consuming theme park entertainments, although whether this is work or pleasure seems debatable! It is this awareness, and people's admiration of the technical achievement exemplified, that encourages people to buy such 'leisure experience'. To engage in commodified pleasure requires in itself a knowing engagement in popular culture and its iconography. Its success relies on detailed knowledge of the symbolic world drawn into being through the artefacts: without familiarity through film and other media with the techniques used to create a sense of other periods and cultures, the consumer cannot recognise the theme or interact imaginatively with it.

A further strand of the sociology of consumption has shown the active use of products as markers of social differentiation. The classic study was that by Veblen (1899) of the conspicuous consumption activities of the leisured class, where particular objects were used to express superior social status. The most detailed and extensive studies of cultural and social expressions of class differentiation, however, stem from the work of Bourdieu (1984), who analysed the expression of taste in cultural goods, such as art, clothing and food, and their use as a key means of differentiation of social classes in France. Amin and Thrift (2003) also give an account of the growth of USA sales in sport utility vehicles (SUVs) to affluent consumers, noting their use as markers of power, status and security, despite their social and environmental costs. People with low incomes may be excluded from such 'luxury goods markets', but are nevertheless depicted as adapting niche market products to the articulation of positive social identities.

Critique – the Indivisibility of Production and Consumption

Ethnographies of consumption have demonstrated the expressive, dynamic and active qualities of practice, and the considerable sophistication and complexity of consumption as an expression of social relations. Such studies have also shown that consumer culture cannot be 'read off' from the meanings of products defined by capital, and that consumption has not been reduced to the pursuit of an individualised, stylised and fragmented self.

It would however be a mistake to conclude from this that the social relations of consumption are not framed by the logics of profit and consumerist values. The shopper who chooses one product or another in a supermarket as an expression of love for family is making choices devised by the rationalised structures and concentrated retail power of the food industry. The pleasures of consumption and the play of hybrid identities are creative within the bounds set by the relations of production. The weakness of a focus on the micro-practices of consumption is that consumption is treated as a self-sufficient entity, which is disconnected from the forces of production. A fuller account of personal and social identities, and agency, needs to recognise the indivisibility of production and consumption, and the continuous interaction between the activities of working and consuming in the formation of identity. Organisations do not determine consumers, nor are they dominated by a sovereign consumer, but there is a 'dialectic' between producing and consuming (de Certeau, 1984). Consumption is situated in global capitalist production arrangements where the pattern of mergers and acquisitions has resulted in enormously powerful corporations with huge marketing and advertising budgets, but such producers also have to respond to the uncertainty generated by the improvisatory, flexible and creative tactics deployed by consumers.

Contemporary sociological theory has treated the expansiveness and indeterminacy of markets, and the experienced contradictions between the demands of consuming and producing, as creating the potential for a more critical awareness of consumerism (Giddens, 1991; Lash and Urry, 1994). Giddens analyses the risks of a self-identity framed by market choices, but nevertheless argues that the growth imperatives of markets continually challenge established ways of doing things and open up new spheres of choice and new ways of living. The organised expansion of the public realm, through the rights of civil society, employment and citizenship, has widened access to knowledge about society and enabled more control over relationships and social identity: women's increased economic independence, for example, has been associated with the greater freedom in relation to marriage, child-bearing and living arrangements. Reference points and sources of meaning outside consumerism therefore provide alternative ways of responding to consumer capitalism and its values.

Recognition of the interdependence of production arrangements and consumption practices indicates that consumption is never solely a realm of free choice, governed by its own expressive logics. As a 'mode of domination' (Bauman, 1987) suggests, the market is seductive, rather than repressive: through the appeal of promotional and advertising activities, we are drawn in knowingly. Hence the expertise of marketing, advertising and promotion is instrumental in constituting the forms of social relations that it aims to manage (Lury and Warde, 1997), and it constitutes identity in terms of lifestyles, brand images and market segments. Such expertise shapes public policy and service provision, as well as private markets, and is part of the general knowledge about society, contributing to a conception of ourselves as 'consumers'. Access to the financial and cultural capitals that enables a degree of reflexivity about consumption is however manifestly unequal. Commercial organisations, for example, can effectively exclude people from participation: 6% of the population have no bank account, excluding them from many routine transactions, and around 8 million people, or 21% of adults, in the UK are unable to obtain credit from mainstream lenders (Jones, 2003). Those who lack the economic and cultural means to participate in consumption are likely to experience control through repression in the form of state regulatory authority, benefits, policing and surveillance (Bauman, 1987).

Although the deterministic argument that identity is entirely captured by consumerism can be rejected, the network of market institutions and its predominant values of materialism and individualism frame who we are. A familiarity with promotional culture results in habitual sensitivity to the symbolic meaning of goods, and the messages they are meant to convey about our attitudes and values. Critics such as Fjellman have argued that there is something more insidious about 'consumer enchantment' than simple diversion and entertainment. The more explicitly ideological aspects of theme parks, for example, celebrate the achievements of science, technology and private enterprise, but these are sanitised accounts of culture and history, with difference, conflict, power and inequality smoothed out. This increasingly provides, Fjellman argues, the basis on which many American citizens understand themselves and their pasts: 'our relations with other people and with ourselves are mediated increasingly by the commodity form' (1992: 401). History becomes little more than pastiche and undemanding entertainment, heroic stories of individualism and the unified advance of technical solutions to human problems. The seductions practised by global corporations, such as Disney, shape values and beliefs: '[we are taught that] it is good, reasonable, just and natural that the means necessary for life are available only through the market' (p. 402).

Even deliberate reductions in consumption and the purchase of 'utility' goods, in opposition to the idea that products convey status and style messages, are interpreted within a market frame as 'identity statements'. The UK Future Foundation (www.futurefoundation.net), a market research organisation, recently produced a report on a new 'identity category', which it labelled the 'New Puritans'. This group is identified primarily in terms of attitudes and values, and is meant to denote a social trend towards active opposition to the conspicuous consumption and hedonism of the 1980s and 1990s, and support for notions of a collective good and the regulation of markets. Oppositional identities, whether derived from youth subcultures or other social movements, are susceptible to being co-opted by the creativity of markets, and provide sources of new market ideas: the New Puritans will no doubt be targeted with a branded range of 'must-have' goods before too long.

Collective Consumer Identities and the Politics of Resistance

The critics of an overly deterministic model of consumption, although creating space for agency, have continued to treat consumers as individuals, thus contributing to a normative account of social relations as dominated by market values. This neglects the significant development of the organised, 'collective consumer', which provides a countervailing power to that of the market. The politicisation of consumption dates back at least to the 1950s, expressed through organisations such as the US National Consumers League, cooperative movements in Europe and the Consumers Association in the UK (Cohen, 2003).

Aspirational values and ideologies of self-improvement do not have a determined content, and have encouraged more critical, vocal and organised consumer identities. Awareness of the limits of an ideology of self-improvement and of inequality in access to resources for self-fulfilment have also stimulated a politics of identity concerned with gender, ethnicity, sexuality and the ethics of consumerism itself (Lury, 1996). The 1950s–60s' southern US civil rights movement was, for example, triggered by organised consumers: the racial segregation of lunch counters and buses rather than the absence of the right to vote stimulated social change (Nava, 2002).

Such consumer movements have become increasingly organised in their own right, to press for better standards of goods and services, to challenge the inflated promises made by producers, and to limit corrupt and anti-competitive practices. The internet and online access to user networks are facilitating significant change in product innovation and markets, with users actively developing, designing and modifying products (www.computer-weekly.com; von Hippel, 2005). A rival to Microsoft's market domination of computer operating systems, for example, is the collaboratively developed Linux system, reliant on the unpaid input of users and programmers. Independent consumer organisations scrutinise the claims made for commercial products and services, and public demands have ensured that government standards bodies monitor and regulate trading standards and advertising claims. In the USA, activists such as Ralph Nader have led prominent consumer rights campaigns, and in Britain consumer organisations such as the Consumers Association have represented consumer interests. Sheila McKechnie, during her time as director of the Consumers Association, attributed the rise of organised consumers to neoliberal economic policies and government retreat from regulation, leaving people to make complex decisions over key areas such as education, personal finance and health, with limited independent advice on offer.

Resistance to the power of corporations is exemplified by global debate about the balance between democratic control in societies and corporate interests (Bakan, 2004; Vidal, 1999). Coalitions of large and small organisations scrutinise producers' claims about the benefits of branded products, and investigate the conditions of production and labour exploitation. Large corporations, for example, have frequently moved production to developing countries such as Mauritius, Indonesia, Morocco and China, where labour costs are low and employment rights absent or limited (Klein, 2000). In the case of the fast-food chain McDonalds, activists have demonstrated through the courts the exploitative labour practices and the damage to health and environment caused by the corporation (Vidal, 1997), and adverse publicity generated by films such as Morgan Spurlock's account of the health costs of consuming nothing but the 'super size' option resulted in changes to product ranges.

Non-profit social movement organisations, such as Corporate Watch, Greenpeace and Friends of the Earth, have used the techniques of rationalised organisation to facilitate forms of resistance. They have deployed the same promotional and persuasive techniques developed by the corporations to raise awareness of corporate scandals, or the environmental and social costs of deregulated global markets. Although corporations have large budgets dedicated to responding to criticism and defending their actions, they are not immune to the influence of the collective consumer. Recent campaigns by coalitions of voluntary sector organisations, for example, have responded to well-financed tobacco industry strategy with health evidence and information, to create momentum for tobacco control policy and legislation (see for example ASH Scotland, 2005). The World Economic Forum, which represents powerful business and political interests, has itself produced survey findings showing that public trust in large corporations is lower than ever (Juniper, 2003), and indicating that people are far from captured by the promotional messages of business. European public perceptions of brands marketed by global corporations, such as Coca-Cola, are of uncaring organisations, selling poor quality products (Beckett, 2000). The pressure for social and environmental responsibility is evident in corporate attempts by businesses such as BT, Shell and BP to respond to the loss of public confidence in them. Consumers have, through collective organisation, reappropriated the expertise of 'consumer choice', and at least discovered an alternative form of market power.

Conclusion

This chapter has highlighted the interdependence of processes of production and consumption in the context of globalising markets, and the forms of agency exercised by organised, collective consumers. In the latter part of the twentieth century, deregulated finance and more competitive markets have resulted in significant organisational restructuring, centring on the marketing techniques of branding, advertising and PR, and the segmentation of markets through the construction of lifestyle categories. Through the invention of specialist knowledge bases in marketing, sales and advertising, organisations have played a key role in redefining modern identity in terms of the image of an active, sceptical consumer, choosing individualised means to continuous improvement and self-fulfilment.

While choice is framed by the market context, with its organised corporate interests, it is structurally impossible to evade the identity of the consumer. The market relies on the generation of unlimited needs and desires for goods, which by definition must not satisfy wants, making people susceptible to unstable assessments of self-worth and stimulating dissatisfaction. There is disagreement about the consequences of this process. More pessimistic analyses present a vision of a passive self, determined by the power of large corporations that seduces us into a preoccupation with superficial choices about shopping and entertainment, while disabling a capacity for engagement in politically informed choices about the kinds of societies we live in. More optimistic analyses suggest that selfhood and social interaction in consumer capitalism retain their indeterminate and improvisatory character. The chapter has demonstrated that the organisations of consumer capitalism are more internally fluid and contradictory than Marxist-informed accounts of consumerism recognise, resulting in less tightly structured and determined connections between corporate enterprise and self-identities than pessimistic analyses suggest. Deterministic theories are based on an inadequate account of human agency on the one hand, and neglect the essential indeterminacy of markets and of social relations on the other. The result is a misreading of the connections between the macro-level of markets and the micro-level of everyday life and its meanings (Giddens, 1991). Rather than passively or uncritically accepting the identity of consumer, people reflect on consumerism and make sense of it in the light of their own circumstances and biographies.

Voluntarism, although not overridden by corporate power, is not sufficient as a counter to the force of organised consumer markets. The provision of effective control of corporate activity is unlikely to emerge out of individualised choices. An emphasis on the collective consumer, and the political activism of collective consumer organisations, does however provide a basis for democratic renewal. These issues are taken up in the next chapter through examination of the implications of markets, consumer identity and notions of choice for public service reorganisation, work and citizenship.

4

Public Service Reorganisation, Work and Consumer Citizenship

The public domain in a democratic society is a powerful source of social and personal identities beyond those of the market, consumption and work. In spite of enduring inequalities of social and economic status, social citizenship in the shape of a socialised provision of welfare has contributed significantly to a sense of social identity and moral worth. The public domain does not refer simply to public services or forms of social protection, but to an array of educational, health and welfare provisions that have been central to post-war democratic states and social identities. Such services are central to the claims of welfare states that they can provide security and social justice as the foundations of citizenship and human rights. Organisational analyses of public services in such societies have been relatively limited compared with the attention given to macro-level institutional theories about the origins of welfare states, the causes of variation in the range and types of social provision, and their general impact on economic growth and employment (see Huber and Stephens (2005) for a review of this literature).

This chapter instead makes the connections between macro-level developments in global financial markets and middle-range theoretical issues concerned with organisational change and the identities of public servants and citizens, which are critical to the quality of life in advanced capitalist societies. The context for change is set by examining, first, the assumptions about identity that informed social democratic principles of universal welfare, and, second, the dual crises of welfare states stemming from neoliberal political economy on the one hand and a politics of identity on the other. I argue that the organisational solutions to such crises have centred on forms of managerialism. I give an account of the application of managerial principles and discuss their implications for the changing identity of public servants. Lastly, I return to a consideration of the risks of the emerging identity of the consumer-citizen for the public domain.

The foundations for modern welfare states began to take shape in demo-cratic countries from the early part of the twentieth century. It was however the post-war compromise between organised capital, labour and nation states that gave political momentum to the development of more compre-hensive public services, as a means of ameliorating poverty and destitu-tion, improving education, health and well-being, and stabilising social order. Esping-Anderson's (1990) concept of welfare state regimes is useful in distinguishing the broad differences in political values and orientations that characterised such modern states. He distinguished between three categories: social democratic, corporatist or Christian democratic, and lib-eral or residual types. Social democratic regimes aim for universal welfare benefits and service provisions based on citizenship (or sometimes simply residence), with services provided by a public sector workforce. Christian democratic regimes aim for universalism in coverage, but tend to provide differential rights based on employment categories, combined with pub-licly financed but privately provided services. Liberal regimes provide 'safety net' or residual coverage only, with rights to benefits decided by means-testing, and there is usually limited provision of publicly funded services. Each of these regimes reflects a different political ideology of the interrelations between state, market and public domain. Social democratic models emphasise the values of social solidarity and equality, and treat the state as a means of regulating markets to achieve these goals. Christian democratic regimes tend to hold more conservative values about the social order, and while aiming to ameliorate poverty, they place greater emphasis on the family and civil society as foundational. Liberal regimes assert that individuals are responsible for their own well-being in a free market enabled by a state that provides only essential services.

In practice, these categories are less clear-cut: different countries vary the emphasis and levels of service provision, depending on the influence of different political parties, the role of organised labour and the power of capital (Huber and Stephens, 2005); the distinctions operate along a con-tinuum rather than as discrete categories. Nevertheless, they serve as a heuristic device to identify different approaches to welfare and to charac-terise contemporary political projects to reconfigure public services. After the Second World War, the UK and the Nordic countries tended towards social democratic models of public services, while Continental European countries were closer to the corporatist or Christian democratic regimes and the USA was closer to the liberal model. While the Nordic countries have typically provided the most socially progressive welfare, the USA has been the most extreme example of an advanced industrial democracy with a liberal welfare regime (Huber and Stephens, 2005).

While these types of regimes have evolved over time, I focus here on the main debate since the 1970s, which has centred on the promotion of a neoliberal model of welfare as a means of stimulating higher rates of economic growth and employment. In those countries with relatively generous welfare provision, the consensus that disciplined markets in the interests of a public domain of citizenship, equity and service faltered in the face of 1970s' budget deficits, limited economic growth and high unemployment. Questions of the costs of public services, relative to calculations of their economic efficiency, have been dominant, affecting all types of welfare state (see for example *The Economist*, June 2003, 'Is the much loved welfare state still affordable?'). Advocates of liberal welfare regimes have argued that public spending is an unproductive cost, rather than a collective investment in a social good. Markets are deemed to be more efficient than states in the provision of services and in creating individual choice (Marquand, 2004). Squaring the circle of public service quality, choice and accountability, on the one hand, with market principles and private sector involvement, on the other, is however proving to be a difficult proposition. Democratic governments, spanning countries from Australia to France and Sweden, have, to differing degrees, reoriented their welfare provisions towards the liberal model, but not without public opposition. The most dramatic systemic shifts have taken place in the UK and New Zealand, where conservative governments of the 1980s were instrumental in introducing wide-ranging market-oriented reforms across public services, driving forward a neoliberal regime of welfare (Huber and Stephens, 2005). The focus here is on the UK as a source of insights into changes in public service organisation, and work and citizenship identities.

The Context: Social Democratic Welfare States and Social Identity

The social democratic ideal of universal welfare, free at the point of use, was founded on a particular substantive rationality informed by values of social reciprocity, mutual dependence and generalised exchange: each person contributing according to their ability and receiving, not just according to need, but as a matter of right (Hoggett, 2000). This ideal of *social* exchange is distinct from principles of rationalised, calculative *economic* exchange, where precise (typically monetary) terms are specified for every transaction (Fox, 1974). Principles of social exchange emphasise a social identity based on integrative, solidaristic social values and assertions of mutual interdependence. Social reciprocity may entail a generalised expectation of future benefit, but on the whole, participation is seen as an end in itself and is oriented to a sense of a common good (Gouldner, 1960).

In the UK, the social solidarity engendered by the experiences of the Second World War consolidated support for a welfare state whose foundations had been laid in the early 1900s. Institutionalising a social identity based on the ideals of reciprocity and mutual dependence was however problematic. In particular, social democratic values proved unable to resist the pressures of modern capitalism to prioritise economic growth and the supply of disciplined labour. The result was a compromise between the calculative principles of economic exchange and ideals of social reciprocity and collective responsibility (Hoggett, 2000). Although welfare was significantly decommodified (Esping-Anderson, 1990), its effects were never as redistributive as might have been anticipated, and the use of means-tested eligibility for many benefits meant that claimants tended to be stigmatised as 'scroungers' (Deakin, 1993; Morris, 1994), rather than construed as citizens entitled to support.

In practice, welfare states also institutionalised particular assumptions about the identity of the ideal typical individual, and these reflected prevailing social divisions rather than enlightenment ideals of equality. Feminist scholarship has drawn attention to the ways that welfare provisions were founded and costed on the assumption of a sexual division of labour, which gave men breadwinner status and prioritised their full employment, while allocating to women the primary role of wife, mother and carer. This made women effectively 'lesser citizens', dependent on men for many welfare benefits (Hoggett, 2000; Sainsbury, 1999; Williams, 1989). Studies of the experiences of first generation Asian and African-Caribbean migrants to the UK have also concluded that post-war welfare citizenship was marked by neocolonial, paternalistic attitudes towards 'race' and immigration, which resulted in inequalities in access to services and benefits (Clarke and Newman, 1997).

The Dual Crises of Welfare States: Neoliberalism and Identity Politics

Since the 1980s, the governance and organisation of welfare has become a highly contested terrain, with divided political and academic positions on its underlying values, what forms it should take, how universal its benefits should be and how it should be paid for. There are two distinct sources of this crisis, which pull in opposite directions. In the context of global financial markets, much of the institutional debate centres on a neoliberal economic rationality, which treats welfare as a social cost. The second strand of the crisis stems from a politics of identity itself, which contests the calculative rationality of neoliberalism, and argues for a more thorough-going, participative welfare society, building on ideals of social solidarity and interdependence. These demands are expressed through politically and socially diverse civil and social movement organisations, which have cohered in claims that the tacit assumptions built in to post-war public services tended to reinforce, rather than ameliorate, social divisions, and that services became unresponsive and unaccountable to their users.

In the context of a continuing dispute about the goals and priorities of welfare, restructuring has been embedded within the calculative rationality of economic globalisation. Neoliberalism regards welfare spending as an unproductive and inefficient use of society's resources, rather than a collective investment in a social good. The social democratic welfare model is seen as hampering economic growth and employment, and creating poverty by encouraging a 'dependency culture'. Market competition, reduced employment protections, lower unemployment benefits and reduced taxes are prescribed instead as an efficient means of allocating limited resources, disciplining the 'undeserving poor', and expanding low wage employment. Neoliberal prescriptions have included the deregulation of financial markets (discussed in Chapter 2), greatly increasing the mobility of finance capital. This places new constraints on national governments' use of public borrowing to finance welfare: a high level of debt is treated as risky by financial markets, adversely affecting the value of domestic currency and the cost of public borrowing (Huber and Stephens, 2005). The greater mobility of capital, and the prioritising of short-term return on investment, results in corporations moving investment to regions with low corporate tax regimes and a cheaper labour supply. In this scenario, taxation is perceived as an inhibitor of competitiveness and enterprise, and public employment is seen as a 'cost' on the economy.

Public services and welfare are consequently embedded in a calculative economic rationality of competition between states to attract capital investment and employment. Regardless of political colour, governments internationally have converged around common neoliberal policies, based on prioritising economic competitiveness in a globalising market, a view of the state as enabling rather than providing, and of the market as a means of limiting public expenditure and passing responsibility for welfare to individuals, families and households (Brennan, 2003; Clarke et al., 2000; Flynn, 2000). The evidence for and against the neoliberal thesis is complex and contested. The OECD *Jobs Study* (1994) concluded that the liberal model *is* associated with higher economic growth and employment, but other studies using similar economic performance data have concluded that social democratic models perform better, even within the calculative rationalities of economics (Huber and Stephens, 2005). The main concern here, however, is with the measures that have developed out of neoliberal ideology, and the analysis of their organisational and social consequences. Three main types of initiatives have been pursued. First is the lowering of direct taxes. Second is the associated reduction in welfare benefits, particularly for the unemployed, and reduced employment protections (Brennan, 2003).

The third is the opening up of public services to private firms. Public services paid for by taxes are potentially a very large source of low risk profit for corporations (Leys, 2001; Pollock, 2004). The prime responsibility of corporations is however to shareholders, not to governments or citizens. The corporate need to maximise profit sits uneasily with the demands on government from an identity politics for equity and participation, and poses considerable problems of presentation and legitimation. Hence the public justification for market mechanisms and private sector involvement is generally made in terms of claims of greater efficiency, affordability and choice, which is presented as making services responsive to a proactive 'consumer-citizen'.

Democratic governments have not been able to assert a calculative economic rationality for welfare without encountering and responding to resistance generated by a values based politics of identity, built on ideals of social reciprocity and interdependence. Wide-ranging social changes in post-war capitalist societies resulted in shifts in the relationships between the very social categories tacitly assumed by modern conceptions of welfare, posing some fundamentally social questions about appropriate provision, its organisation and the role of the state. Women's demands for gender equity (Sainsbury, 1999), in part stimulated by improved access to education and health services, have been associated with the increased autonomy of women and further demands for more participation in service provisions. In Britain, for example, the sexual division between a male breadwinner and female homemaker applies to a declining percentage of households, and men's and women's economic activity rates are converging. Seventy-one per cent of married and cohabiting women with dependent children are in paid work, albeit 61% of these work part-time (EOC, 2005), whereas the proportion of 16–64-year-old men in paid work has declined from 94% in 1960 to 79% in 2004. Cohabitation before marriage is common, divorce laws are more liberal, there are fewer marriages and more women are remaining childless (*Social Trends*, 2005).

Anti-racist social movements, civil society organisations and disability rights groups have also promoted recognition of the diversity of social identities in advanced capitalist states (Castells, 1997), as well as the inadequacy of taken-for-granted presumptions about the identity of the ideal-typical citizen. Social movements and civil society organisations have campaigned for devolved government, social justice and anti-discrimination laws. Demands have also been made for more participation in defining needs and shaping services, in areas spanning health, education, crime, disability, housing and domestic violence (Clarke and Newman, 1997).

The crises engendered by the global infrastructures of deregulated finance, on the one hand, and changing social identities, on the other, pose major problems for the legitimacy of democratic governments and institutional politics. The main device relied on in the attempt to reconcile the competing goals of economic rationalisation with socially accountable services has been resort to managerialism and markets. In the UK, for example, the New Labour government, elected in 1997, aimed to transcend the gulf between a neoliberal preference for market solutions and social demands for collective provision with a politics of the 'Third Way', adapted from Clinton's Democratic presidency of the USA. This claimed a commitment to modernising government and decision-making through the application of management tools, which are represented as above politics and value-based disputes. The Third Way attempts to articulate new identities for citizens and public servants, and is used as a device to mobilise alliances, stimulate change and limit potential opposition (Blair, 1998; Clarke et al., 2000; Giddens, 1998; Williams, 1999). The extent to which Third Way politics generates substantively different policies from those of neoliberal economics is disputed. On the one hand, New Labour has been publicly accepting of the legitimacy of a politics of identity of gender, sexuality, nationality and ethnicity and disability. Policies have recognised the need to tackle social exclusion, even in the absence of a radical commitment to the redistribution of wealth. Devolved government has also enabled local control and divergence in social policies relating to health, education and communities. Its concept of 'the citizen' is, however, informed by markets and the idea of the individualised 'consumer-citizen', who has both rights to efficiency, value and choice in public services, and responsibilities to contribute to society through paid work (Lister, 2003). The New Labour Working Families Tax Credit, for example, channels benefits through taxation to reward those in paid work.

The Reorganisation of Public Services: from Professional Bureaucracy to Management Tools and Markets

Management and markets have been the central organising principles of change in public services, as is evident from the burgeoning international interest in emulating private business. Government is meant to become more businesslike and public servants less like administrators who follow rules, and more like leaders who use resources strategically to address priorities and solve problems (Hood, 2000). Efficiency is itself regarded, not as a matter of different political values, but as amenable to technical solutions, using a 'management toolkit'. Devices such as business planning, performance measurement and results-based service provision have been introduced, alongside competition through internal and external markets and league tables. The global consultancy firm McKinsey has, for example, been used by the UK government as a means of engineering change in Whitehall and the NHS. Unsurprisingly, given the complexity of services and the variety and range of devices introduced, the effects of managerial reform measures are disputed (Hood, 2000).

The complex demands of mass provision of services charged with alleviating poverty and improving health and education, combined with political accountability and the expectation that public services should also contribute to economic growth, pose severe problems of organisation. Modern welfare states relied on centralising, bureaucratic solutions (Marquand, 2004). Competing goals and priorities were regulated through hierarchical authority, while service provisions entailed the development of differentiated specialist knowledge and expertise in the welfare professions. The structure of a professional bureaucracy is characterised by tensions between professionalisation, which is associated with indeterminacy, discretion and judgement, and bureaucratisation, which is associated with standardisation and control (Clarke and Newman, 1997). Professional power is embodied in particular persons, while bureaucracy is formally indifferent to persons. In theory, such tensions are productive of effective organisation. While bureaucratic control represents the guarantee of universality, fairness and citizenship rights, professionalisation represents the goal of disinterested authority and expert knowledge in the service of the public good.

A commitment to bureaucratic administration has some advantages. It disciplines policy and protects welfare provision from political fashion or unconsidered change (Clarke and Newman, 1997). Its officers are required to strive for impartial and predictable decisions, derived from a rational-legal framework of rules that are formally indifferent to personal characteristics such as skin colour, sex or family background, wealth and status. If the outcomes of welfare reproduce, rather than ameliorate, systematic inequalities, then at least the formal rules enable legitimate public challenge. Although the potential for various forms of corruption is never eliminated, because areas of discretion are never eliminated, bureaucratic regulation protects the integrity of democratic government by discouraging improper conduct by officials, and is associated with greater impartiality, less patronage and nepotism (Du Gay, 2000).

The ideal-typical professional bureaucracy has been the target of criticism from both a politics of identity agenda and a neoliberal welfare reform agenda. Advocates of neoliberal reform argue that professional bureaucracy is inflexible and expensive, and that welfare professionals are self-serving rather than welfare-oriented (Marquand, 2004). Among welfare users, perceived failures of 'expert solutions' and the attributed arrogance of bureaucratic office have eroded trust in expert judgement: 'senior professionals . . . now have to prove their trustworthiness on a regular basis and on an increasingly changed set of criteria' (Hanlon, 1998: 54).

Governments' prescribed remedies have coalesced around the increasing use of managerial tools and markets (Clarke et al., 2000; Pollitt and Bouckaert, 2000). The neoliberal US text *Reinventing Government* by Osborne and Gaebler (1992) has been internationally influential in the formation of a new orthodoxy, centring on market mechanisms, a view of citizens as customers, and output-driven performance targets, as a means of ridding governments of excessive bureaucracy. Markets are regarded as replacing the attributed 'producer agenda' with a consumer one. The power of welfare professionals is constrained by exposing them to the pressures of budgetary constraints and controlled costs:

> The tools and techniques of markets and managerialism are promoted as able to tackle bureaucratic and professional self-interest, through deregulation, performance targets, incentives for entrepreneurialism and flatter organisation. (Marquand, 2004: 3)

The central facet of managerialism is the idea that, when twinned with market principles, management tools are the instruments of a 'hands-off' enabling state, rather than a direct, providing state. 'Executive government' places politicians in the position of steering the direction of policy, but its operation and implementation become the responsibility of public servants, who in theory exercise discretion over the means devised to achieve policy goals (Hood et al., 1999). The model is derived from business boards of directors, who set strategic direction and review performance, and executive officers who produce business plans and carry operational responsibility (Farrell, 2005). Common organisational solutions have relied on simplifying committee structures, and creating a corporate management team with responsibility for identifying priorities, assigning budgets and setting output targets in line with centrally directed objectives (Newman, 2000). The result is public services controlled through outcomes and performance targets, rather than inputs and processes. Such 'blunt instruments', Young (1996) argues, reduce the scope for compromise and mediation, and make management increasingly directive. Performance measurement and target-setting become the focus of bargaining between politicians, public servants and agencies set up to implement policy, since the measures come to define what counts as success and failure, for public servants and politicians alike (Hoggett, 1996).

Outcome-oriented performance measurement opens up discretion over the choice of means to deliver specified outcomes and is the key to market rationalisation. In the UK, for example, restructuring has entailed significant use of market mechanisms, through the use of private finance arrangements and competitive tendering for services. Public private partnerships (PPPs) are the means used to raise commercial loans for new schools, hospitals and health centres. Private businesses have been able to contract for publicly funded services, from cleaning and catering to prisons, medical treatment centres, the management of schools, financial audit and government consultancy. Instead of services provided and coordinated by public servants, working in bureau-professional structures, a variety of partnership arrangements between private, public and voluntary organisations are increasingly common. Such organisations are linked through networks of contractual relationships and monitored by non-elected agencies (Clarke et al., 2000; Clarke and Newman, 1997). Private involvement has grown rapidly to become a majority of annually managed public expenditure:

> In 1977, when most public services were carried out in house, general government purchase of external goods and services (gas, electricity, office supplies etc) accounted for 28 per cent of annually managed current expenditure (ie. excluding welfare payments and debt servicing). By 1991 it had risen to 38% and in 1999 . . . to 57 per cent. (Pollock et al., 2001: 13)

The effects of the growth of business involvement in public services are disputed. Governments defend the use of private providers on the grounds that it is a means to more efficient and lower cost, responsive services and innovative developments. Critics argue that the use of market mechanisms is motivated by political affinity with a neoliberal ideology, rather than evidence of its value rationality in relation to both cost-efficiency measures and social goals of equity and responsiveness. Defenders of a social democratic politics, represented by 'think tank' organisations such as Catalyst Forum (www.catalystforum.org.uk), for example, argue that private sector provision produces *higher* costs, new inefficiencies and inequitable services, because it necessarily prioritises profitability and shareholder interests over those of stakeholders. The increase in private provision of publicly funded services also entails new transaction costs associated with managing competitive procurement and contractual compliance. In the NHS, for example, administrative costs were 6% of total spending before the introduction of internal markets in the 1980s, rising to 12% by 2001 (Pollock, 2004). In the American private health system, administration costs account for 31% of health expenditure (Woolhandler et al., 2003). Combining claims of pragmatism with promises of accountability to citizens thus remains problematic, given the different, and contested, social values that underlie the debate.

Discretion over the means devised to pursue performance targets, and the extensive use of subcontracting, has however created new concerns with the accountability of public servants. The growing use of subcontracting for services with private and voluntary sector providers entails higher risks of fraud and corruption (Maesschalck, 2004). The FBI estimates the costs of fraud in the US privately financed healthcare system, for example, at $418 billion for the years 1991–95 (Leys, 2001). Discretion has consequently been accompanied by forms of re-regulation, which replace trust-based systems with intensified inspection, quality assurance reporting, audit and risk management (Hood and Scott, 2000). This rule-driven apparatus of information audit extends bureaucratic regulation beyond financial probity to include all organisational processes (Power, 1997). New forms of external accountability are also increased through the institutions of complaints commissioners such as the new police complaints body, public services ombudsmen, accounts commissioners, information commissioners and standards and public appointments commissioners. The combination of discretion over the means to achieve performance targets with a new regulatory regime has produced some extraordinary results. In the UK, for example, a secondary school headteacher, who was praised by government and honoured for the improved performance of the school, was subsequently accused by the Audit Commission of nepotism, mismanagement and making illegal payments to staff. The headteacher has publicly justified her actions in terms of the requirements of leadership and pragmatic problem-solving in a target-driven system (Revell, 2005), but audit measures, it seems, drew the opposite conclusions. Power (1997) argues that authentic quality assurance judgements cannot be provided by such regulatory instruments, because they mistake the ritualised monitoring of internal control procedures for real engagement with organisational practices. Minimally, the new apparatus of regulation and control represents an intensified rationalisation of services, where bureaucratic means displace substantive ends: the reporting requirements of the regulatory regime drive activities, rather than the substantive goals of service improvement.

Public Management and a New Identity Project for Public Servants

The transformation of welfare services through practices of managerialism and markets ultimately relies on the day-to-day conduct of public servants. Public service professionals in particular have been depicted as resistant to change, providing a rationale for incorporating them into management by making them responsible for meeting budgetary and performance targets. Public sector professionals have been shown to be a politically and socially distinctive group, typically having critical attitudes to advanced capitalism and a moral commitment to a fairer society (Bagguley, 1995; Heath and Savage, 1995). Loyalty and a sense of vocational commitment have typically been rewarded with favourable terms and conditions of employment, and the expectation of secure career progression, within a trust-based service class contract (Goldthorpe, 1995). The claimed self-serving 'producer interests' of the welfare professions, which this trust-based contract was deemed to allow, were however regarded as detrimental to the neoliberal project of market reforms. The ambition, reflected in policy documents, reports and political speeches, was to construct a new public service identity modelled on values, attitudes and self-understanding derived from a business-oriented discourse of entrepreneurialism, empowerment, innovation and risk-taking. Structurally, the public service contract would be remade, creating more individualised opportunity structures, with rewards tied to performance in competitive quasi-market conditions (Broadbent et al., 1997; Sayer, 1996). Flatter structures would reward flexibility, initiative and generic management skills, rather than loyalty and commitment (Halford et al., 1997, Hoggett, 1996; Webb, 1999).

Structural changes are however represented as insufficient; cultural change, leadership and results-oriented efficiency are seen as the key:

> Reform of our planning and performance management processes will not be enough. If the changes we plan are to happen, we need to create a culture and climate for change. (NHS Scotland, 2005: 69)

For some, the prescribed changes represent a new normative 'discourse of enterprise' and empowerment (Du Gay, 1996; Hoggett, 1996), reflected in the idea that improved performance will stem from and reinforce an improved self-identity, through thinking differently, taking initiatives and breaking down professional barriers and conventional mindsets. The pre-scribed changes have sometimes been given quasi-religious connotations, with the deliberately emotive condemnation of a 'failed' bureaucratic past contrasted with a 'reinvented' new entrepreneurial future (Du Gay, 2000):

> In government, in business, in our Universities and throughout society we must do much more to foster a new entrepreneurial spirit. (Blair, 1998: 5)

The move beyond rationalistic appeals to economic efficiency into the realms of emotional identification with the 'project' of cultural transform-ation has stimulated analysis of a new discourse of public management. Most accounts have used a postmodernist concept of identity, which treats agency as subordinated to the internalised disciplinary powers of discursive regimes of truth: welfare professionals are expected to identify with and intern-alise a new managerial identity. Such assertions neglect evidence derived from the practical experiences of culture change initiatives, which show that identity cannot be read off from discourse. There are multiple sources of identity in any setting, which result in similar neoliberal prescriptions being interpreted differently in different national, local and institutional contexts: public services in the UK differ from those in Australia, which differ from those in France, and within any given state, benefit offices differ from schools, which differ from hospitals and so on (Flynn, 2000).

Particular tensions centre on the degree of local autonomy and discretion, as opposed to the central control of standards and performance targets. Within the UK, devolved government is resulting in different policy emphases, with greater recourse to collaborative solutions in Scotland and Wales, and more reliance on markets in England. The pressure for partnership and collaboration also intersects with the interests of specialists in directing provisions, and the pressures of meeting short-term targets, such as those for hospital waiting times, are set against goals of longer term change (Newman, 2000). Agency is situated in the contingencies of government, business, political parties and communities of interest, and public servants derive their logics of action from them in a struggle for control, resulting in considerable indeterminacy over the shape and quality of services (Clarke et al., 2000).

Whatever their theoretical orientation, studies providing systematic evidence of the practices of public management have repeatedly shown that prescribed cultural changes in identity do not operate in a deterministic fashion. Entrepreneurialism, empowerment and self-reliance are cultural constructs subject to multiple and shifting interpretations. As symbolic resources they are inevitably used by different groups for ends other than those intended by their originators, and are variously politically contested, resisted, adapted and complied with (Halford and Leonard, 1999; Leonard, 2003; McDonald, 2004). Representatives of police, social services and secondary education, for example, gave different emphases to new public management identities, when reflecting on their experiences of change (Thomas and Davies, 2005). Formal definitions of managerial and leadership competences emphasised qualities such as strategic thinking, financial control and market awareness. These were, however, given different emphases by different informants, and competing logics of management were also deployed at the same time. In the police and in education, a masculine-identified, competitive and aggressive interpretation was evident, with references to ruthless competition to meet targets, and to put in long hours in the quest for visibility. A feminine-identified management discourse existed alongside this, however, emphasising communication, coaching and support for diversity. Social work also reflected a sense of compliance and submission to a hostile culture, as opposed to active engagement. Particular professionals moved between these vocabularies, according to their position, and its responsibilities and opportunities. They were not passive recipients of an imposed, dominating identity, so much as generating, contesting and performing its meanings, within the power relations existing between different levels of government, politicians and public servants.

In a comparison of Home Office immigration officers and officials in a new agency, Work Permits UK, designed to epitomise flexible, responsive government, Duvell and Jordan (2003) found that political changes in policy towards migration affected the performance-related identity of public servants differently:

> Despite the claim of 'joined-up' approaches, there was little evidence of a common public-service identity or a coherent sense of what the rules they implemented were trying to achieve. Both managers and staff themselves made strong claims about the competence of front-line practitioners, who were well-educated and trained, sophisticated and able to take responsibility. However, they also shared the identity of stressed, hard-worked and under-resourced public servants, working in conditions that seldom allowed them to give a high-quality service to immigrants. (Duvell and Jordan, 2003: 334)

Although both organisations defended their activities in terms of a strategic, performance-oriented public service identity, the perceived positive status of the new agency-style 'solution' to regulating immigration meant that enforcement staff generally presented themselves as more 'user-friendly' and able to respect the rights of immigrants as well as responding to business needs for labour. Home Office employees, in contrast, were more likely to feel demoralised and disempowered by changes in immigration policy, and held a more negative view of performative management, which meant a more defensive–aggressive identity. In each case, interviewees drew on other sources of identity as a resource in maintaining a degree of critical awareness of the contradictions and inadequacies of practice. Counter to the rhetoric of empowerment, however, this awareness derived from the practical experience of new managerialism was not taken up by their organisations to improve performance or adjust practice.

Studies of culture change initiatives have also found that people adopt shifting positions in relation to the discourses of empowerment and continuous improvement, drawing on multiple sources of identity, including personal values and desires, gender ideologies and wider occupational, professional and ethical norms (Baxter, 2002; Leonard, 2003; McDonald, 2004). In Ruth McDonald's (2004) account of culture change in primary care, a programme presented as aiming to empower staff focused on techniques designed to remake identities around ideas of continuous improvement through self-development and more effective use of working time. The results of this attempt to manufacture a subjective alignment with managerial measures were however quite different from those intended. Some participants, particularly those promoted to higher paid jobs, did internalise messages about accountability and self-reliance, and accepted that it was their responsibility to find a way of handling a heavy workload, rather than a problem of the environment and resources. Others took the 'positive thinking' messages on board superficially, in a form of 'self-surveillance', which had the effect of suppressing explicit dissent about the impact of primary care reforms on either the quality of services or workloads and responsibilities. Such dissent was not eliminated however, but was channelled instead into searching for other employment. Yet others took the messages of performance improvement and used them to challenge the authenticity of senior managers' claims that new arrangements were oriented to a better quality of care. Among this group, the reinforced messages about self-accountability and responsibility were used, not to internalise a sense of personal deficiency in performance, but to re-emphasise the structural problems and contradictions of current service provisions and to resist self-blame.

Experiencing the Contradictions between Empowerment and Rationalisation

Agency and critical awareness are thus not captured by such identity projects, but reinterpreted through them, often in complex and contradictory ways. The postmodernist perspective regards identity as situated in the workings of power, and treats resistance as inherent in the relations of power, embodied in this case in discourses of entrepreneurialism and empowerment. Research within this conceptual framework is limited, however,in its ability to identify the social sources of critical reflection and insight into the practices of power. In the studies discussed above, such insightis derived from practical experience of the contradictions between the promise of empowerment and the processes of rationalisation. It is this struggle to reconcile the pressures for rationalisation with operational discretion over the shape of services and a belief in the value of welfare that frames the identities of public servants. Two axes of experience are centrally relevant. The first relates to the tension between the economistic logic of markets and performance measurement, in contrast with promises of operational 'empowerment' and discretion to improve the quality of services. The second relates to the tension between pressures to rationalise labour, in contrast with promises of empowerment and partnership in employment relations.

A new 'moral calculus' sets the instrumental rationality of financial and performance targets in uneasy relationship with claimed operational empowerment and the value-based rationalities of improved public service (Sayer, 1996). Performance measures, Hoggett (1996) suggests, reduce the validity of work that is non-measurable:

> the care and attention given to service users or fellow members of staff suffers as it fails to contribute directly to the immediate output measures upon which the organisation's success stands or falls. (p. 24)

Targets create perverse incentives and opportunism, and encourage people to erect boundaries around responsibilities rather than thinking innovatively about services (Hood and Scott, 2000). Nevertheless, aspects of performance measurement may be treated pragmatically as a means to substantive improvements in services. Public service managers in the Canadian province of Alberta, for example, at first treated such tools as a basis for the reasoned justification of services, and saw them as creating new opportunities to engage in informed dialogue about values, goals and priorities. Instrumental priorities, however, became dominant, and commitment to wider public engagement faded (Townley et al., 2003). The authors imply that there is an inevitability about the processes of rationalisation, but it seems likely that 'local discretion' was in this case constrained by wider power relations, which prioritised the external, political uses of performance measures over their internal validation and control.

Similar tensions are evident in other professional groups. In the restructuring of Scottish and Welsh local government, promises of empowerment were regarded as a positive means to tackle the 'politics of patronage' and to improve services and local democracy (Webb, 1999). New public management techniques were seen as facilitating less status consciousness and better working relationships across specialist boundaries in solving problems. The benefits were however perceived as compromised by the experience that empowerment mainly entailed the requirement of 'doing more for less', in a system that centralised accountability and control. In the NHS, senior nurses are regarded as critical to the success of managerial changes. Responses to new 'nurse manager' roles again show nurses' awareness that they can use aspects of the role to innovate and improve services, but they also 'show a critical appreciation that beyond the vision of nurses as empowered managers are tight budgetary controls and performance measures and targets' (Bolton, 2005: 6). The experience of the contradictions at the heart of new public management in each of these cases is turned to a critical engagement with its tenets and the maintenance of a degree of detachment from it.

New Contracts for Public Service: Empowered Partners or Rationalised Labour?

The second dimension of experienced contradiction emerges from the tension between economic rationalisation and espoused workforce empowerment through partnership in employment relations. Current best practice in public management prescribes workforce partnership and describes labour as a stakeholder in public sector governance. Processes of rationalisation, however, rely on reducing labour costs through intensification, flexible contracts or the replacement of labour with a cheaper manufactured product and incentives for self-service. Although there are considerable continuities in patterns of work in public services, these are matched by greater variability and less predictability in careers, increasing emphasis on individual opportunism and initiative, and new forms of gender segregation, which locate more women in caring roles and more men in control of resources (Halford et al., 1997; Webb, 2001). More use is being made of lower paid, part-time labour, in an increasingly feminised workforce. There is also evidence of the intensification of work and a sense of heightened insecurity (Webb, 1999, 2001). In the UK, for example, lower paid nurses are increasingly trained in tasks previously carried out by higher paid doctors, while nurse assistants in turn take over more routine nursing tasks. Costs are also reduced by raising productivity: hospitals see more patients, lecturers teach bigger classes, social work caseloads are increased, but personal contact and continuity are lessened, and mistakes and failure rates tend to increase.

It is however the lowest paid manual workers who experience the highest costs of market measures. Competition and privatisation have tended to reduce pay and worsen conditions. Through participant observation in routine manual work in hospitals, Toynbee (2003) found that pay had declined in real terms over the last thirty years. Most of the cost savings made by private companies taking over public services have been achieved not through managerial efficiency, but by cutting pay and reducing the terms and conditions of the workforce. In private prisons in the UK, for example, average basic pay is 30% lower, contracted work hours are longer and holiday and pension provisions poorer (Sachdev, 2004).

As recognised in policy prescriptions, the quality of services depends critically on the willingness of labour to work constructively and take responsibility for solving problems. Yet culture change programmes seem to be targeted at changing attitudes and 'identity', rather than dealing directly with management practices and low trust relationships that discourage employees from applying their, often tacit, knowledge and experience to tackling problems and obstacles. Extensive workforce involvement in the restructuring of jobs, the allocation of work and the routine management of budgets has been shown to improve both the quality and efficiency of services. In Indianapolis, for example, the municipal employees' union, seeking security of employment, persuaded a pro-privatisation mayor to work with them on the reform of services, resulting in a manual workforce with better knowledge and participation in managing services and lower costs (Martin, 2002). Current measures to rationalise labour make it less, rather than more, likely that workers' knowledge and experience will be used to improve services, as Toynbee (2003) confirmed in her study of portering, cleaning and catering staff employed on privatised labour contracts in hospitals. The discourse of workforce partnership and empowerment is in sharp contradiction with an instrumental model of the public service workforce as labour commodities.

The Identity of Consumer Citizenship

The neoliberal rationale of welfare is also articulated through the extension of a consumer identity to citizenship. The 'cult of the customer' has increasingly been promoted as the basis for all social relations (Du Gay and Salaman, 1992), privatising and individualising responsibility for welfare, rather than socialising and democratising it. Competition between service providers is argued to empower users through creating choice, counterbalancing the power of the professionalised producers (Clarke et al., 2000; Maquand, 2004). The consumerist orientation is exemplified in UK Labour government notions of the demanding, 'sceptical citizen consumer' (Green Paper on welfare reform, 1998), which suggests that the impetus for consumer citizenship comes from a more confident, independent population, who expect value for money and choice, while being less inclined to trust government and politicians. The rise in home ownership is drawn on as evidence that people prefer private solutions to social and welfare needs. Services, by implication, have to be rebuilt as 'adaptive, responsive, flexible and diverse rather than paternalist, monolithic and operating on a model of "one size fits all"' (Clarke et al., 2000). In England, for example, Prime Minister Tony Blair forecast the end of 'the bog standard comprehensive' in a speech designed to launch policy advocating more specialist schools (Taylor, 2001), although his former policy adviser, turned classroom assistant, has since suggested that the government lacks commitment to improving all schools through more investment in teaching (Hyman, 2005).

A consumer-citizen identity relies on an economic model of a self-interested individual and is abstracted from the particular conditions of people's lives (Clarke et al., 2000). It replaces an ethic of entitlement with one of obligation, in a motif that is echoed across OECD welfare systems (Townsend, 2002). The disciplining role of the market is seen as removing the 'moral hazard' of benefits and replacing this with incentives for self-reliance and personal responsibility. Its individualising assumptions weaken the social reciprocity pursued by a politics of identity, and make it more difficult to gain public recognition of systematic inequalities between social categories. In an extension of Weber's theory of rationalisation, Ritzer (1999) argues that consumer citizenship in the USA results not in more authentic choice and control over the intimate life events of birth, marriage and death, but in its replacement with a calculative version of 'choice' and standardised services. Rationalisation through fixed budgets andperformance targets means that calculative criteria define those in most need as 'high-cost users' and 'risks' to be 'managed' rather than supported (Williams, 1999).

Choice is limited in practice by the lack of 'exit' options for most people. But there is also a risk for governments that a privatised, consumer-citizen identity encourages withdrawal from a shared responsibility for civil society and the public domain. Bauman points to the paradox that people feel freer to live their own lives, but are also inclined to believe that they cannot change anything:

> Once the state recognises the priority and superiority of the laws of the market over the laws of the polis, the citizen is transmuted into the consumer, and a consumer demands more and more protection while accepting less and less the need to participate in the running of the state. (Bauman, 1999: 156)

Consumer identity is inherently self-regarding, encouraging people to specify individualistic preferences, to act instrumentally and to enact accountability through mechanisms of complaint rather than civic engagement (Needham, 2003). Consumer citizenship in these terms produces a self-fulfilling cycle of disappointment and cynical withdrawal, weakening a public domain where debate about the proper place of markets in social life could take place.

Conclusion

This chapter has argued that macro-level developments in global financial markets, in particular the deregulation of capital, its increased mobility and the dominance of speculative capital, have driven global change in the public domain of social and welfare services in democratic states. These are changes that are critical to the quality of life and social identities in advanced capitalist societies. They are exemplified here through a middle-range theoretical focus on organisational change in public services, the managerialisation of public service identities and the promotion of an individualised consumer-citizen identity. The context for change was set by examining the assumptions about identity that informed social democratic principles of universal welfare. Such principles of social exchange emphasised a citizenship identity based on integrative, solidaristic social values and assertions of mutual interdependence. Post-war social democratic welfare states have however increasingly faced dual crises stemming from the neoliberal political economy of deregulated finance on the one hand

and a new politics of identity on the other. In the context of global financial markets, neoliberal economic rationales treat welfare as a social cost, and aim to individualise responsibility for well-being. The resulting identity is one of a consumer-citizen, acting calculatively to maximise self-interest, in a competitive market. The risk for the public domain of such an identity is that it creates incentives for people to withdraw from a sense of shared responsibility for social cohesion and civil society. The politics of identity expressed in new social movements contests the calculative rationality of neoliberalism, and argues instead for a more thorough-going, participative welfare society, building on ideals of social solidarity and interdependence.

In the UK case, the government has tried to reconcile the demands of a politics of identity with the pressures of mobile capital and financial markets through movement towards a neoliberal model of welfare and promises of greater choice in public services. This has been brought about through the organisational application of market competition, managerialism and performance measurement. These instruments have had a significant impact on the experience of public servants striving to reconcile promises of improved services, discretion over service organisation and empowerment in employment relations with the economic calculus of neoliberal political economy. The resulting discourse of new public management has in some cases been argued to result in the subordination of agency and critical insight to the internalised disciplinary powers of discursive regimes of truth: welfare professionals are expected to identify with, and internalise, a new managerial identity. Such accounts fail to see the ways in which agency works through professional and personal identities to ensure that the discourse is evaluated in the light of experience and enacted selectively according to its perceived opportunities and costs. The contradictions between promises of empowerment and experiences of centralised financial control, performance targets, culture change programmes and intensification ensure that identity is far from aligned with the discourse. Similarly, in employment relations, promises of partnership sit uneasily with labour rationalisation, individualised opportunity structures and the worsening of terms and conditions of work, particularly for those in the lowest paid jobs.

Neither has the construct of an individualised consumer-citizen, as the counterpart to a managerialised public sector, satisfied a politics of identity expressed in social movements challenging sexism and racism, or articulated by disability activists, carers' groups and alternative service providers. Such activism is evidence of resistance to a privatised consumer-citizen identity and a neoliberal system of rationalised welfare. It also represents the sources of an alternative, participative democratic agenda for reform through the pursuit of well-being, dignity and autonomy in a welfare society (Williams, 1999). A public domain, distinct from the market sphere, enables meaningful choice about the conduct of markets and their place in society. It offers a vital means to establishing the common interest in tolerant and civil societies.

The reorganisation of welfare, and the individualisation of responsibility, is one part of a bigger picture of social and economic restructuring, contingent on the operation of global, deregulated finance, which makes it more difficult for governments to meet their obligations for social well-being. In the next chapter I turn to an examination of the wider restructuring of work and occupations stimulated by the rationalities of financial markets, and consider the implications for the social identities of advanced capitalist societies.

5

Organisations and Global Divisions of Labour

The organisation of work is fundamental to the structuring of societies and social identities, and recent changes in the employment and occupational structures of major capitalist economies suggest that the operation of deregulated, mobile capital, at a global level, is stimulating a new global division of labour, new forms of social relations and new conditions for the making of social and personal identities. Although the broad contours of change are discernible, their social significance is less clear. The evidence is sometimes obscured by the rhetoric of apocalyptic change, and claims about 'the end of work' in postindustrial societies (Beck, 2000; Bridges, 1995; Rifkin, 1995). An informed understanding of change depends on using available evidence to evaluate prominent theories, while acknowledging the limitations of what we know. This chapter begins by outlining the main theoretical conjectures about the restructuring of work in what have been described as postindustrial (Bell, 1976) or information (Castells, 2000) societies. The key theoretical assertions are then evaluated using comparative labour market statistics showing the changes in employment and occupations in four OECD countries – the UK, Germany, USA and Japan. Understanding these changes is in turn dependent on understanding how they fit into the bigger picture of an emerging global division of labour, marked by increasing socioeconomic inequalities within and between countries.

The broad contours of employment and occupational change raise further questions about the organisational dynamics of social identities, which cannot be addressed through the examination of labour market data alone. Trends in the restructuring of work have often been interpreted as indicating the end of job security and lifetime employment, and as challenging the secure sense of personal identity that continuity of employment and bureaucratic career paths sustained. The consequence may be the 'gradual undermining of the coherent system once formed by occupational identity, career development and personal identity' (Kallinikos, 2003: 600). The destandardisation of labour, it is argued, leads to the decline of stable work and occupational identities associated with modern divisions of class and gender (Beck, 1992, 2000; Sennett, 1998). New organisational forms, it is claimed, are associated with intensified processes of individualisation and fragmentation, making a sense of self more tenuous. Chapter 6 therefore links the broad trends of restructuring of work and organisations discussed here with an evaluation of their significance for personal and social identities.

Theoretical Conjectures: the Restructuring of Work and Organisations?

In the 1960s and 1970s, social theorists argued that new technologies, the growing industrialisation of the Pacific rim countries, and the declining competitiveness of western mass manufacturing were resulting in the emergence of a postindustrial society (Bell, 1976). A new social structure was said to be emerging in advanced capitalist economies, characterised by a series of interrelated changes in the main axes of social organisation:

- In the sphere of economic activity, the production of goods was being surpassed by services

- In employment, manufacturing jobs were declining as managerial, professional and technical occupations increased to form the core of the new social structure

- In parallel with this occupational shift, the information and knowledge content of work was said to be increasing

- In relation to economic growth, it was argued that the major source of wealth creation was therefore shifting from manufactured goods to knowledge creation.

Implicitly, postindustrialism asserted a single, universalising and inevitable trajectory of development for capitalist societies, much as earlier grand narrative theorists of modernisation had done. In this case, it was American society that provided the template, and postindustrial theory can be subject to the same criticisms as those levelled at Marx and Weber, and rehearsed in Chapters 1 and 2. In brief, particular economic rationalities are not the result of natural laws, but are politically and culturally shaped through the workings of different global, regional and local institutions and actors. Shared trends in economic change are the product of particular political ideologies and decisions.

Although postindustrialism overstated its claims about the universality of change and the convergence of societies, it nevertheless proved influential in attempts to understand broad trends in the reorganisation of work, and Castells (2000) adapts its premises to a more nuanced account of the inter-relations of capital and labour. He suggests first that 'the appropriate distinction is not between an industrial and a post-industrial economy, but between two forms of knowledge-based industrial, agricultural and services production' (p. 219). In other words, there is considerable continuity and interconnection between past and present economic relations in industrialised societies. Castells attributes the underlying common dynamic of economic change to a new global production system, facilitated by deregulated, highly mobile finance capital, and organised around 'the principles of maximising knowledge-based productivity through the development and diffusion of information technologies' (2000: 219) across all areas of activity. This does not inevitably lead to the convergence of societies around a particular social structure, because systems of production do not dictate social relations. Historical variation between cultures, institutions, organisations and political environments ensures that the technical and economic rationalities of globalising markets are differently enacted through employment structures and occupational change. By extension, the implications for change in social identities are also indeterminate.

Work and Occupational Change in Advanced Capitalist Countries: an Evaluation of Theoretical Assertions

Insight into structures of work and occupational change, and continuing social diversity in the organisations of advanced capitalism, can be gained from a comparison of OECD economies. In this case, I summarise changes in the UK, Germany, the USA and Japan over a period of approximately thirty-five years. The USA has been the template for theories of postindustrialism, and latterly it has adopted the most aggressive approach to deregulating financial markets, privatisation and the prioritisation of economic individualism. The UK has also pursued a neoliberal economic agenda, but against a very different historical backdrop of organised labour and a social democratic welfare state. Germany provides a counterpoint to the UK, with its Christian democratic welfare provisions, commitment to maintaining a strong manufacturing and engineering base, employment protections, and state-regulated markets. In the 1970s, Japanese manufacturing competitiveness was regarded as a major catalyst of restructuring in the West; its government has strongly regulated its economy in the past, but economic recession has prompted a degree of neoliberal reform. These four examples cast light on the articulation of global, deregulated financial markets with the institutions of culture and political economy at state level, and the restructuring of employment and occupations at organisational level.

Assessing change in employment and occupational structures is not an exact science. The tables and figures presented here and in Chapter 6 are derived mainly from government employment statistics, publicly available from the International Labour Organisation website (http://laborsta. ilo.org/) and the Organisation for Economic Cooperation and Development (http://www.oecd.org/). (Detailed information about sources is given in the footnotes to each table.) All tables are given in appendices at the end of Chapters 5 and 6. This is to avoid interrupting the flow of the argument in the text, where the evidence from the tables is presented in the form of bar charts (Figures 5.1–5.11 and 6.1–6.2). These illustrate the patterns of employment and occupational change more powerfully for the reader. Caution is necessary in the interpretation of the data, because of the differential availability of longitudinal records for different states, and the differences in survey conventions and classificatory schemes used. Nevertheless, where there are consistent patterns over time, and in different countries, there are grounds for some confidence in the general validity of the trends observed.

A Services-dominated Economy?

The conjecture that advanced economies are dominated by employment in services has almost become a truism. In each society, the most marked change since the 1970s is the common decline in manufacturing employment and the commensurate rise in services. The further development of the trends noted by Castells (2000) is evident, as illustrated in Figures 5.1–5.4 and Tables 5.1–5.4. Within the overall shift towards service-dominated economies, there remains significant variation in the speed of change and in the resulting balance between sectors, indicating the operation of different political processes and historical trajectories.

The most radical decline in manufacturing employment has taken place in the UK, with the numbers of people employed falling by approximately 45% between 1970 and 2004. At present only 13.5% of the workforce are directly employed in manufacturing, while the numbers employed in service industries have increased by around two-thirds, to comprise three-quarters of all employment (Table 5.1). The UK is not unusual in this shift to an economy dominated by services. European labour force statistics show that service sector employment in the UK is slightly higher than the European average, but similar to that of France and Sweden, while the Netherlands and Luxembourg employed an even higher proportion of people in services (Eurostat, 2005). The USA and UK economies have shared a particularly rapid decline in manufacturing, combined with increasing employment in all services. Both Germany and Japan remain distinct from the UK and the

USA, with the transition to services taking place more gradually (comprising around two-thirds rather than three-quarters of employment), and a slower decline in manufacturing (Tables 5.3 and 5.4). In Japan (Table 5.4), the social and personal services sector remains small in comparison with the USA and the UK, and has still not reached the proportions that it was in the USA in 1970.

It is producer services that are regarded as the key to claims about the transition to a knowledge-based economy, because these are seen as providing the support and information necessary to improve the efficiency of firms (Castells, 2000). In each country, there has been rapid expansion in this category of producer services, suggesting that the sector is increasing in its strategic importance. The latter employed 5% of people in the UK in 1970, but 15.5% by 2004, while in the USA producer services expanded to 17.3% of employment, in Germany to 12.8% and in Japan to 13.3%. Producer services remain a relatively small proportion of total employment, however, suggesting that much of the work entailed in providing information, knowledge and support for business remains internal to firms. The growth that has taken place seems likely to be the result of a deregulated financial market, which has prompted more vertical disintegration of organisations, and greater use of subcontracting and supply chain networks (discussed in Chapter 2).

The common trend towards services-dominated economic activity, combined with a continuing differentiation between societal interpretations of the trend, is illustrated in Figures 5.1–5.4. The distinctiveness of the rapid shift

Figure 5.1   UK: distribution of employment by industrial group, 1970–2004

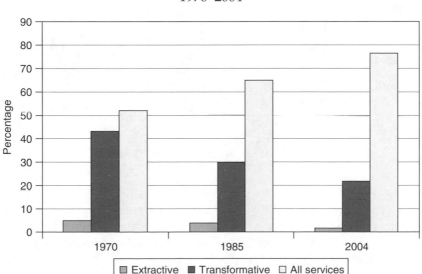

Figure 5.2   USA: distribution of employment by industrial group,
1970–2004

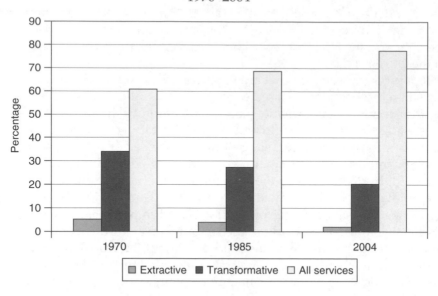

Figure 5.3   Germany: distribution of employment by industrial group,
1970–2004

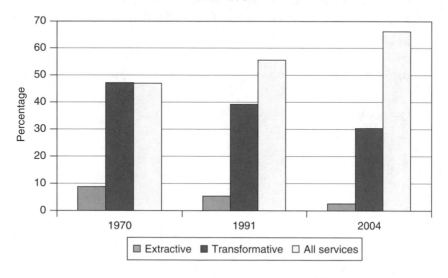

to services in the USA and UK, and the visibly steep decline in manufacturing in the UK, compared with the more gradual changes in Germany
and Japan, reflect differences in political ideologies and decisions about
economic and organisational restructuring.

Figure 5.4 Japan: distribution of employment by industrial group, 1970–2004

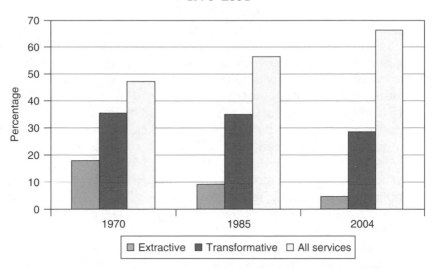

Why the Rise in Services Does Not Mean a Postindustrial Society

To equate sectoral shifts in employment with postindustrialism would be misleading for a number of reasons. First, it ignores the continuing import-ance of manufacturing and its related activities, in both the advanced cap-italist countries and across the globe. Second, it relies on an overly simple notion of the definition of 'services', which is increasingly outdated by social and technological change. In a different political-economic context, at least part of the growth of business and producer services would appear as manu-facturing employment, internally integrated into the firm. The OECD *Jobs Study* (1994) found that the restructuring of manufacturing had resulted in the growing use of outsourcing, subcontracting and external business services. Each of these gives manufacturers enhanced flexibility in controlling costs, and cuts the numbers of direct employees, relocating them broadly into busi-ness services. The study estimates that, if all those contracted to provide serv-ices to manufacturing were included in the manufacturing sector, the decline of manufacturing employment since 1991 would be cut by two-thirds.

Manufacturing-related activities, as opposed to absolute levels of direct employment, continue to be critical to the wealth of capitalist countries. The operation of global finance, as discussed in Chapter 2, means that the labour strategies of corporations increasingly operate at a global, rather than a regional or national, level. The result is not 'postindustrialism', but the reorganisation of industrial activity on a global level, including the trans-fer of much manufacturing employment to the industrialising economies of developing countries, where there is a vast supply of cheap and disciplined labour. The scale of development of manufacturing and related activities in China alone is phenomenal. The Chinese government estimates that eight million jobs were created in 2003 (US Chinese Embassy website), and more than 100 million rural Chinese have moved to cities, the largest ever recorded movement of people, with over half of them in the new manufacturing area of Guangdong (Ash, 2002). Since 1977, official recorded levels of employment have increased by over 300 million, to around 740 million, and estimates of employment by industrial sector give a glimpse of a social revolution, as China makes the transition from an agrarian to an industrial economy. In 2002, 45% of those in employment are recorded as working in agriculture, fishing and forestry, but 11% are now in manufacturing, 5% in construction and a further 9.3% in trade, transport and communication (www.laborsta.ilo.org). Manufacturing employment is not disappearing; it is being reorganised at a global level.

The category of 'services' itself is also increasingly unhelpful as a concept for the analysis of work organisation in advanced economies. Designed as a 'catch-all' residual category for everything that was *not* manufacturing, mining, construction, utilities or agriculture, it has become *the* major category of employment. Advanced economies with growing biotechnology, IT, media and communications industries blur the boundaries between the 'informational' or knowledge-based and the 'material' content of goods, making the conventional manufacturing/services distinction increasingly redundant (Castells, 2000). One of the most successful new consumer and business products of the last decade, the mobile phone, relies on a combination of material artefact, information technology, high-tech communications and leisure and entertainment services. The organisation behind this and other ICT-hybrid artefacts is invisible to most consumers and reflects the underdeveloped conceptual framework for understanding the transformation of work organisation.

The typical advanced capitalist economies of the early twenty-first century therefore demonstrate considerable continuities with their early twentieth-century industrialised forms, and remain 'industrial' in important ways. The organisation of manufacturing and services has changed, however, with more diversity of economic activity, growing emphasis on new forms of producer, and social, personal and leisure services, more disaggregated organisation forms and more globalised production strategies.

A Knowledge-based Occupational Structure?

It is inherently difficult to evaluate claims that work and organisations are *increasingly* dependent on the production of knowledge and the maximisation of its economic value, since it is clear that industrialisation itself depended heavily on the exploitation of emerging scientific knowledge. Nevertheless, patterns of occupational change suggest that a growing proportion of work in each of these societies relies on the use of specialist knowledge as part of the calculation of economic value. In each country, there is a common trend towards increasing proportions of the workforce being employed in the 'knowledge-based' managerial, professional and technical occupations (Castells, 2000). Some caution is necessary in interpreting such statistical evidence, because the use of occupational titles, such as 'manager' or 'professional', is likely to differ from place to place. Consistency of change over time within data for each country and the similarity of overall trends between countries nevertheless give some confidence in the general validity of the results.

Variation between countries in the balance between these occupations and in their level of concentration may partly reflect different conventions of categorisation, but also suggests that differences in policy and organisational strategies produce different proportions of managerial, professional and technical and associate professional jobs. Japan shows the most significant increase in the proportion of managers, from 5.8% of the workforce in 1970 to 14.5% in 2004 (Figure 5.9 and Table 5.8). In Germany, in contrast, it is technical and associate professions that have grown fastest, from around 7% to 20.5% of occupations (Figure 5.11 and Table 5.7). In the USA, managerial and professional occupations increased from a quarter to over one-third of jobs, while technical work declined from 17.4% to 13.3% (Figure 5.10 and Table 5.6). In the UK, managerial, professional and technical occupations have all increased markedly from 18% to 40% of jobs (Figures 5.5 and 5.12 and Table 5.5). In the USA, the knowledge-based occupations comprise close to 50% of jobs; in other cases, they are around 40%. In every instance, however, these occupations represent a larger proportion of jobs than all manual categories combined (Figures 5.5–5.8 and Table 5.9).

Moreover, the rise of knowledge-based occupations is matched by a consistent decline in manual labour (Figures 5.5–5.8). This is particularly marked in the UK and Germany, where the proportion of manual jobs has fallen from around 50% to 30%. In the USA, manual occupations comprise less than a quarter of the total. There has been consistent growth in the proportion of more routine jobs in offices, retail, entertainment facilities and personal and social services, providing around one-quarter of occupations in each case (Figures 5.5–5.8).

Although the increasing proportions of managerial, professional and technical occupations suggest that specialist knowledge is integral to economic activity, the organisational division of labour also continues to rely on significant numbers of routine and semi-skilled workers. Forms of work, and normative experiences of work, have changed considerably in the

Organisations, Identities and the Self

Figure 5.5   UK: occupational groups, 1971–2004

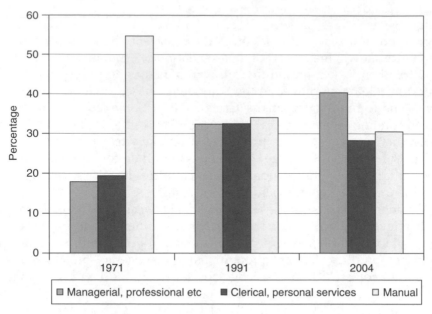

Figure 5.6   USA: occupational groups, 1970–2002

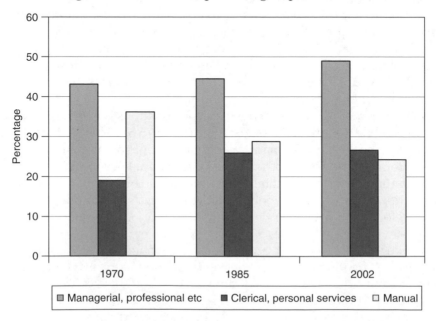

Figure 5.7   Germany: occupational groups, 1976–2004

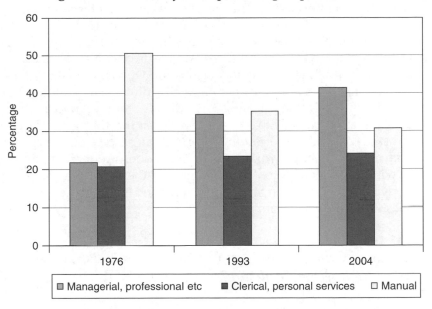

Figure 5.8   Japan: occupational groups, 1970–2004

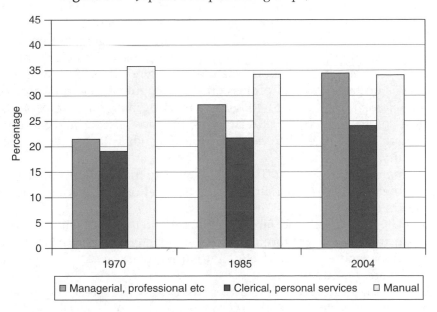

past half-century, to focus more on social interaction and the production and processing of information. The most common form of technology used in work is likely to be some form of computerised equipment, and work is likely to require both a degree of computer literacy and considerable communication skills used in shops, offices and leisure facilities. In Britain, for example, around 80% of those in the leisure and welfare industries, 59% of those in national or local government and 53% of those in banking, insurance and finance said that 'dealing with people' took up at least half of working hours, compared with 30% of those in manufacturing (Gallie, 2000). If social skills and the more routine information-processing are included in the idea of knowledge work, then organisations are increasingly concerned with the exploitation of knowledge, but the majority experience is not the high-value knowledge creation activities envisaged by the early theorists of postindustrialism.

Are Advanced Capitalist Societies Converging around a Common Occupational Structure?

The mobility of deregulated capital in a global market has not overridden the cultural, institutional and political distinctions between societies, as is evident from Figures 5.9–5.12 (detailed in Tables 5.5–5.8). In line with Castells' (2000) findings, the four countries represent two contrasting trajectories of change. The USA and the UK approximate to a 'service economy' model, with manual work declining sharply, and jobs in personal services and sales, clerical, secretarial, professional and managerial categories all increasing. Japan and Germany approximate to a production economy, showing greater continuity in occupational structure, higher rates of skilled manual work maintained over time, and a greater emphasis on technical and professional development. Japan (Figure 5.9 and Table 5.8) and the USA (Figure 5.10 and Table 5.6) represent the biggest contrasts, with the USA showing the most *dis*continuity in types of occupation between 1970 and the present, while Japan shows most continuity.

Germany (Figure 5.11 and Table 5.7) is close to the Japanese pattern, but with a higher proportion of professional occupations (14.1%) and a lower proportion of managers (6.8%).

The UK (Figure 5.12 and Table 5.5) is similar to the USA, with a marked increase from one-tenth to one-quarter in managerial and professional occupations, and a marked decline in manual work, resulting in a more even spread of occupations.

Despite the large decline in manual jobs, the UK still has similar proportions of people in manual work to Germany, but Germany has more skilled

Figure 5.9   Japan: employment by occupation, 1970–2004

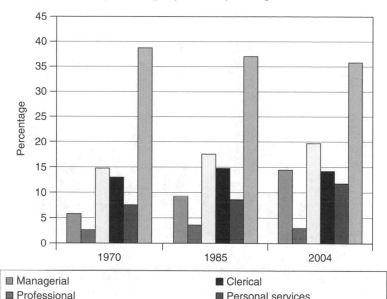

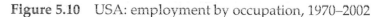

Figure 5.10   USA: employment by occupation, 1970–2002

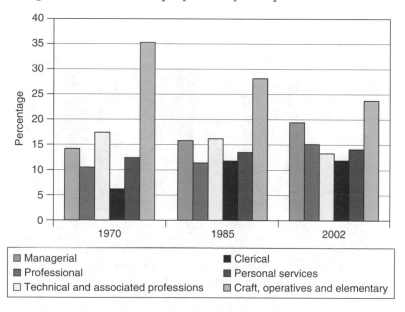

Figure 5.11   Germany: employment by occupation, 1976–2004

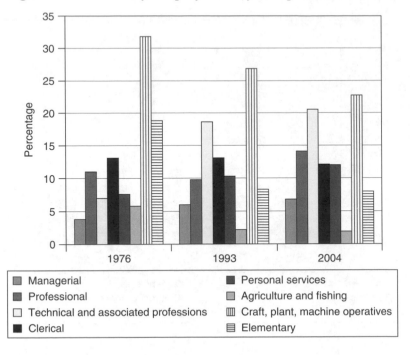

Figure 5.12   UK: employment by occupation, 1971–2004

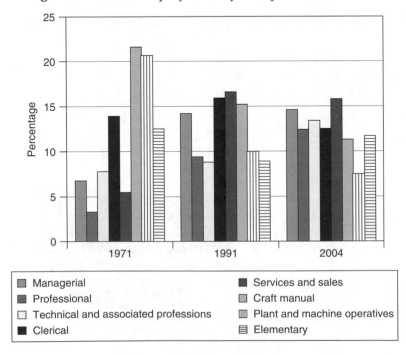

manual jobs (15.5% compared to 11.3% in the UK), and less unskilled (15.2% compared to the UK's 19.2%). The UK also has a higher concentration of managers, and a lower level of technical and associated professionals, indicating the long-established contrast between the engineering base of German industry and the managerial and finance orientation of the UK. The figures indicate a more polarised occupational structure in the UK, with more people drawn in to lower paid services work, in a more deregulated labour market.

While the predominance of technical occupations in Japan and Germany has increased, in line with greater continuity in a production economy, managerial and professional occupations are predominant in the USA and the UK, reflecting the emphasis on business, and personal and social, services in these economies. Setting aside questions about differences between countries in the ways that occupations are allocated to categories, the differences between the proportions of managerial occupations (which range from 19.4% in the USA to 6.8% in Germany) suggest that science and engineering knowledge is more highly valued, and correspondingly more developed, in Japan and Germany, while management is more elaborated and diversified in the USA and the UK. These represent two different models of knowledge-based economies, and two different orientations to the same underlying logics of mobile, deregulated capital markets.

Upgrading of the Occupational Structures of Advanced Capitalist Societies?

The more pessimistic prognoses about the future of work in developed economies predicted an increasing polarisation of occupational structures, anticipating the growth of deskilled, routine and low-level service occupations at the bottom of the occupational hierarchy, and a declining 'middle level' of skilled work. Common trends in occupational change over the last thirty years suggest instead that a degree of upgrading of the occupational structure has taken place, reflected in the increasing proportions of managerial, professional, and technical and associate professional occupations, which have expanded faster than routine service and labouring jobs. Routine services, sales and elementary occupations have declined as a percentage of occupations in Germany, remained relatively stable in the USA, increased slightly in Japan and increased somewhat more in the UK. It is notable that the UK has experienced the most expansion in routine personal services and sales work since the 1970s, although at 15.8% of employment, this category is similar to the USA, and is only marginally higher than in Japan (11.8%) and Germany (12%).

Overall, occupational structures have been marked by a degree of upgrading, with between 40–50% of people in managerial, professional and associated occupations, around a quarter in semi-routinised, white-collar office and shop work, a smaller group of skilled manual workers, and between one-quarter and one-third (depending on the classification used) of unskilled service and general labouring work. It could be argued that this apparent upgrading is an artefact produced by sectoral shifts towards services employment, which perhaps inflate the estimate of 'knowledge work', simply because work itself is less likely to involve manual labour. In a 'shift share' analysis differentiating the two effects in the Scottish labour market, Paterson and Ianelli (2004) conclude that upgrading is due mainly to a change in the nature of work itself, across all sectors. In other words, whether someone works in manufacturing, commercial or public services, they are more likely to be in a more skilled job now than twenty years ago. Given that the Scottish labour market is similar to that in the rest of the UK and Europe, it is reasonable to infer that the process of occupational upgrading is a general one.

Upgrading of the Knowledge Content of Work?

General assumptions that the knowledge content of work has increased, alongside the upgrading of occupational structures, however, need to be treated with a degree of scepticism. The knowledge content of any job is not an absolute or fixed attribute, but is the result of a managerial process that produces a particular division of labour. Where judgement, discretion and autonomous problem-solving are requirements of any job, then the knowledge content is considerably higher, but recent evidence from the UK suggests that organisational responses to competitive pressures are to impose tighter controls over labour in the belief that this leads to higher productivity. The result is less discretion at work, even among those in highly skilled occupations (Gallie et al., 2004). Higher levels of educational attainment and rising numbers of graduates do not therefore necessarily lead to a higher level of knowledge or skills used in the jobs done.

There is also a danger that an increase in credentials expected by employers is confused with the upgrading of skills used by employees (Kumar, 1995). Although it is difficult to judge the relationship between qualifications and job content, the OECD *Jobs Study* (1994) and Brynin (2002) also conclude that substantial numbers of people are overqualified for the jobs they do. Conversely, job titles may be inflated to imply more knowledgeable or prestigious jobs, without any increase in skills or authority: sales staff become 'sales consultants', routine clerical and call centre workers become

'managers' and 'associates' and so on. In other cases, organisational restructuring may have the effect of deskilling jobs, even though they retain their
old title: in banking, for example, branch management has feminised at the
same time that it has been downgraded by the centralisation of corporate
control over strategy (Halford et al., 1997).

Nevertheless, surveys of work experience during the 1980s and 1990s
found that the majority had experienced an increase in the skills required
in their jobs over the last five years, and this applied to all occupational
groups, other than semi- and unskilled manual workers (Gallie et al., 1998;
Gallie, 2000). Those in professional and managerial occupations were
particularly likely to experience increasing skill requirements, with only
9% reporting any decrease. The process of upskilling had accelerated
between the 1980s and 1990s, leading Gallie (2000) to conclude that 'with
the exception of non-skilled workers, the overall picture is one of a
substantial rise in skill levels across the greater part of the workforce'
(p. 290). Organisationally, there are contradictory processes at work:
increasing skills are accompanied by decreasing levels of discretion,
implying low levels of trust in employment relations, even at higher occupational levels, and a mechanistic model of organisational knowledge, as
operating without the need for judgement and autonomy in a network of
social relations.

Increasing Polarisation of Income in an Upgraded Occupational Structure

The upgrading of occupational structures and skills, and evidence of the
growing significance of formal knowledge in organisational strategy, has
paradoxically been accompanied by increasing inequality of incomes and
wealth. In the USA and the UK, where neoliberal economics have been
pursued most aggressively, inequality has risen particularly sharply. In
December 2003, the conservative US journal *Business Week* created a flurry
of concern when it published an article entitled 'Waking up from the American Dream'. The article used Thomas Piketty and Emmanuel Saez's (2001)
US Census Bureau data to show the decline of upward mobility since the
1970s, the decline in average incomes, and the growth of inequality. Between
1973 and 2000, the average real income of 90% of US taxpayers fell by 7%,
while the income of the top 1% rose by 148%, and the income of the top 0.01
percent by 599%. Simultaneously, public spending on education and welfare has been reduced and government functions have been privatised,
both of which tend to reduce opportunities for upward mobility and well-
paid employment. In the UK, in the 1980s, average household income
increased by 27%, but there was a large redistribution of resources in favour

of the wealthiest and hence growing social polarisation. The top 10% gained an average increase of 38% and the bottom 10% an increase of 7% (*Social Trends*, 2001). Since the election of a Labour government in 1997, relative poverty has been reduced, mainly by drawing people back into employment and linking benefits to work. 'In-work poverty' has however increased from around 3 million a year between 1994 and 1997, to 3.5 million a year between 1999 and 2002 (www.poverty.org.uk), and the level of inequality, measured by the Gini coefficient, is at its highest level since the 1960s (Brewer et al., 2004).

This disconnection between upgraded occupational structures and rising social inequality suggests that social polarisation is not an inevitable outcome of a new information- and knowledge-based division of labour, but the result of a capitalist logic, which is enacted in processes of political decision-making and organisational restructuring. Deregulated financial markets make economies more interdependent at a global level, which means that occupational structures, and the associated pattern of social divisions and opportunities, increasingly have to be understood in terms of a global division of labour, shaped and controlled by large organisations and their shareholders. Different countries continue to have different relationships to shared economic and technical rationalities, reflecting both their cultural, institutional and organisational diversity and their interdependence in a globalising economy. The route that is followed by the USA or the UK as opposed to Japan or Germany, or China or India, depends on the political policies adopted by governments and the organisational strategies pursued, as well as that country's position in a global economy (Castells, 2000).

The Globally Organised Interdependence of Labour

The occupational structures of advanced capitalist economies are best understood in the context of an emerging global division of labour, in 'a process of hierarchical, segmented, inter-dependence of the labour force, under the impulse of relentless movements by firms in the circuits of their global network' (Castells, 2000: 252). This is not equivalent to a global labour market, but is a result of the mobility of deregulated capital. Constraints on labour mobility derive from culture, borders, taxation policies and government restrictions on asylum and immigration, and although there has been increasing migration of people in need of work, much of this results from the effects of war, famine and poverty.

The operation of mobile capital, through globally oriented supply chains and organisational arrangements, managed at the apex by multinational corporations, underlies the new global division of labour. Deregulated capital gives organisations increasing autonomy over the range of strategies available to them to control costs, increasing their power over labour, and putting more pressure on governments to lower employment protections. Although a significant proportion of skilled labour in the developed economies retains good terms and conditions of work, more routine work and tasks have been subject to a range of strategies to increase short-term return on investments to shareholders, in a financial market that prioritises shareholder value over long-term development. In relation to labour, this means reducing costs and enhancing the potential for flexibility in the use of labour in every aspect of economic activity.

First it is evident that mass production activity is increasingly being relocated to areas where labour costs are low, as illustrated by the case of China. As a result of subcontracting and FDI in factories, China now manufactures significant proportions of most consumer goods, including 70% of toys, 29% of colour TVs and 70% of clocks and watches. Twenty million migrant workers, for example, are estimated to live in the Pearl River delta area of Guangdong province, adjacent to Hong Kong. The province accounts for 10% of China's economy, one-third of its exports and has received one-third of total FDI (Hennock, 2003). Labour conditions and safety are poor, and hours of work very long (Ash, 2002; Hennock, 2003). In 2004, the pay of a Chinese factory worker averaged $0.92 per hour, in comparison with $21.80 in the USA (*Guardian*, 7.11.05). The rising economic power of China, indicated by its growing trade surplus and foreign currency reserves, and rapidly developing consumer markets, means that its position in a global division of labour is evolving rapidly, with uncertain implications for the future.

Network technologies also enable organisations to capitalise on the availability of educated, but cheaper labour to provide services or process data from remote offices. In relation to call centre and data-processing work, for example, financial service businesses including Barclays, Abbey, Lloyds TSB and HSBC are all exporting jobs to India, China and Malaysia (West, 2004). Skilled labour in Bombay and Bangalore has made these cities global subcontractors for software development, with pay between 20% and 50% of the rate earned for similar work in the USA. The availability of accountancy, law and finance graduates in India means that a proportion of professional services are also expected to move there (Khan, 2003).

A global labour strategy is also evident in the organisation of supply chains to outsource parts of production, data-processing or services. Supermarkets such as Wal-Mart or Tesco, for example, influence wages and working conditions globally, indirectly through their supply chain practices, and directly through their employment standards. Research by Oxfam (2004), spanning 12 countries and based on 1,000 interviews with workers, business owners, government officials and trade unions, concluded that the large-scale retail organisations used their buying power through the supply chain to impose tighter production targets and lower prices. Inspection systems and ethical trading codes, designed to enforce minimum protections for labour, were evaded by factory managers seeking to meet production targets (Lawrence, 2004). The effects are felt most severely at the bottom of the chain, as price cuts result in lower rates of pay and increasing overtime.

The mobility of capital may be used as a bargaining lever over existing workforces to extract a more intensive wage–effort bargain in exchange for retaining their jobs. This feeds through into organisational strategies to increase direct control over labour in the advanced economies, and creates perceptions of insecurity and intensification at work, with negative effects on morale and motivation. In a UK study of organisational restructuring (Burchell et al., 1999), over 60% of those interviewed reported increases in the speed of work and in the effort required to do their jobs; three-quarters reported increased responsibility, but only 19% reported an increase in promotion prospects and 27% reported a decrease. Perceived insecurity seems likely to reflect perceptions that employers are acting more instrumentally towards labour, increasing uncertainty over the employer's next move, heightened distrust and greater pressure on work productivity.

Increasing flexibility in the organisation of labour is reflected in the increased use of fractional or part-time contracts to manage seasonal variation or changes in levels of demand. Part-time work has increased across the developed economies, with the exception of the USA, from 10–15% of employment in 1979 to as much as a quarter in 2004 (Figure 5.13 and Table 5.10).

By 1998, 44% of UK workplaces had one-quarter or more part-time employees, whereas in 1980, only 32% of employers met this criterion (Millward et al., 2000). Although much part-time work is routinised and poorly paid, and is a poor substitute for the disappearance of large numbers of skilled jobs in the manufacturing sector, it encompasses an increasing range of occupations, from domestic help to professional practice and business services (Hoque and Kirkpatrick, 2003). Part-time work remains poorly conceptualised, however, because of the continuing assumption that work is done in at least eight hour blocks for at least five days a week. This was itself a construct of large-scale modern organisations in the twentieth century, one which is declining as a result of globally oriented labour strategies.

Organisations may also seek greater flexibility over labour by increasing the use of temporary contracts and self-employed freelancers. Skilled labour may be bought in on short-term contracts for specific, time-limited

Figure 5.13　Changes in part-time work, 1979–2004

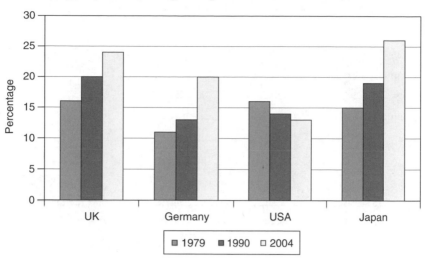

tasks requiring specialist expertise, such as software engineering, website development, research, design, corporate marketing, head-hunting, financial management and so on. This small group of people is likely to operate in a labour market at global level, where they are able to command a high price for their labour (Rosenberg and Lapidus, 1999). The most extreme contrast is in the use of routine labour to respond to variations in seasonal production or demand. Food production, for example, uses temporary and migrant labour, often in the least regulated sectors of the economy, with poor terms and conditions of employment (Lawrence, 2004). At its worst, the result is the exploitation of the most vulnerable migrant labour, as illustrated by the death of 20 Chinese people, treated effectively as bonded labour by gang organisers, picking cockles on Morecambe beach, northwest England, in February 2004. On average, temporary work is disadvantageous to labour: it is worse paid, even when age, education and industry are controlled for, and attracts fewer benefits such as pensions, sick pay and paid holiday (Rosenberg and Lapidus, 1999). Recorded statistics, which probably underestimate low pay, show that, in the worst case, pay is 47% less than the average (in Spain) and even in the best case is 17% less (in Germany) (OECD, 2003). Such work tends to be concentrated amongst younger people, women and those with fewer credentials, and in the USA there is some evidence that ethnic minorities are more likely to be in temporary work, with African-Americans, for example, comprising over 20% of temporary domestic help (Rosenberg and Lapidus, 1999).

Counter to pessimistic predictions about the wholesale casualisation of work, however, temporary labour has not increased universally and there

Figure 5.14   Temporary employment as % of total employment in
selected OECD countries

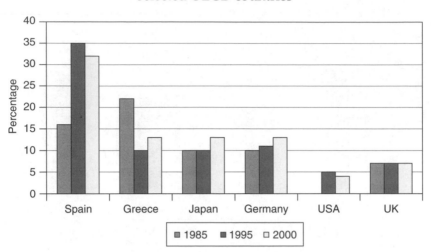

are persistent differences between countries in its use. Between 1985 and
2000, there were significant increases in France, Italy, the Netherlands,
Portugal and Spain, but a decline in Greece and Luxembourg, and limited
change in Japan, Germany, the UK and the USA (OECD, 2003). In Spain,
for example, almost a third of employment was temporary in 2000, compared with 4% in the USA and 7% (1.6 million) in the UK, showing little
change over time (Figure 5.14 and Table 5.11). There is also considerable
mobility out of temporary jobs: between one-third and two-thirds of
people move into permanent jobs within two years, although up to a quarter also become unemployed within the same period (OECD, 2003).

Issues of definition make reliable assessments of the extent of temporary work difficult. It seems, for example, that although temporary contracts
may not affect a large proportion of the workforce, a growing proportion
of employers are using them. Millward et al.'s (2000) analysis of time series
data at UK workplace level shows significantly increasing use of fixed-
term contracts of less than 12 months. In 1998, 35% of workplaces with
more than 25 employees used short-term contracts, compared with 19% in
1980. Such arrangements are not necessarily short term for the employee,
who may work long term with the same agency but in a number of different organisations, or work for the same organisation for many years but as
a subcontractor rather than employee. Nor are they inevitably exploitative. Skilled workers in occupations such as teaching and nursing may
choose to work as short-term labour supply, because of personal responsibilities or better short-term pay rates. Overall, there is considerable variation
in the organisational use and worker experience of temporary or short-term

contracts, depending both on cultural and institutional contexts and the skills exercised by labour.

Conclusion

The organisation of work, and the structuring of societies and social identities, increasingly has to be understood at global level, where a new hierarchy of capital and labour has been brought about through the mobility of finance capital in a deregulated market. In an enactment of the calculative economic logics of markets, technology and expertise, the manual work of mass manufacturing, once concentrated in Europe and North America, is increasingly being transferred to areas of cheaper labour. The wealthier countries seek to retain competitive advantage by retaining control over the strategic direction of enterprise, but their position remains tenuous in a globalising economy where all forms of capitalism are changing. The relative upgrading of occupational structures in the wealthier countries thus has to be seen in the context of a global division of labour, rather than interpreted as a new form of postindustrial society, and will not necessarily be an enduring feature of working life in these societies.

The global economic logic of deregulated markets has been articulated through different cultural and political institutions, resulting in the diverse work and occupational profiles described here, with differences in the balance of occupations, the rates and directions of change and the degree of inequality. The USA and the UK approximate to a service economy model, with rapid declines in manufacturing and increased diversity of services, especially those linked to business and finance, as well as social welfare. In the UK, whereas two-thirds worked in manual jobs in the1950s, managerial, professional and technical workers alone now outnumber those in manual work. In the USA, half the workforce is employed in managerial, professional and technical occupations, with less than a quarter in manual jobs. Japan and Germany have maintained a production economy, following a more gradualist model of change, and maintaining higher levels of manufacturing employment, as well as restructuring through greater emphasis on skilled producer, rather than personal or social, services.

At the same time, the mobility of capital, together with socially regressive taxation policies in the neoliberal regimes of the USA and the UK have resulted in an increasing polarisation of incomes, both within and between countries. In the context of weakened labour organisation, organisational restructuring and disaggregation are creating a 'two tier' system. The highly skilled are relatively advantaged by a global division of labour that profits firms at the high value end of production and services. Those who are unqualified or unskilled appear increasingly disadvantaged, as global supply chains and global production arrangements enable corporations to drive down prices, cutting the costs and worsening the conditions of labour, in both the developed and the industrialising economies. In the wealthiest country, the USA, average incomes have declined and inequality increased, concentrating wealth in fewer hands, despite an upgrading of the occupational structure. Employment protections in the wealthier societies are under pressure from a universalising logic of cost-cutting, even for those in the advantaged knowledge-based occupations, who perceive themselves as working harder, having less discretion and less security (Devine et al., 2000; Gallie et al., 2004). Economic recession in Japan also stimulated new flexibility strategies. Traditional employment protections for the core workforce, entailing regular wages increases, promotion and lifetime security, have been weakened, and the size of the peripheral workforce, without security or prospects of wage rises, has grown (Kyotani, 1999). In poorer countries, such as India and China, rapid economic growth has gone hand in hand with increasing inequality, and enormous sections of the population remain excluded from the benefits of increased GDP (UN, 2005). The global division of labour has thus subjected those in the industrialising economies to the worst of the deregulated, flexible labour market. The polarisation of incomes is not inevitable, but is a result of neoliberal policies and the associated short-termist strategies of organisations.

The significance of changes in work and organisations for social and personal identities in the advanced capitalist countries is disputed, and the next chapter turns to an examination of these processes. The main contention is that the destandardisation of labour is leading to the decline of stable work and occupational identities organised around modern divisions of class and gender (Beck, 2000; Sennett, 1998). The result is expected to be greater individualisation and fragmentation of experience, and the loss of a coherent sense of self, as organisational restructuring, subcontracting and externalisation affect routes into, and progression within, labour markets. In the wealthier societies, however, there are significant continuities in work and employment, and rising rates of economic activity suggest that paid work remains a central source of social organisation and identity. Pessimistic prognoses of rising insecurity and the end of a stable sense of self may thus be overstated. Levels of temporary employment have not risen dramatically in most countries. In the UK, job tenure has remained stable over the last twenty years, and women's average tenure has increased (Nolan, 2003). Changes in personal and social identities cannot therefore be read off from changes in occupational structures and divisions of labour. Instead, their interconnections have to be traced through assessments of changing experiences of work and organisations.

Appendix

Table 5.1   UK: percentage distribution of employment by industrial sector 1970–2004

Industry	1970	1985	2004
I Extractive	**4.9**	**3.8**	**1.6**
Agriculture, forestry and fishing	3.2	2.5	1.3
Mining and quarrying	1.7	1.3	0.3
II Transformative	**43.1**	**29.9**	**21.8**
Construction	6.8	6.1	7.7
Utilities	1.6	1.2	0.6
Manufacturing	34.7	22.6	13.5
III All services	**52**	**64.9**	**76.5**
Transport and communication	6.7	5.8	6.8
Wholesale and retail trade, restaurants and hotels	16.4	19.9	19.9
Producer services (finance, insurance, real estate, business)	5.0	9.5	15.5
Social and personal services	23.9	29.7	33.5
IV Unclassified	**0**	**1.3**	**0.8**
Total employed	**24,381,000** (100%)	**24,539,000** (99.9%)	**28,008,400** (99.9%)

Source: ILO Labour Statistics, www.Laborsta.ilo.org/UK Office of Population Censuses and Surveys; all in employment aged 16 and over. Based on International Standard Industrial Classification (ISIC) Rev.3.

Table 5.2   USA: percentage distribution of employment by
industrial sector, 1970–2004

Industry	1970	1985	2004
I Extractive	**5.2**	**4.0**	**2.0**
Agriculture, forestry and fishing	4.5	3.1	1.6
Mining and quarrying	0.7	0.9	0.4
II Transformative	**34.0**	**27.4**	**20.3**
Construction	6.1	6.5	7.7
Utilities	1.5	1.4	0.8
Manufacturing	26.4	19.5	11.8
III All services	**60.9**	**68.7**	**77.6**
Transport and communication	5.3	5.7	4.2
Wholesale and retail trade, restaurants and hotels	19.1	20.8	21.5
Producer services (finance, insurance, real estate, business)	6.8	10.3	17.3
Social and personal services	29.7	31.9	34.6
IV Unclassified	**0**	**0**	**0**
Total employed	**78,678,000** (100.1%)	**107,150,000** (100.1%)	**139,252,000** (99.9%)

Source: ILO Labour Statistics, www.Laborsta.ilo.org/US Census Bureau; all in employment aged 16 and over. Based on ISIC Rev.3.

Table 5.3 Germany: percentage distribution of employment
by industrial sector, 1970–2004

Industry	1970	1991	2004
I Extractive	**8.7**	**5.3**	**2.6**
Agriculture, forestry and fishing	7.5	4.2	2.3
Mining and quarrying	1.2	1.1	0.3
II Transformative	**47.1**	**39.2**	**30.4**
Construction	7.7	7.0	6.8
Utilities	0.8	1.1	0.8
Manufacturing	38.6	31.1	22.8
III All services	**46.9**	**55.6**	**66.3**
Transport and communication	5.4	6.2	5.5
Wholesale and retail trade, restaurants and hotels	15.2	14.2	17.4
Producer services (finance, insurance, real estate, business)	4.5	7.5	12.8
Social and personal services	21.8	27.7	30.6
IV Unclassified	**0**	**0**	**0.5**
Total employed	(100%)	37,445,000 (100.1%)	35,659,000 (99.8%)

Source: 1970 percentages from Castells (1996); 1991 and 2004 from ILO Labour Statistics, www.Laborsta.ilo.org German Federal and Land Statistical Offices; all in employment aged 15 and over. Based on ISIC Rev.3.

Table 5.4   Japan: percentage distribution of employment by
industrial sector, 1970–2004

Industry	1970	1985	2004
I Extractive	**17.8**	**9.0**	**4.6**
Agriculture, forestry and fishing	17.4	8.8	4.5
Mining and quarrying	0.4	0.2	0.1
II Transformative	**35.2**	**34.7**	**28.3**
Construction	7.7	9.1	9.2
Utilities	0.5	0.6	0.5
Manufacturing	27.0	25.0	18.6
III All services	**46.8**	**56.0**	**65.9**
Transport and communication	6.4	5.9	6.2
Wholesale and retail trade, restaurants and hotels	19.9	22.7	24.3
Producer services (finance, insurance, real estate, business)	2.6	6.8	13.3
Social and personal services	17.9	20.6	22.1
IV Unclassified	**0.1**	**0.4**	**1.1**
Total employed	**50,940,000** (99.9%)	**58,070,000** (100.1%)	**63,290,000** (99.9%)

Source: ILO Labour Statistics, www.Laborsta.ilo.org/Japanese Statistics Bureau; all in employment, aged 15 and over. Based on ISIC Rev.3.

Table 5.5   UK: percentage distribution of employment by
occupation, 1971–2004

Occupational category	1971	1991	2004
Managerial	6.8	14.2	14.6
Professional	3.3	9.4	12.4
Technical and associate professions	7.8	8.8	13.4
Clerical/secretarial	13.9	15.9	12.5
Personal services and sales	5.5	16.6	15.8
Craft and related manual trades	21.6	15.2	11.3
Plant and machine operators	20.6	10.0	7.5
Elementary workers and labourers	12.5	8.9	11.7
Armed forces	N.A.	0.4	0.6
Unclassified/other	8.1	0.7	0.2
Total employed	**25,021,000** (GB)	**26,399,600** (100.1%)	**28,008,400** (100%)

Source: 1971 figures are for Great Britain only, adapted from Gallie (2000); 1991 and 2004 figures from ILO Labour Statistics, www.Laborsta.ilo.org/OPCS Labour Force Survey; all in employment aged 16 and over. Based on International Standard Classification of Occupations (ISCO) 88.

Table 5.6   USA: percentage distribution of employment by
occupation, 1970–2002

Occupational category	1970	1985	2002
Managerial	14.2	15.8	19.4
Professional	10.5	11.4	15.1
Technical and associate professions	17.4	16.2	13.3
Clerical/secretarial	6.2	11.8	11.9
Personal services and sales	12.4	13.5	14.1
Crafts, operators and elementary	35.3	28.1	23.7
Total employed	**78,678,000** (100%)	**107,150,000** (100%)	**136,485,000** (100%)

Source: ILO Labour Statistics, www.Laborsta.ilo.org/OPCS Labour Force Survey; all in employment aged 16 and over. Based on ISCO 1968.
Note: 2002 figures used because these give a breakdown between professional and technical and associate professional categories. Breakdown into craft, operators and elementary occupations not given in ISCO 1968. But Castells' (1996) data suggests that the decline is among craft and operators' occupations.

Table 5.7   Germany: percentage distribution of employment
by occupation, 1976–2004

Occupational category	1976	1993	2004
Managerial	3.8	6.0	6.8
Professional	11.0	9.8	14.1
Technical and associate professions	7.0	18.6	20.5
Clerical/secretarial	13.1	13.1	12.1
Personal services and sales	7.6	10.3	12.0
Agriculture and fishing	5.8	2.2	1.9
Craft and related trades	–	19.0	15.5
Plant and machine operators	31.8 (includes crafts)	7.9	7.2
Elementary workers and labourers	18.8	8.3	8.0
Armed forces	N.A.	1.3	0.8
Unclassified	1.1	3.4	1.2
Total employed		**36,380,000** (99.9%)	**35,659,000** (100.1%)

Source: 1976 figures from Castells (1996); 1993 and 2004 from ILO Labour Statistics, www. Laborsta.ilo.org/German Federal and Land Statistical Offices; all in employment aged 15 and over. 1993 and 2004 based on ISCO 88.

Table 5.8   Japan: percentage distribution of employment by occupation, 1970–2004

Occupational category	1970	1985	2004
Managerial	5.8	9.3	14.5
Professional	2.6	3.6	3.0
Technical and associate professions	14.8	17.6	19.7
Clerical/secretarial	13.0	14.8	14.2
Personal services and sales	7.6	8.6	11.8
Crafts, operators and elementary	38.7	37.0	35.8
Unclassified	0.2	0.4	1.0
Total employed	**50,940,000** (100%)	**58,070,000** (99.9%)	**63,290,000** (100%)

Source: ILO Labour Statistics, www.Laborsta.ilo.org/Japanese Statistics Bureau; all employed aged 15 and above. Based on ISCO 1988.

Table 5.9   All managerial, professional and technical occupations compared with all manual occupations as a percentage of total employment, 2004

Occupational group	UK	USA	Germany	Japan
All managerial, professional and technical	40.4	47.8	41.4	37.2
All manual occupations	30.5	23.7	32.6	35.8

Table 5.10   Changes in part-time work, selected OECD countries, 1979–2004

Country	Part-time as a percentage of total employment			Percentage of women in part-time employment 2004	Women's share of part-time employment 2004
	1979	1990	2004		
UK	16	20	24	40	78
Germany	11	13	20	37	83
USA	16	14	13	19	68
Japan	15	19	26	42	67

Source: OECD *Employment Outlook*, 2005.

Table 5.11   Temporary employment as a percentage of total employment, in selected OECD countries, 1985–2000

Country	1985	1995	2000
Spain	16	35	32
Greece	22	10	13
Japan	10	10	13
Germany	10	11	13
USA	–	5	4
UK	7	7	7

Source: OECD *Employment Outlook*, 2002.

6

Organisational Restructuring, Work and Social Divisions

In the previous chapter, I highlighted the different emphases given to common underlying trends, contrasting the more managerial and services-oriented occupational structures of the USA and the UK with the more production-oriented economies of Germany and Japan. In every country examined, we saw a pattern of decreasing employment in manufacturing, increasing employment in all forms of services, both highly skilled and more routine, and across all sectors, increasing proportions are employed in management, professional and technical work. The mobility of global capital, combined with the power of network technologies and the increasing global interdependence of labour have created a growing uncertainty about the future of work and social divisions in the advanced capitalist countries.

The restructuring of manufacturing according to the economic instrumentalities of global capital and rapid change in occupational structures have generated concern that employment, the prime source of income for the majority, will become far less predictable and secure. Neoliberal economic policies have resulted in downward pressure on employment protections and greater emphasis on self-reliance. In the USA and the UK in particular, this has been associated with growth in routine services occupations at the lower end of the hierarchy of jobs, creating greater social polarisation. Continuity of work in the same organisation and a stable occupational identity were once seen as enabling a secure sense of self, but new organisational forms are expected to rely on more diversity in working hours and more fragmented opportunity structures, with more frequent changes in jobs, location, tasks and responsibilities.

Work, it is argued, is becoming more individualised. The decline in manual work is seen as fracturing working-class identities, centred on occupational community. The stability of a middle-class identity secured by bureaucratic career hierarchies is expected to be undermined by organisational disaggregation, delayering and subcontracting. The anticipated changes have been presented both positively and negatively. In the latter case, individualisation is seen as damaging to both the fabric of society and selfhood. The most pessimistic scenarios have prophesied the end of work and secure careers, mass unemployment and increasing exploitation through the informal economy (Bridges, 1995; Rifkin, 1995). In a more nuanced argument about the interrelations between flexibilised capitalism, work organisation and selfhood, Richard Sennett (1998) argues that short-termism in work and organisations requires an infinitely malleable, calculative, risk-taking individualism, which undermines the values of mutual care and interdependence. In a competitive and hierarchical system, most will feel relative failures and will bear the psychic as well as the material costs of their relatively disadvantaged position.

More positive interpretations of change, often advanced by business organisations and governments seeking acceptance of less regulated labour markets, have suggested that more individualised work and employment relations create the conditions for greater choice and discretion over work and life. Management writers such as Charles Handy (1994) suggested that the numbers of permanent jobs would decline, but that more self-reliance and 'portfolio working' would enhance the quality of work life by giving people more control over the location, time and type of work they do. Change in organisations also creates an opportunity for challenges to a stratified and divisive system of class, gender and ethnicity. If organisations are increasingly dependent on knowledge and expertise, then it might be expected that there would be increasing emphasis on rewarding people according to their skills, knowledge and competence, rather than whether their face fits. The result should be fairer, more open-minded employment practices, more social mobility between classes, and the atrophying of sexism and racism, in a more inclusive society.

The debates about work restructuring have been marked more by sweeping generalisation and dogmatic assertion than they have by systematic evidence about actual changes in work and identities at organisational level (Taylor, 2002). This chapter evaluates the claims critically, building on the evidence of organisational and occupational restructuring discussed in the previous chapter, and focusing on the significance of the changes for class, gender and ethnic divisions. Changes in employment and occupational structures are effected at the level of organisations, and influence personal and social identities through experiences of work and employment relations. It is at this level that the global reorganisation of capital feeds into the economic opportunity structures of everyday life. Such structures embody occupational hierarchies and boundaries, and different contractual conditions of employment, which constitute socioeconomic class categories and contribute to the structuring of gender and ethnic divisions. As argued in Chapter 1, class, gender and ethnicity are not 'fixed' or singular identities that define who someone is, but social processes expressive of power relations and inequalities. Such processes are importantly exemplified in the ordinary practices of organisations, in which divisions of class, ethnicity and gender are mutually reproduced (Acker, 2000: 192). In the process, agency is conditioned and constrained, but not eradicated, as people reflect on their circumstances and act in relation to them.

Theoretical Conjectures about Employment and Occupational Change

Does the emerging global division of labour result in a series of interconnected changes in work organisation? These can be described along two interrelated dimensions: first, those predictions concerning the terms of the employment contract, and second, those concerning the content of job tasks and responsibilities that are embedded in particular forms of management control over labour. The latter issues are mainly discussed in the next chapter, although they are introduced and set in context here. The focus in this chapter is on changing forms of employment contracts, in relation to the occupational hierarchies characteristic of advanced capitalist countries.

Contemporary patterns of organisational change, driven by the pursuit of enhanced profitability in deregulated financial markets, are seen as intensifying the pressures for self-reliance and the individualisation of labour (Beck, 2000; Castells, 2000; Sennett, 1998). This means that more of the responsibility for economic well-being falls on the individual, rather than the organisation or the institutions of the welfare state. For some, such as Castells and Sennett, these are structural *economic* relations, which fragment labour and undermine forms of social solidarity and security. Others have associated new work orientations with a wider *cultural* shift in contemporary societies towards valuing individualism in itself (Beck and Beck-Gernsheim, 2002; Kallinikos, 2003). The latter position disconnects culture from economic change, suggesting that individualism is itself a result of cultural change, independent of the instrumental sphere of economic relationships.

The 'destandardisation' of labour, Beck (1992) predicted, would proceed through the organisational dismantling of stable work, occupations and career hierarchies in deregulated labour markets, constituting a race to the bottom and mass insecurity. According to Rifkin (1995), new technologies would be the main cause of such changes, rather than the loss of manual jobs to areas of cheaper labour. Such technologies would create advances in productivity and 'jobless growth', increasingly displacing even those in the knowledge-based occupations, and affecting management jobs in particular. The development of flexible and fragmented employment contracts would enable employers to extract higher value from labour. Lifetime, or at least continuing, contracts of employment would be superseded by temporary or time-limited and fractional-time contracts for all occupational groups, including the professional and highly skilled. The counterpart to more temporary contracts is increased self-employment and freelance working. Responsibility for the costs of 'managing' and sustaining work would pass to the individual, rather than the organisation. Two different predictions have been made about new forms of self-employment. The information society, Castells (2000) suggests, creates more rewarding forms of freelance professional work, and writers such as Leadbetter (2000) have seen this as leading to greater self-determination and independence in a more entrepreneurial economy. In contrast, Beck (2000) predicted more precarious, low-quality, exploitative self-employment as the norm.

Challenging the Myths of Mass Casualisation of Work, Short-termism in Employment and the End of Careers

In practice, sweeping generalisations about the 'end of work and careers' are not substantiated. Indeed, although the occupational structures of advanced capitalist societies have undergone dramatic change since the 1970s, there is also considerable continuity in employment patterns.

Relative Continuity in Employment

Most of the workforce of advanced capitalist societies continues to be in stable, long-term employment (Auer and Cazes, 2003), and in the UK and the USA, the numbers in employment have risen, confounding expectations that paid work would cease to be central to life. In the UK, which is not out of line with other countries, trend data from the UK Labour Force Survey shows considerable continuity between 1986 and 2004: for example, there was no decline in the percentage of employees with 10 and over years of service and no sharp rise in the percentage of those with less than one year's service. Systematic survey evidence comparing the experience of work in Britain in 1992 and 2000 also shows that average job tenure has increased slightly from just over six years to seven years and four months (Nolan and Wood, 2003), although this hides the notable fall in job tenure for men over 50 (Moynagh and Worsley, 2005).

Career Hierarchies Continue

There is also ample evidence that the claimed demise of careers is overstated. The rise in managerial, professional and associated technical work in the advanced capitalist countries was demonstrated in the previous chapter, and despite restructuring, middle management remains a significant group. In the USA, Gordon (1996) estimated that around 17 million people were employed solely to supervise subordinates. In the countries examined here, the proportion of people in managerial jobs has increased steadily since the 1970s, and recent evidence from the ESRC *Future of Work Programme* confirms the increases in managers employed in the UK in the last decade (www.leeds.ac.uk/esrcfutureofwork/). Changing employment and occupational structures have also resulted in a growing similarity between the occupational trajectories of managers and professionals, with management itself becoming more professionalised (Li, 2002).

Employment contracts are more diverse in form, and there is evidence of the erosion of trust, increasing individualisation of career opportunities, less certainty about progression and a lower ceiling on expected job level for many (Beynon et al., 2002; Halford et al., 1997; Webb, 2001). Nevertheless, this group of managers and professionals retains a relative advantage in internal and external labour markets. White et al.'s (2004) survey of human resource managers in 2,000 organisations in Britain found a high proportion of workplaces looked to retain employees through creating career and promotion opportunities, which they sought to fill mainly through internal progression. Around half of managers thought their organisation had a well-defined career ladder. In the largest establishments, this rose to three-quarters. It was also notable that service sector organisations, particularly in financial and business services (54%) and public services (60%), were more likely to have career ladders than those in manufacturing (33%), suggesting that the move to services has reinforced the use of career progression as a means to retain labour, rather than undermined it. Most organisations describing themselves as having career hierarchies also saw progression as accessible to the full range of occupations, rather than managerial or professional work alone. Although human resource managers might be expected to put the best gloss on the situation in their organisation, nevertheless these findings suggest considerable commitment to continuity in employment relationships, rather than encouragement to more job moves and fragmentation.

Temporary Contracts and Self-employment are not the Norm

The vast majority of the employed population continue to have permanent contracts. The Working in Britain Survey 2000 found that such contracts have increased by 4% since 1992 to 92% (Nolan and Wood, 2003; Taylor, 2002). In the same survey, only 5% described themselves as working on a temporary contract of less than twelve months and the proportion employed on fixed-term contracts of one to three years was just under 3%. Overall, temporary employment has shown little change since the 1980s (Spain being the notable exception), and typically remains at 15% or less of the workforce (see Table 5.10). Neither has there been a sharp rise in self-employment: in the UK, rates of self-employment have fluctuated between 11% and 13% since the 1970s, while long-term trends in the USA show self-employment at around 8.5% (Moynagh and Worsley, 2005). Other evidence suggests that opting for self-employment is likely to be the result of constraint, rather than opportunity: the majority believe that they have no choice other than self-employment, because they are older, lack the skills for the jobs on offer or are constrained by domestic responsibilities (Smeaton, 2003).

More Diversity in Employment Contracts

Evidence to support the claim of mass casualisation and short-termism in employment, or the death of careers and the rapid growth of 'portfolio working' among highly skilled 'e-lancers' (Leadbetter, 2000) is thus lacking. There are however some significant changes. For example, a greater proportion of UK organisations reported using temporary contracts, with an increase from 19% in 1980 to 35% in 1998 (Millward et al., 2000) (based on workplaces with more than 25 employees). The survey of human resource managers cited above found that four-fifths of organisations used temporary, freelance, casual staff, or outworkers in some capacity (White et al., 2004). Agency labour is also increasingly being used in public services such as health and education and in financial services (Beynon et al., 2002; Nolan, 2004). This qualifies the picture of continuity, and suggests that employers are making use of such contracts as a short-term means of controlling labour costs (Beynon et al., 2002), and in some cases as an extended form of job selection, moving most employees onto permanent contracts after a short period (Meadows and Metcalf, 2006). White et al.'s (2004) survey also found that plans for recruitment centred on increasing the numbers of permanent employees, and not on increasing temporary contracts or agency workers.

Rising average economic activity rates disguise changes in the character of the employed population. In particular, an increasing proportion of men of working age are economically inactive: ONS Labour Force Survey data for the UK, for example, shows that since 1971, men's activity rates have fallen from 91% to 84%. There is gradual convergence between men and women, with 67% of women now economically active compared to 51% in 1970 (see Table 6.1). For both younger men and women, employment is affected by the expansion of further and higher education, and among 16–24-year-olds there is evidence of frequent job moves, with people today holding an average of four jobs in three years, as opposed to two jobs in three years in the 1970s (Meadows and Metcalf, 2006). Most remarkable is the sharp decline in economic activity among men aged 55–64: 34% of men aged 55–64 were inactive in 2002 compared to 9% in 1972–6 (Faggio and Nickell, 2003). This signals a marked change in working life for many men. Although a proportion of men over 50 have been able to retire early, with pensions and severance packages from professional and managerial occupations, a larger proportion have lost jobs because of the relocation of manufacturing, and have either withdrawn from work, and are classified as sick or disabled, or have become long-term unemployed (Taylor, 2003).

Above all, it is the increase in fractional-time contracts that marks changing forms of employment, and it is this which constitutes the main growth in 'non-standard' work (see Table 6.2). It is only in the USA that the proportion of part-time jobs has declined over time to less than 15%. In the UK, around 4.5 million new part-time jobs have been created in the last twenty years (Nolan, 2004), mostly in public and private sector services, and it is predominantly women who occupy them, with 41% of women working part time. In the OECD countries, on average 26% of women work part time, compared with 7% of men, although the rate of increase in part-time working is higher among men. Women's share of part-time work is typically between 68% and 85% (Figure 6.1 and Table 6.2). Much of this is low-paid work, with little opportunity for training and progression, but it is not necessarily insecure or short term.

Figure 6.1   Women in part-time employment, 2004

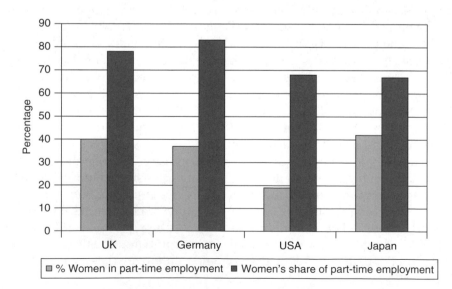

% Women in part-time employment   Women's share of part-time employment

The Power of Finance Capital and the Intensification of Work

Apocalyptic predictions of mass casualisation of work, short-termism in employment, the end of careers and the rise of self-employment are therefore misleading. They have, paradoxically, distracted attention from the very significant changes that are happening, but which relate far more to the content of work and forms of organisational control over labour than they do to 'the end of work' and employment. The dependent wage–labour relationship, which Marx identified as peculiar to capitalist work relations, remains central to the organisation of economic life in the twenty-first century.

Forms of employment are however more diverse, as reflected particularly in the growth of fractional hours contracts. Moreover, there is growing and consistent evidence that the work–effort bargain characteristic of employment relations is being restructured around expectations that labour will be deployed more flexibly, taking on a wider range of tasks and responsibilities and working more intensively (Beynon et al., 2002; Grimshaw et al., 2002; Moynagh and Worsley, 2005; Nolan, 2004; White et al., 2004). The Working in Britain Survey in 2000, for example, included interviews with 2,466 people from the full spectrum of occupations, and found that at every level work was experienced as more stressful, more intensive and demanding, and less satisfying, in comparison with the Employment in Britain Survey conducted in 1992 (Gallie et al., 1998; Taylor, 2002). Job satisfaction had declined in every aspect: although there were only small increases in dissatisfaction with the nature of work, its variety and use of skills, there were much larger increases in dissatisfaction with pay, prospects and training, and the biggest change was in dissatisfaction with the amount of work and the increased time spent doing it. Comparing the situation across advanced capitalist countries, Auer and Cazes (2003) also conclude that despite broadly stable employment, levels of perceived insecurity and dissatisfaction were high. All this evidence points to a decisive shift in power relations between capital and labour, to the detriment of labour.

Changing Class, Ethnic and Gender Divisions in Organisations?

Prognoses about the end of class and the death of work (Beck, 2000; Gorz, 1999; Pakulski and Waters, 1996) are therefore particularly ironic, since these have coincided with polarising occupational structures, rising inequality in incomes, and the intensification of effort. Claims that we were experiencing 'the end of class' at best unintentionally pinpoint the sense that economic class relations have become so taken for granted in the emerging global capitalism that questioning the legitimacy of class-based economic exploitation, which is increasingly organised at global level, has become more difficult than ever.

The misunderstanding has arisen out of contested and competing uses of the same concepts. Conjectures about the end of class, which have been prevalent in deindustrialising societies, have typically related to the claimed demise of a working-class *consciousness* or class *identity*, as a salient social dynamic, and not to the ending of capitalist labour markets that differentially allocate economic advantage, privileging those in the upper levels of occupational hierarchies relative to those in more routine jobs. In the UK, the massive decline of manufacturing, mining, steel-making and shipbuilding in the 1970s has led to the decline of geographically concentrated, white, male, working-class communities. Such manual work was dominated by men and associated with mass membership of trade unions, the Labour Party and social clubs, also dominated by men. Rising unemployment among male manual workers and the increasing concentration of employment in services, which drew more women into jobs, was seen as eroding solidaristic, class-based occupational identities, while making other sources of identity, including consumption and lifestyle, increasingly important.

The assertion of a shared 'working-class identity' owed a lot to Marxist-informed theoretical conjecture about the potential emergence of a working-class consciousness out of the experience of exploitation and class struggle. In practice, the assumption of a unified working-class identity also contained some implicit sexist and racist assumptions that white men were the primary agents of class solidarity. Moreover, systematic connections between economic class (defined by labour market position and employment relations), cultural class-consciousness, or identity, and collective class action were always very difficult to show (Crompton, 1998). Until the 1970s, much sociological analysis of inequality centred on class relations, but research on working-class cultures and attitudes showed people's ambivalence towards identifying themselves with an economic class position. Connections between economic position and expressions of class identities, cultural beliefs and values were fluid and often contradictory (Devine and Savage, 2005). Marshall et al.'s (1988) survey of class in Britain, for example, found that although class was a salient feature of life to respondents, it was not an attribute of individual subjectivity, so much as a feature of social relations expressed in employment relationships and political organisations. Most people had an understanding of a class structure related to economic position and the relative prestige of occupations, but distanced themselves from it, in a pragmatic evaluation of their circumstances and the lack of probability of a political commitment to the redistribution of wealth. Growing critical awareness of the inability of class-based analyses of inequality to account for sexism and racism, without either simply reducing these to class divisions or treating them as 'add ons', provoked further critiques of class theory and contributed to arguments that social and cultural change meant that class was no longer socially significant.

During the 1980s and 1990s, much sociological research on inequality moved away from direct attempts to connect class-consciousness, or identity, and action to economic position, concentrating instead on social structural analyses of class relations and social mobility, measured in terms of the employment relationship (Goldthorpe, 1987; Goldthorpe and Marshall, 1992). This work was based on a Weberian, rather than a Marxist, model of class and stratification, treating class primarily as an economic category derived from differential labour market positions that confer relative advantage or disadvantage in life chances. The dynamic character of capitalist labour markets, where the relative value of different kinds of skills and experiences constantly changes, results in increasingly fragmented classes and complex patterns of differentiation between different groups of employees, from corporate managers to lawyers, police officers, clerical workers, sales assistants and so on. Economic class position in these terms does not necessarily result in any commonality of class identity or expression of common interests; it merely provides one significant basis for shared interests to be articulated. Weber also argued that the differentiation of economic classes was made more complex through interaction with other sources of stratification based on status or social standing. Membership of status groups continues to affect life chances in modern societies, because it positions people differentially in relation to labour market opportunity structures, privileging some and marginalising or excluding others. Some analysts have argued that the Weberian concept of status, involving culturally defined categories of social actors, can be used to develop a better understanding of the disadvantaged position of women and minority ethnic groups, through the intersections of class relations, constituted in economic terms, and status relations, constituted historically, culturally and socially (Crompton, 1998; Fraser, 2000). This gives a more fluid and dynamic picture of social stratification, whose dimensions change as economic organisations and status hierarchies change.

In practical rather than theoretical terms, it is not possible to make a clear-cut distinction between economic class and social status, because economic relations are culturally and socially embedded. The relative economic worth attached to particular skills in the labour market, for example, reflects the social evaluation of different groups: caring skills conventionally attributed to women are valued lower than technical skills conventionally attributed to men. The irreducible social dynamic at work in structuring economic relations is particularly evident when processes of social division are examined at the organisational level. Organisations reflect the intersections of class and status, indicating processes of racism and sexism embedded in market hierarchies of economic worth, despite the espousal of individualised opportunity structures (Halford et al., 1997; Modood et al., 1997). Although in theory the instrumental rationalities of market organisations are indifferent to such personal characteristics as sex or skin colour, in practice, ideologies of gender and 'race' have been central to the allocation of resources, to routine interaction and to the legitimation of material inequalities. In this sense, cultural values, beliefs and understanding comprehensively infiltrate economic relations: the attribution of 'cultural' difference in a status hierarchy of skin colour, sex or religion, for example, is closely connected to economic inequality in routine organisational practices of recruitment, selection, training, performance appraisal and promotion. Such processes of division position men and women and 'racialised' groups in relation to intersecting divisions of class in occupational hierarchies. Although the precise contours and relations of division have changed since the 1970s, with the increasing dominance of business, consumer and public services over manufacturing and the polarisation of occupations, they remain significant (Acker, 2000; Cox, 2004).

Organisations and Restructured Gender Divisions

One of the key social changes taking place in advanced capitalist societies since the 1970s is the increasing employment of women in organisations in increasingly diverse roles. The combination of the decline in factory work, the shift to more service-oriented economies, and their association with employers' demands for flexible labour, has created more routine, low-paid jobs in areas of work that were already feminised, in offices, domestic and personal services, and leisure and entertainment industries. Occupational upgrading, women's demands, educational attainments and equality initiatives have also resulted in women gaining increased access to professional and managerial occupations (Caiazza et al., 2004; Moynagh and Worsley, 2005).

In North America and the EU, the increasing dominance of business, consumer and public services over manufacturing has prompted arguments that work itself is becoming culturally 'feminised', although this is a feminisation that men as well as women are expected to perform (Adkins, 2002; Adkins and Lury, 1999; Jenson et al., 1988; McDowell, 1997; Witz et al., 2003). The performative ethos of service work entailing intensive interaction with peers and customers (such as those in financial and business services, tourism and travel, the cultural industries and retailing) is accompanied by heightened concern with self-presentation, sociability and communication. These are qualities conventionally attributed to women in a dualistic ideology of masculinity and femininity (Cockburn, 1991; Halford et al., 1997; McDowell, 1997). The result is an organisational revaluing of 'feminine' empathy and communication, while masculine 'virtues' of heroism, virility and will power are sometimes now interpreted as 'vices' of aggression, inflexibility and emotional detachment (MacInnes, 1998). The increased emphasis on a work culture of targets and results (Du Gay, 1996; Halford et al., 1997; Webb, 1999) has also stimulated images of management that are less overtly tied to a dualistic ideology of gender: bank managers no longer have to be 'father figures' and nurses are not necessarily 'motherly' (Halford et al., 1997). The changes are reflected in a degree of convergence between the organisational trajectories of women and men, as well as the increasing polarisation of class and ethnic divisions between women, suggesting that ideologies of gender and 'femininity' are also racialised. In the USA, for example, African-American, Native American and Hispanic women have lower earnings and are less likely to work in professional and managerial jobs than white or Asian American women (Caiazza et al., 2004). Class and ethnic divisions have thus been made even more salient in the experiences and self-understandings of women.

Organisational and occupational restructuring has thus reconfigured work inequalities, but not overcome them. At a basic level, there are continuing differences between countries in the overall level of women's employment, indicating the influence of different family policies, social attitudes and the balance between services and manufacturing work. The Mediterranean countries have traditionally had fewer women in paid work and these differences are persisting: in Spain, women are still less likely to be in paid work now than women in Japan were in 1970. A higher proportion of manufacturing-oriented activity in Japan and Germany is also combined with lower participation among women than in the more services-oriented economies of the USA or the UK (Figure 6.2 and Table 6.1).

Although most employers no longer explicitly create jobs for one sex only, at every occupational level men and women remain concentrated in differentially valued jobs and many jobs continue to be 'sex-typed'. In the organisational survey carried out as part of the ESRC *Future of Work Programme*, half the workplaces still had jobs exclusively occupied by men or women, and managers had no plans to change this (White et al., 2004). Women continue to be seen as specifically suitable for some jobs, while men are seen as particularly fitted for others, suggesting the adaptability of an ideology of gender difference to changed occupational boundaries and hierarchies.

Occupational structures continue to be marked by horizontal and vertical segregation. Patterns of horizontal segregation mirror the wider sexual division of labour. Women continue to dominate the more routine support and service work in secretarial and clerical jobs, personal services and sales, with little prospect of training or upward mobility. They are also concentrated in

Figure 6.2   Women's economic activity rates as % of female population,
aged 15–64

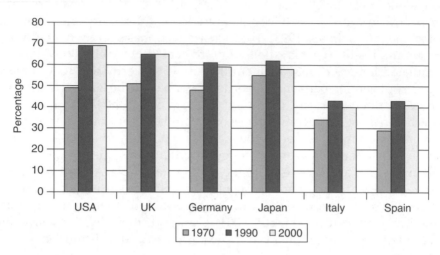

the 'caring professions' in health, education and social welfare. Men, on the
other hand, continue to dominate skilled manual work, engineering and
technical occupations (Moynagh and Worsley, 2005). Although women have
established themselves in managerial and professional careers, vertical segregation remains the norm, with men more likely to dominate senior management, and senior levels in the public and private professions. In the EU,
while women are approximately 30% of managers, fewer than 5% of women
occupy senior management roles, with little change over the last decade
(Davidson and Burke, 2000). In local government in Britain, women make
up half of senior officers, but only 10% of chief executives (Webb, 2001). Most
positions of power and authority in organisations continue to be the preserve of men who

> dominate the old institutions of power, ranging from the judiciary to the board-
> room, and . . . the new institutions of power, ranging from the media to the
> informal networks of the ICT revolution. (Hutton, 2001)

Women remain marginal in global economic and financial policy-making.
There are, for example, 24 men and no women on the board of directors of
the IMF and 22 men and 2 women on the board of directors of the World
Bank (Women's Environment and Development Organisation, 2002).

Women's increased access to professional and managerial occupations
does not reflect a simple process of movement into what were previously
'men's jobs'. Restructuring has significantly affected organisational career
ladders and hierarchies, with new gendered spaces being created and a

degree of internal resegregation taking place. The progressive displacement of the conventional association between managerial authority and paternalism has helped women gain greater acceptance in supervisory and lower management jobs (Beynon et al., 2002; Halford et al., 1997), but many of these would not have been defined as 'managerial level' in the past (Breugel, 2004). In other instances, the job retains the same title, but has been downgraded by restructuring. Women have, for example, moved into branch management in banking at a time when branch managers have been disempowered by centralisation. Career restructuring in banking, nursing and local government reproduced men's dominance in senior posts and continued to give men access to organisational careers that allowed them to progress from junior to senior positions (Halford et al., 1997). Women with comparable backgrounds were likely to remain in entry-level jobs. Data from the British Household Panel Survey also shows that women in comparable occupations to male peers receive smaller pay increases and are likely to remain at the lower end of the pay scale (Booth et al., 1999). The experience of women who gain promotion suggests that new forms of gender distinctions are emerging within occupational categories: women are more likely to be in specialist support roles while men dominate line management and the control of organisational resources (Beynon et al., 2002; Halford et al., 1997; Moynagh and Worsley, 2005). The costs of promotion have also increased, 'as even lower level managerial or supervisory jobs are requiring even longer hours spent at work' (Beynon et al., 2002: 305).

Not surprisingly, the earnings gap between men and women has persisted: in OECD countries, women earn 16% less than men, on average, for every hour worked. The differential is widest in countries where the wage structure is most unequal. Hence in the USA and the UK, women earn around 20% less than men per hour (OECD, 2003). In the UK, the narrowing of the pay gap has occurred only in relation to full-time work (Bottero, 2000), while part-time work continues to be paid at 36% less on average (Robinson, 2003), indicating the particular economic disadvantages of many of the new 'flexible' jobs in the service sector, which are low paid, with limited earnings growth and poor terms and conditions of employment (Jenkins, S., 2003). In a process of levelling down and a sharpening of class, rather than gender, divisions, men and women doing routine jobs have become equally disadvantaged, with men experiencing downward mobility and increasingly subject to the downgraded terms and conditions of employment more commonly experienced by women. For young men with few educational credentials, polarised occupational structures have decreased their chances of upward mobility, in comparison with their fathers' (McDowell, 2002). In Beynon et al.'s (2002) comparison of seven organisations, routine and semi-skilled jobs done by men such as printing assistants, drivers, field engineers and park wardens were subject to worsening terms and conditions of employment, making them comparable with routine jobs done largely by women.

The extent and continuity of women's employment has eroded assumptions that women are destined for a 'domestic identity' and motherhood but not displaced assumptions of a continuing sexual division of labour, which attributes primary responsibility for children and caring to women, and assumes that women (rather than families) will fit paid work around domestic responsibilities. Women make more transitions between full- and part-time contracts, with the impact of childbirth on women's paid work status particularly notable in the UK and Germany (Yeandle, 1999). Halford et al.'s (1997) study of banking, local government and nursing careers (all sectors that are seen as having made great progress in equality measures) found that motherhood and promotion continued to be diametrically opposed. Young, single women are also made aware of managerial attitudes to them as a potential 'liability' and feel that their chances of promotion are hampered (McDowell, 1997). Women in managerial jobs are less likely than their male peers to have children, and women in professional occupations often remain at 'practitioner' level rather than progressing into strategic or leadership roles (Crompton, 1997). In recruitment and promotion decisions, preconceptions about domestic responsibilities continue to be central to judgements of suitability: for men, marriage and children are seen as positive, indicating stability, motivation and reliability, whereas for women they are interpreted as indicating unreliability, short-termism and as conflicting with careers and organisational requirements (Halford et al., 1997; Halford and Leonard, 2001; Wajcman, 1998).

The economic instrumental rationalities of organisations therefore continue to be shaped by the cultural and social legacy of men's historical dominance in the family, in business and in civil society (Hearn and Parkin, 2001), and by an ideology of gender difference that is deployed to justify and legitimate the relative material disadvantage of women and dominance of men (MacInnes, 1998; Siltanen, 1994). Simultaneously, greater polarisation between women in organisations makes the lack of a singular identity among women more evident: inequalities are marked by intersecting relations of class and ethnicity, as well as gender.

'Racialised' and Ethnic Divisions in Organisations

Organisational and occupational change is also associated with increasing diversity in the employment experiences of people historically subject to racist forms of occupational segregation and exclusion from the upper tiers of organisational hierarchies. In the organisational context, such ethnic divisions are produced by discriminatory practices of recruitment, appraisal and promotion, resulting in systematic disadvantages, which intersect with class and gender. The historical consequences of colonialism and slavery continue to mark the organisational trajectories of people of minority ethnic backgrounds. In the USA, people of African-American, Hispanic and Native American origin continue to be overrepresented in the poorest paid jobs (Caiazza et al., 2004; Castells, 2000), while in Britain there are marked economic inequalities between people of South Asian and African-Caribbean origin and the white population (Modood et al., 1997; Platt, 2005). In European cities, first and second generation immigrants are generally overrepresented in the poorest groups, and are more likely to lack basic protections of citizenship, resulting in continuing exclusion from primary segments of the labour market and organisational hierarchies (Castells, 2000).

The production of ethnic divisions in organisations continues to reflect a postcolonial ideology of 'race', which positioned black and brown skin as inferior to white. In post-war Britain, labour migration was actively encouraged, bringing people from the New Commonwealth countries in South Asia and the Caribbean to solve labour shortages. Women from the Caribbean were recruited into routine occupations in the health service, while Caribbean men were recruited into public transport in London, and manual jobs in factories. South Asian men worked in metal manufacture and textiles, and South Asian women, who were least likely to work outside the home, also worked in textiles. The reversal of relatively liberal immigration policies in the 1960s means that most migrants from outside the EU have since required work permits, which are granted only for industries where there is insufficient domestic labour, such as the health service and hotels. Migrants from the New Commonwealth countries were 'racialised' according to attributed cultural traits, influencing their acceptability in different occupations, regardless of their skills and experience (Jenkins, 1986). Such beliefs enabled employers to rationalise the racist exclusion of people from jobs where they were judged socially 'unacceptable', regardless of competence or skills, or the employer's own equal opportunity policies (Jewson and Mason, 1994).

Occupations of first destination have continued to predict the employment experiences of second and subsequent generations, but change is also evident, with people of different minority ethnic backgrounds increasingly differentiated by organisational class and gender divisions. This reflects the interaction between occupational restructuring, anti-racist campaigns, the different backgrounds of the first generation of migrants and subsequent educational credentials. The children and grandchildren of migrant groups originating from more affluent backgrounds, with higher levels of formal education, have been more upwardly mobile. Census data shows that people of Indian, African and Chinese background have similar average incomes to the white population, and younger people are well represented in higher education, with professional qualifications in accountancy, law and medicine acting as routes into organisational careers (Berthoud, 1998; Peach et al., 2000; Platt, 2005). The decline of many of the manual jobs that first employed unskilled men from more rural backgrounds in Pakistan and Bangladesh, however, has been associated with higher unemployment and high levels of self-employment in catering, restaurants, shopkeeping and taxi driving among these men (Modood et al., 1997; *Social Focus on Ethnicity*, 2002). Men of African-Caribbean origin are more likely to be in manual occupations, while half of women of African-Caribbean background work in public administration, education and health sectors, comprising the highest proportion of any ethnic group. Around 10% of these work as nurses, in a medical occupational hierarchy of class, 'race' and gender, where black women are overrepresented in the lowest paid, hardest jobs (Anderson, 2000). Within professional occupational hierarchies such as those of social work, where black women have made some inroads, ideologies of gender and 'race' cut across superficially similar class situations to produce implicit racialised status hierarchies, which intersect with occupational status (Lewis, 2000, 2002).

Class, ethnicity and gender also intersect in patterns of differential disadvantage in relation to exclusion from organisational hierarchies and unemployment. Men of African-Caribbean background are almost twice as likely to be unemployed as white men with similar qualifications (Berthoud, 1999), but men of Bangladeshi origin have the highest unemployment rate – 20% – four times that of white men. Young men of African origin, men and women of Pakistani origin, and men and women of African-Caribbean origin had unemployment rates in excess of 20%. This compares with an unemployment rate of 12% for young white men and 9% for young white women. It is overwhelmingly the Pakistani and Bangladeshi households who are poorest, with high unemployment and the lowest average earnings of any group (Berthoud, 1998).

Restructured organisations thus continue to differentiate between people of different ethnic groups, with historical economic, educational and cultural backgrounds influencing opportunities and employment trajectories. Occupational upgrading, combined with anti-racist campaigns and equal opportunity initiatives have resulted in increasing diversity in the organisational trajectories of people of minority ethnic origin in advanced capitalist countries. Educational and professional credentials have provided a route into the increasing managerial and professional occupations in organisations, but there remains a continuing perception of a lack of organisational commitment to the proper implementation of initiatives (Creegan et al., 2003), and too little is known about the organisational production of ethnic and racialised divisions (Acker, 2000; Cox, 2004), which are increasingly articulated at a global level through the production arrangements and supply chains of multinational corporations.

The Restructuring of Class Divisions in Organisations

Occupational restructuring in affluent societies has gone hand in hand with increasing social polarisation, producing growth in the higher paid managerial, professional and technical jobs, as well as in low-paid services. The mobility of capital in the circuits of global finance has polarised labour through the 'internal fragmentation . . . between informational producers and replaceable generic labour' (Castells, 2000: 346), leaving a significant divide between professional, managerial and technical work reliant on skills and qualifications, and more routine work with limited access to training and routes to progression (Beynon et al., 2002). Middle-level jobs in organisations have declined, resulting in divergence between the 'top' and 'bottom' of occupational structures and reduced opportunities for upward social mobility (Goos and Manning, 2003; Moynagh and Worsley, 2005; Nolan, 2004). Routine work has changed dramatically with the restructuring of manufacturing according to a global logic of capital accumulation, but it remains a very large proportion of jobs, and is at least partly reliant on the relatively high disposable incomes of households with adults employed in professional, managerial and technical jobs. Routine work is now more likely to be in personal and social services in retail, distribution, tourism, entertainment and domestic settings, rather than factories, and is typically poorly paid, with few prospects and the likelihood that job mobility will entail circulation between similar routinised occupations rather than predictable upwards progression (Beynon et al., 2002).

Although position in an occupational hierarchy is only a rough proxy for class, the 'hour glass' occupational structure (Nolan, 2004) in advanced capitalist countries suggests not 'the end of class', but its restructuring as a principle of economic division on a global scale, in complex interaction with gender and ethnic divisions, which are used as additional means to the goal of higher profit. The fragmenting of economic classes, in a Weberian sense, has produced a more complex and shifting picture. Greater diversity of occupational position among women and people of minority ethnic background means that there are less homogeneous social categories of the kind that generated assertions of a male, manual working class, unified by the ideology of a working-class masculinity. But class, as a principle of economic division, has consequently become more important as an indicator of differential life chances:

> Thus at the end of the twentieth century in the United States, class exploitation and inequity have far more legitimacy than gender- and race-based exploitation and inequity, which are illegal and defined as discrimination. The legitimacy of class is, at the present time, so self-evident that no one with any political or economic power, at least in the US, discusses eliminating wage labour. (Acker, 2000: 200)

The same could be said of Britain, 'where class differences remain of crucial importance to our understanding of employment' (Taylor, 2002: 8), and other advanced capitalist countries. Occupational classifications and employment relations are limited as a means of understanding class relations, because they exclude some significant sections of the population, notably the very wealthy (Scott, 1997) and the non-employed poor. They also give only a broad overview of economic divisions, which glosses over processes of fragmentation, along racist and sexist lines, and of social identification. Nevertheless, it is clear that there is a significant, and if anything less permeable, economic divide between routine and semi-skilled workers, and professional, managerial and technical groups. The latter groups are more likely to have an employment relationship based on a 'service contract', where salary and benefits such as paid holiday, pensions and promotion prospects are exchanged for specified services and expertise. Routine workers are more likely to be employed on a labour contract, where they are paid a wage for set tasks, carried out under direct supervision. This division in the employment relationship and relative levels of direct control, supervision and benefits reflects considerable continuity with the 1980s' divisions of class in modern societies (Erikson and Goldthorpe, 1992). If anything, the gap in benefits and related terms and condition of work has increased (Nolan, 2004; Taylor, 2002).

Although those in the intermediate and higher levels of occupational structures have retained relatively favourable employment relations, they have not escaped the overall intensification of work. Both survey evidence and organisational case studies (Beynon et al., 2002; Dickens et al., 2003; White et al., 2004) point to more intensive, stressful working, longer hours, more direct performance monitoring and appraisal, a lower value placed on loyalty, reduced scope for upward mobility within the organisation, and more individualised career-oriented competition, alongside senior management expectations of 'unlimited liability' to the organisation.

The meanings for social and personal identities cannot be read off from changes in economic classes, but widening inequality suggests that it is now more, not less, important to analyse the organisational specificities of reordered class, gender and ethnic relations.

Social Divisions and Processes of Cultural and Social Identity

As features of organisational hierarchies, divisions of class, ethnicity and gender are 'implicated in claims and attributions of identity, social practices and social action' (Anthias, 2005: 39), but it would be a mistake to assume that the social divisions produced and reconfigured in organisational processes of resource allocation *determine* identities. Indeed, people resist being defined by an essentialised, categorical social identity, whether this is one marked by ideologies of class, 'race' or gender (Devine et al., 2005; Lewis, 2000; Skeggs, 1997). Instead, they make resourceful and pragmatic adaptations to such ascribed identities and, in a work context, draw on multiple sources of identity in a process of negotiation directed at maintaining personal agency and dignity, however routinised and disempowered the work (Adib and Guerrier, 2003).

In order to avoid the idea that identity is an object conferred on someone by economically determining relations, and to expose the power relations behind attributions of a fixed or categorical identity, postmodernist writers have emphasised the significance of culture as an autonomous sphere, not dependent on economic relations. This use of a concept of identity emphasises the relational qualities of subjective, culturally mediated claims of recognition, which are contested and ambiguous, and refuse to be defined by external labelling of a position (Anthias, 2005). Such work is critical of social structural analyses of categorisation and inequality, which assumed either economically determined or 'additive' models of social divisions, or uniformity of identity, rather than fluid and contradictory processes, which enable reflexivity and challenge to exclusion (Anthias, 2005; Gherardi, 1995). It has provided an alternative way to explore the articulation of class with gender and ethnicity, this time emphasising the ambiguity and ambivalence of multiple, intersecting and often contradictory sources of identity. The result is a greater focus on struggles to reclaim marginalised or devalued identities, and on the complex and contradictory power relations of class, gender and ethnicity (see for example Skeggs, 1997).

Nevertheless, the concepts of identity and social division, and the non-equivalence of class, gender and ethnicity as bases for such divisions, continue to be disputed. Sociology is itself caught up in theoretical disputes about the relative primacy to be given to the economic, as opposed to the cultural, in analyses of identity (Devine et al., 2005), ironically during a period of widening inequality. Postmodern cultural analysis has in turn been criticised on the grounds that it fuses the cultural and the economic in such a way that the capacity to explain social and economic inequalities is significantly reduced, if not lost altogether (Crompton and Scott, 2005; Ray and Sayer, 1999). Prioritising culture and identity, for example, reduces capitalist organisations to cultural forms, losing sight of the specific power relations of instrumental economic rationalities. Accounts of cultural processes of claiming identity have created insights into the multiple and shifting meanings of being classed, gendered and racialised. The problem, however, remains of how to explain the reproduction of systematic social divisions, and the particularities of organisational power relations in capitalist societies are important to such explanations. An analysis of change and continuities in organisational hierarchies, occupational boundaries and employment relations does not equate to a deterministic treatment of structure on the one hand and action on the other. As argued in Chapters 1 and 2, the structuring of organisational hierarchies and job boundaries is always embedded in social and cultural relationships, which embody divergent interests and power relations, including those of capital and labour. The organisational hierarchy of occupations and authority is a means of differentially distributing resources of symbolic and cultural, as well as economic, kinds. Paying attention to the organisational level therefore casts light on the practical workings of power relations. It uncovers processes of accommodation, consent and resistance, as well as the organisational use of hierarchies and occupational boundaries to produce and legitimate social divisions and inequalities.

A distinction can be drawn between the occupational positions constituted by managerial strategies, and the processes of positioning, which take place as particular people encounter the contradictory experiential dimensions of class, gender and ethnicity, and negotiate their potential meanings (Anthias, 2005). In principle, any of these occupational positions are available to any individual. In practice, organisational recruitment, selection and promotion practices have reproduced cross-cutting and intersecting patterns of social division along the lines of class, gender and ethnicity. The result is a hierarchy of occupational positions, which operates alongside intersecting social and cultural status hierarchies of 'race', ethnicity and gender, producing uneven and contradictory patterns of dominance and subordination. In an organisational context, any person may be simultaneously advantaged by being in a managerial or professional job, but disadvantaged by being female and black; women may be differentiated by occupational level, with particular differences between those in routine jobs and those in professional and managerial work. But at the same occupational level, they may be disadvantaged relative to men, because they are seen as less legitimate. When black and white women are in occupations that give them some authority and control over resources, they tend to receive less work-related support and help than white men (McGuire, 2002), and it seems likely that processes of 'racialisation' tend to result in black women receiving less support than white women in structurally similar occupational positions.

The experience of the partially contradictory power relations of gender, 'race' and class is associated with greater personal and organisational reflexivity over ascribed identities and wider debate about the mutual constitution of 'race', gender and class. According to Giddens (1991), the attribution of agency and responsibility to individuals and sceptical attitudes towards tradition and authority in modern societies have created the conditions for reflexive self-awareness, making identity subject to a degree of choice.

Ascribed class, gender and ethnic identities may be used, refused and remade self-consciously as resources, in claims for recognition, critiques of exclusion and as the basis for challenge to an established class, gender and racialised social order. Such reflexive awareness of cultural represen-tations is part of a critical consciousness, creating pressure for the sub-stantive changes that have already taken place.

It is important, however, to draw a distinction between changes in sym-bolic representations and changes in people's material circumstances. An entirely postmodern, cultural analysis, which treats identity as freely chosen in a reflexive process, exaggerates the extent of transformation and over-emphasises the expressive, voluntaristic possibilities in social relations (McNay, 1999). A greater degree of cultural awareness of the contradictory and partially incoherent nature of ideologies of 'masculinity' and 'feminin-ity', for example, does not necessarily translate into greater equality between the sexes in any direct sense. Neither does a reflexive orientation to ascribed identities necessarily imply a capacity to reinvent ourselves at will, or to live outside conventional norms. The institutional structures of states and labour markets work to constrain the sphere of choice, and economic changes are partial and uneven. Such reflexivity as we have is gained out of the aware-ness of the contradictions between what we might be and what we can be, given the economic and social circumstances in which we live.

Does Economic Individualisation Necessarily Produce Individualism?

Processes of increasing class, gender and ethnic diversity arguably reflect a culture of individualism, but just as it is mistaken to assume any necessary or determining relationship between economic class and social or personal identity, so it is equally mistaken to assume any necessary relationship between economic individualisation, resulting from the organisational restructuring of employment relations, and individual*ism*. What disap-pears when this assertion of an autonomous cultural individualism is made is a focus on the power relations in the employment relationship, which have centred on reducing the power of organised labour and individualising labour market competition (Healy et al., 2004; Kelly and Waddington, 1995; Nolan, 2004).

To the extent that we have a degree of reflexive, critical awareness of social and economic individualisation, which the evidence of increasing dissatis-faction with work suggests, this seems equally likely to provide new bases for the renewal of collective forms of identity, as it does to promote individu-alistic values. Such collective identities may be built out of multiple sources of cultural awareness *and* economic position. In a study of union organisation among black and minority ethnic women, for example, Healy et al. (2004) found that workforce diversity contributed to trade union renewal and creative forms of collectivism, rather than detracting from them: 'collectivism may spring initially from ethnic and gender identifications, as well as those of class and occupation' (p. 463). Consequently, greater diversity in organisations and more individualised forms of management control of labour do not inevitably translate into self-interested individualism. New forms of collective identity can be made from the shared interests in overcoming past experience of inequalities.

Conclusion

The restructuring of occupations and employment in the organisations of advanced capitalism has changed the balance of power between capital and labour, structurally individualising the employment relationship, while simultaneously reinforcing dependence on waged work. Predictions about the end of work, mass casualisation and short-termism are characterised more by overblown assertion than appraisal of the evidence. They have paradoxically distracted attention from the very significant changes in work that are taking place. Global financial markets and mobile capital are driving the intensification of labour, at all occupational levels, producing a common perception of uncertainty and insecurity, rather than the structural casualisation of work per se. The increasing numbers drawn into employment, the rising participation of women, and the increasing movement of people of minority ethnic origin into professional occupations mean that work in organisations 'has an unprecedented place in people's lives' (Moynagh and Worsley, 2005: 11). Such work plays a significant part in structuring life chances in capitalist economies, which means that it is salient in processes of social division, and a key, if indeterminate, influence over social and personal identities.

Organisational restructuring, in the context of mobile capital, growth in services employment and more diverse forms of employment, does not herald the end of class as a principle of economic division, even if the contours of more fragmented and divided classes are harder to discern and less immediately obvious as sources of collective identity. Arguably, we now have not a 'classless society' but globally dispersed, ethnically segmented and gendered class relations, given differential expression through different cultural and social practices at the organisational level. Restructuring has produced a more polarised occupational structure in advanced capitalist countries, with growth in managerial, professional and technical work as well as growth in routine and semi-skilled jobs, while middle-level jobs have declined.

Despite organisational commitments to the use of career ladders to retain labour, the relative upgrading of occupations has been matched by declining opportunities for upward social mobility from routine jobs into knowledge-based careers.

Organisational forms of employment and occupational structures have therefore proved to be both powerful drivers of certain forms of progressive change and contributors to the reinforcement of systematic inequalities. A postmodern, cultural analysis of identity has criticised economically deter-minist theories of class, and emphasised the fluidity and voluntaristic pos-sibilities of the reclaiming of marginalised and devalued identities. The organisational experience of contradiction at the intersections between ascribed identities of 'race', gender and class is a source of reflexive awareness about who we are, and has contributed to the partial unravelling of modern social divisions. People are more able to distance themselves from naturalised understandings of 'gender' or 'racialised' identities, and to view ascribed identities as cultural resources to be deployed flexibly. This provides a basis for the remaking of collective forms of identity, resistant to economic individ-ualisation. A more reflexive orientation to the reworking of such ideologies does not, however, immediately overcome material inequalities, indicating the limitations of a cultural analysis of identity, which loses sight of the spe-cific economic relations manifest in the organisations of advanced capitalism.

The current dualism between knowledge-based work and routinised labour in occupational structures is not inevitable, but reflects neoliberal mar-ket policies and the short-termist strategies of organisations in their pursuit of profitability. There is growing criticism of the failure of organisations in developed economies to capitalise on the skills and knowledge of the work-force in order to improve organisational performance. This would require investment in the development of trust in employment relations, through better organisational democracy and an increased sphere of employee dis-cretion. The next chapter takes up these themes by considering the changing content of work in the context of organisational strategies to extract higher value from labour through making employees responsible for solving prob-lems and working flexibly across task boundaries. In this case, change focuses on claims that employers are making more intensive use of labour, whatever the job or occupational level, through forms of control designed to align self-identities with organisation goals (Alvesson and Willmott, 2004; Casey, 1995, 1996; Thompson, 2003; Thompson and Warhurst, 1998). This includes requir-ing employees to increase their effort at work, to use all their social compe-tences in the doing of their job, to solve problems through teamwork across functions and job boundaries, and to 'love the organisation'. What is dis-puted is whether such raised expectations of employee performance are matched by a higher level of commitment by the employer to commensurate reward and recognition through the employment relationship.

Appendix

Table 6.1 Women's economic activity rates as a percentage of the female population, aged between 15/16 and 64, 1970–2004

Country	1970	1990	2004
USA	49	69	65
UK	51	65	67
Germany	48	61	60
Japan	55	62	57
Italy	34	43	45
Spain	29	43	49

Source: OECD *Employment Outlook*, 2005.

Table 6.2 Changes in part-time work, selected OECD countries, 1979–2004

Country	Part-time employment as a percentage of total employment			Percentage of women in part-time employment 2004	Women's share of part-time employment 2004
	1979	1990	2004		
UK	16	20	24	40	78
Germany	11	13	20	37	83
USA	16	14	13	19	68
Japan	15	19	26	42	67

Source: OECD *Employment Outlook*, 2005.

7

'We Are the Company': Work, Control and Identity in the Organisations of Advanced Capitalism

What are the implications of the restructuring of organisations, according to the logics of deregulated, mobile capital, for work identities? This chapter discusses how organisations have become more interested in regulating the identity of employees, as a means to increasing effort in a revised wage–effort bargain. We have seen in the previous chapter that work remains highly significant to the formation of identity, but the focus there was on the role of organisations in the production of social divisions and on the dynamic renegotiation of ascribed identities. Here, the focus is on the managerial interest in the regulation of self-identity as a means of organisational control over the performance of work (Ackroyd and Thompson, 1999; Alvesson and Willmott, 2004; Casey, 1995; Deetz, 1995; Karreman and Alvesson, 2004), which increasingly entails mental rather than manual effort, and the manipulation of symbols rather than materials. As discussed in Chapters 1 and 3, corporations are investing heavily in the development of distinctive organisational or brand identities as a means to greater profitability (Hatch and Schultz, 2004), and explicit attempts to persuade employees to identify with the brand have become increasingly common (Thompson and Warhurst, 1998). Popular managerial discourses of enterprise and excellence, prescribing visionary leadership, customer care and love of the organisation, link work productivity to engaging 'hearts and minds' in the labour process, from the top to the bottom of the occupational hierarchy (Du Gay and Salaman, 1992; Sturdy, 1998).

This chapter has four aims: to explain why managing employee identity has become a managerial concern; to explore how organisations seek to control employees through regulating identity; to examine the extent to which organisations colonise identity; and finally to provide a critique of the view that managerial control is enacted by a rigorous regulation of identity.

Explaining the Organisational Emphasis on Managing Employee Identity

There are a number of reasons why the organisational regulation of self-identity has become a prominent concern. The first is related to the growing predominance of non-manual work in consumer societies dominated by service sector employment and a high proportion of professional, managerial and technical occupations. There is considerable variation in the occupational status, knowledge content, variety and responsibility of such work, which ranges from highly paid business consultants, through public professions to low-paid personal service workers. Whatever the status, each occupation entails managing self-presentation and social interaction, and requires discretion and judgement. Forms of direct control undoubtedly remain important in non-manual work, with machine-pacing and monitoring through computer systems creating an 'assembly line in the head' (Taylor and Bain, 1998), and performance measurement and appraisal a common feature (Beynon et al., 2002). It is also clear that high-quality service requires committed and socially skilled workers, who are self-managing, well informed and responsible. Social interaction has therefore become central to profitability and the employer has commercial motives to control and direct the feelings of employees about their job and the organisation. In these circumstances, where it may be counterproductive, or impossible, to rely entirely on direct controls, the management of labour has often relied more on indirect control through norms and values (Etzioni, 1964), and attempts to persuade employees to identify with, and internalise, organisation goals. Such forms of control are familiar in professional and higher executive occupations, where there are financial and other benefits attached to a professional identity, as well as considerable status, but until recently they have been less commonly associated with semi-skilled and routine work.

The second set of reasons for the growing concern with the organisational regulation of identity relates to the character of markets and competition in neoliberal economic regimes, and the resulting contradictory pressures for both high-quality and more intensive work. Both survey evidence and case study research point to managerial strategies to increase work responsibilities and the effort put in to work, but also to persuade employees to invest more of themselves in the organisation (Beynon et al., 2002; Burchell et al., 1999; Thompson, 2003; White et al., 2004). The pressures at organisational level do not emerge out of a vacuum, but are connected to the shift in the dynamics of capital accumulation detailed in Chapter 2. These comprise deregulated, shareholder-driven and globalised financial markets, and globally organised production and supply chain networks. Deregulated markets for many goods and services also produce higher competition in domestic markets: supermarkets, for example, now compete with banks as providers of loans, mortgages and insurance; telecommunications and media are characterised by high rates of both disaggregation and mergers; local authorities and health services are involved in extensive market contracting and so on. Businesses are thus subject to greater competitive pressures in markets where similar goods and services are in plentiful supply, and where financial institutions are looking closely at short-term returns on investment in company shares. Public service organisations are not exempt, with the state replacing the City as the source of pressure: 'During the 1990s it seems that the state increasingly acted like the City, regulating local government and health sectors through ever-tighter financial and performance criteria' (Beynon et al., 2002: 266).

Markets are no longer simply the context for economic exchange between organisations, but have increasingly been internalised within them, regulating and informing management strategy and labour control, in an increasingly rationalised system. Corporations have to differentiate their products and services through claims about quality, customisation and distinction (Fuller and Smith, 1991; Leidner, 1993), and customer satisfaction (Frenkel et al., 1998). But these qualities are dependent on the involvement and willing self-management of labour in countless, indeterminate service interactions, often conducted by low-paid employees. The president of the Scandinavian airline, SAS, described such encounters as the millions of 'moments of truth' that decide customer reactions and the success of the enterprise (Lash and Urry, 1994). The effort and commitment of employees are therefore central to profitability, which means that managers have a vested interest in engaging the hearts and minds of the workforce and persuading them to identify with the organisation. At the same time, labour costs create incentives to intensify work, by standardising and scripting encounters, monitoring the quantity of work and the volume of transactions, and setting tight performance targets (Beynon et al., 2002). Labour does not automatically share the interest of management in aligning values and feelings with organisationally defined goals, particularly during periods of rapid change in employment relations and occupations. Intensification and standardisation risk employee cynicism and the withdrawal of goodwill, which undermine management goals of increasing effort and improving service quality. This dilemma redoubles managerial attempts to control employee identity, as a means to gain the willingness of labour to work harder, without encountering the effects of resentment about an overly exploitative work–effort bargain.

Less clear-cut organisational boundaries, resulting from globally dispersed production and supply chain arrangements, mergers, takeovers and joint ventures, raise further uncertainties about identity and affiliation, stimulating struggles over national, local and professional sources of identity. Ailon-Souday and Kunda (2003), for example, discuss the merger of a high-tech Israeli corporation with an American competitor, and argue that employees used national identity as a symbolic resource in resisting a globalised version of corporate identity. Rapid change in organisation ownership and structures is matched by less social and cultural homogeneity in many occupations. From professional and managerial occupations to call centre operators, the changing social identities of labour mean that employers are less able to rely on shared cultural and social norms as a source of shared values: more men have taken up routine work alongside women; call centre operators may be Indians in Bangalore serving black British customers in Birmingham; some managerial roles have been feminised; professionals are less likely to be universally 'pale and male'; and an organisational brand identity may have to find commonalities between managers in the USA, China, India and so on. All this means that employers have to work even harder to manufacture an organisational identity for employees who are likely to be increasingly diverse in values, attitudes and beliefs, less certain about the economic and cultural meanings of the organisation, and less stable in their sense of affiliation.

Organisational Control through Regulating Identity

In this section, I will focus on three aspects of organisational attempts to regulate the identity of employees, exploring first how corporate culture seeks to construct a 'we'; then how teamwork is used to instil identification with organisational goals; and finally, the role of emotional labour in customer service work.

Corporate Culture: Constructing 'We'

Increased normative control over labour, which aims to persuade people to identify with the organisation and thus bring personal commitment to their work, has been sought by investment in an articulated 'corporate culture' (Kunda, 1992; Peters, 1987). In the 1970s and 1980s, the declining profitability of large Anglo-American corporations and the economic strength of Japanese businesses led to enormous interest in emulating models of work organisation used in Japanese corporations. These were seen as demonstrating the potential for improvements in productivity, flexibility and quality through the capacities of labour (Elger and Smith, 1994). The rigid job descriptions, status demarcations and grading hierarchies, with the fragmented, deskilled divisions of labour characteristic of companies such as Ford, were not used in Japanese corporations, and there was more flexibility about work tasks and responsibilities. Nissan, for example, had only two shop floor grades, manufacturer and technician, compared to Ford's plethora of categories (Thompson and McHugh, 2002). The Japanese model emphasised multiskilled labour processes, customer-oriented, just-in-time production, team-working and employee participation in continuous quality improvements (Womack et al., 1990; Kenney and Florida, 1993).

In Japan, large corporations rewarded effort with security of employment, promotion through seniority and benefits designed to stimulate corporate loyalty and trust. The Anglo-American adversarial tradition in labour–management relations was characterised by a work–effort bargain that was the focus of continuous, low-level tension. Rather than identifying low trust employment relations as a major source of the problem, however, management consultants, such as the influential North American McKinsey Consultancy, argued that the effectiveness of Japanese work organisation derived from the presence of a 'strong corporate culture', which produced a committed, motivated workforce who identified with the organisation (Thompson and McHugh, 2002). Culture change programmes, promoted to the entire workforce, became the order of the day. Translated into an Anglo-American business model, the central tenets concerned the need for leadership in the development of a 'shared vision' and 'partnership' between management and workforce, in order to win hearts and minds. Consultancy texts, such as that by Deal and Kennedy (1988), recommended corporations to take on the role of shaping values and fostering social cohesion, drawing implicitly on a Durkheimian model of society. Consultants advocated appeal to the workforce through ritual and symbolic activities, including award ceremonies, orchestrated corporate entertainments and myths of corporate heroism and charismatic founders. The advocates of corporate culture as a means to profitability thus regarded people as 'needing' emotional attachment in order to find meaning in their lives, and aimed to engage such emotional needs in the service of organisations, rather than externalising them through bureaucratic regulation. Carol Ray (1986) described this as the final 'frontier of control' in a calculated move by senior management to generate a sense of belonging and identification, rather than instrumental compliance.

Peters and Waterman's (1982) *In Search of Excellence* proved to be the iconic text of the period. Its authors took the modern understanding of self-identity as an achievement, and wedded it to the perceived need for renewal of US businesses in the face of competition from the industrialising economies of the Pacific rim. Appealing to myths of heroism, Peters and Waterman exhorted managers to become charismatic leaders, conveying the drama and excitement of corporate enterprise to a workforce depicted as needing new challenges and convictions. Traditional, planning-driven management was criticised as 'paralysis by analysis', and as characterised by a 'culture of blame'. The rapidity of economic change required flexibility, adaptability and teamwork, instead of functionalist divisions between specialisms, empire-building and destructive rivalry. 'Excellent' organisations, they argued, were those which engaged people's capacities for creative thinking, giving them scope to take responsibility for the pursuit of organisational goals and allowing everyone to feel part of the 'winning team'. Actively managed corporate culture was the means to align the (attributed) needs of individuals for self-growth with the needs of organisations for innovation and adaptability. Culture would provide the 'social glue' of affective and emotional attachment to organisations, especially in an era of apparent weakening of other social bonds derived from community, religion and family (see for example Ouchi and Johnson, 1978). It would overcome the contradiction between the centralised direction of business strategies, on the one hand, and individual 'empowerment', on the other. Crucially, Peters and Waterman presented the persuasive notion that the organisation not only benefits from engaged employees, but that employees *themselves* benefit from the resources for self-improvement provided through the organisation:

> These [excellent] companies give people control over their destinies; they make meaning for people. They turn the average Joe or Jane into winners. They let, even insist that, people stick out. (Peters and Waterman, 1982: 61)

In other words, organisations should provide the means of enabling people to 'achieve' an individual identity and shape its direction and values. In one move, they suggested an organisational ideology that apparently swept away the conflict between management and labour over the work–effort bargain, making it seem that the harder someone works for the organisation, the more they benefit, not just through their bank accounts, but through the 'currency' of self-identity and achievement.

Management consultancy advocates of corporate culture present such techniques as non-authoritarian and a source of empowerment for labour. Social scientists, however, are sceptical of such claims, arguing that, whatever the presentational packaging, this is mainly a more subtle form of disciplinary control. In Weberian terms, corporate culture programmes represent not a reversal of instrumental reason so much as a further twist in the story of rationalisation, through the explicit integration of emotions within the calculative framework. In these terms, the manager's responsibility has been enlarged to include shaping employees' subjective sense of self in ways that accord with corporate goals.

Using Teamwork to Create Self-managed Identification with Organisational Goals

While corporate media induction programmes and social activities explicate corporate values and set out to gain employee commitment to them, it is teamwork that is expected to deliver the means of translating values into specific rules of conduct. Where traditional management operated top-down through a hierarchy, teamwork is about projects managed across levels and functions, emphasising flexibility and adaptability (Warhurst and Thompson, 1998). At one level, teamwork is concerned with using more of the tacit knowledge of employees to solve problems and make continuous improvements in performance (Aoki, 1988). It is through this means that many employees are drawn into the micro-management of work (Milkman, 1998). This is an era, however, where occupations and task content are continually changing, and occupational identity is less clear-cut. Identification with a team is intended to substitute for occupational or professional identities, which have typically provided an alternative source of identity and a means of challenging a managerially desired organisational identity. Teams work in theory by harnessing peer pressures, mutual control and self-surveillance in the service of organisation goals (McKinlay and Taylor, 1998). Barker's (1993) account of the introduction of self-managed teams in ISE Communications, a US circuit board manufacturer, describes the flattening of a managerial hierarchy to create teams responsible for the entire production process of fabricating, testing and packaging their assigned circuit board orders. Teams managed their own work organisation and were made responsible for productivity and discipline. Barker concludes that teamwork operates by turning abstract corporate values, such as 'customer service is our first priority' into practical rules governing work behaviour, which are derived from a negotiated consensus between team members. In Casey's (1996) study of the Hephaestus Corporation, a computer systems developer and manufacturer, employees increasingly referred to themselves not by occupational title (engineer, physicist), but as Hephaestus employees and team members. Casey concludes that the teams offered a 'simulated sociality' that provided a form of psychic security to those willing to be drawn in. Rather than compliance in a bureaucratic control system, Barker (1993) argues that the result is a form of 'concertive control', which produces identification with, and internalisation of, corporate goals. The self-managed teams were both stressful and powerful sources of control, because it became a matter of self-esteem not to let the team down. Identification produces a sense of emotional satisfaction and 'belonging', enabling members in theory at least to suspend personal responsibility for decisions about 'who they are' or 'how to act', because team rules provide a sense of purpose and guide to conduct:

> Being a team member and/or a member of the wider corporate family may then become a significant source of one's self-understanding, self-monitoring and presentation to others. (Alvesson and Willmott, 2004: 449)

The metaphor of the team is itself closely allied with the positive value placed on being 'a team player' in sports, competing, striving to win as an 'us' against 'them', and carrying on to compete again. The team analogy constructs the idea that there is no conflict between managers and workers, as everyone is presented as part of a corporate 'we' who are 'in this together'. The boss becomes a 'coach' for the 'players', as in the Subaru-Isuzu plant studied by Laurie Graham (1995), where discussion of problems had to be couched in the language of team cooperation, not confrontation, thus obscuring the power relations of manager and workers. The effect, Sennett (1998) argues, is one of a sham or feigned community, which hides the real power relations of flexibilised capitalism.

Emotional Labour in Customer Service Work

In service-dominated economies, dealing with customers has become central to the work of large numbers of employees, many of whom are in relatively routinised and intensively paced and monitored jobs in call centres, supermarkets, theme parks and leisure and entertainment industries (Beynon et al., 2002; Fuller and Smith, 1991; Gallie et al., 1998; Korczynski et al., 2000). Extensive normative controls have been associated more in the past with professional and managerial work. Competitive and financial pressures in both commercial and public services, and the critical role of labour in customer service, have resulted in a new focus on the regulation of employee identity among the large numbers of people working at the interface with customers. This takes the form of an intensive investment in recruitment, selection and coaching in the required self-presentation and monitoring of performance.

Selection processes aim to identify people with the 'right personalities' and a 'pro-customer attitude', as exemplified by attitudinal and behavioural characteristics (Callaghan and Thompson, 2002; Crouch et al., 1999; Korczynski, 2003; Redman and Matthews, 1998). In Callaghan and Thompson's (2002) study of recruitment and selection in call centres, although numeracy, keyboard and problem-solving skills were assessed, more emphasis was placed on personal and social characteristics and the way people spoke, including tone, pitch, energy, fluency and enthusiasm. A sense of humour and insight into its appropriate use was also desired. Above all, a 'positive attitude' was regarded as the essential personal quality, but was seen as something unteachable.

Despite claims that people are selected for their 'natural personality', employees are generally subject to intensive coaching on the organisationally desired forms, style and content of communication and interaction with customers (Bolton and Boyd, 2003; MacDonald and Sirianni, 1996; Taylor et al., 2002; Taylor and Tyler, 2000; van Maanen, 1991). Coaching aims to shape, sometimes in considerable detail, how employees should behave, in order to 'design' a workforce that embodies an organisational aesthetic and 'brand identity'. In a study of retail and hotel employers, for example, Witz et al. (2003) describe organisational attempts to regulate employees' appearance, posture, gestures and language. 'Aesthetic labourers', they conclude, 'are the animate component of the material culture that makes up the corporate landscape' (p. 44), drawing customers and employees into an emotional and imaginative engagement with the organisation, as a way of delineating it from competitors. Self-identity is deliberately implicated in the work: routine workers in Disney World, for example, are referred to as 'cast members' or 'crew', and work presented as an aspect of lifestyle (Bryman, 1999). In settings such as themed restaurants, employees are expected to act out the part of fun-loving, sociable assistants (Crang, 1994). Such work entails self-consciously dramatised performance, requiring impression management, adaptability and a commitment to improvement (MacDonald and Sirianni, 1996).

Concern with controlling labour costs means that the performance is enacted in the context of intensively paced and often repetitive work. Employees are expected to present a consistently friendly, competent social persona, even when they are tired, bored, irritated or harassed by customers. In the airline industry, for example, customer service training is given equal prominence with safety and emergency training, but training in how to deal with violence or abuse or maintaining staff well-being is minimal (Bolton and Boyd, 2003; Boyd and Bain, 1998; Boyd, 2002).

Unlike professional and managerial work, the emphasis is placed less on specific knowledge or expertise, than on social competences. Hochschild (1983) described this type of work as the performance of 'emotional labour'. She argued that emotional labour is a subset of a wider category of emotion work, which we carry out when we try to fit appropriate emotional expression to a situation. In using the notion of emotional labour, however, Hochschild argued that feelings are increasingly subject to the calculative logic of the market. Emotional labour is a specific form of emotion management, which is carried out in the commercial sphere as paid labour. Moreover, she argues, such commodification of feeling is invasive and exploitative, because the employee is required to 'perform to order', to meet customer demands and to appear courteous, concerned and willing, regardless of the circumstances or the behaviour of customers. The social smile, produced for commercial purposes, is central to face-to-face service work, as in the case of the flight attendants that she studied, and employers insist that such smiles must be regarded by customers as sincere. (There are apparently consumer comparison guides to airlines, which include a ranking of the effectiveness of smiles, greetings and care of customers.) Emotional labour in these terms is a further step in the intensive invasion of self-identity by the organisation.

The Organisational Colonisation of Identity?

The managerial ambition to enhance productivity by developing strong and cohesive cultures and persuading employees to 'buy into the message' is clear, but assessing the effects of such strategies is more complex. Although initially sceptical of the potential for corporate culture programmes to capture employee identity (Smircich, 1983), radical postmodern accounts of such programmes, influenced by Foucault's concepts of disciplinary and discursive forms of power/knowledge (see Chapter 1), have treated the devices of corporate culture as effective in silencing dissent or conflict. This is said to be because cultural controls produce the willing internalisation of corporate values and the identification of the self with the organisation (see for example Dandeker, 1990; Smith and Wilkinson, 1995; Townley, 1993; Willmott, 1993). Deetz (1995) argues that such discursive controls enable management to mould the 'insides' of employees, channelling hopes, fears and aspirations in the service of the corporation. In his study of engineers in the US firm Tech, Kunda (1992) argued that sophisticated corporate policies of openness, visibility and involvement superficially enabled people to give vent to their criticisms of Tech, but effectively disarmed them in the process, producing cynicism among the engineers. This cynicism, Kunda suggests, perversely reinforced their 'entrapment' within corporate discourse, because it prevented people from uncovering a common interest in opposing an exploitative employment relationship. Similarly, Casey's (1995) account of the Hephaestus Corporation concludes that self-identity was colonised by a totalising corporate discourse, with cynicism the only remaining, and self-defeating, defence.

Teamwork and peer review processes have also been regarded as highly effective in colonising self-identity, through seductive appeals to self-improvement and empowerment. McKinlay and Taylor's (1998) account of the teamwork practices used by the Motorola plant in Scotland, for example, depict the ambitious construction of pro-company values through self-managed teams. Barker's (1993) argument that teamwork creates concertive control leads him to conclude that employees become willingly engaged in an exploitative labour process from which they are unable to extricate themselves.

Although not couching her analysis in Foucault's concepts, but drawing on Erving Goffman's (1959) analysis of the presentation of self, Hochschild (1983) also concluded that emotional labour results in self-estrangement. Constant employer pressures to 'be yourself', in a work setting that directs you how to 'be yourself', make it difficult to avoid corporate purposes insinuating themselves into self-evaluations. The organisational 'feeling rules' become part of an inner dialogue about acceptable standards of conduct, with the result that people struggle to maintain alternative sources of self-esteem and experience self-alienation. Survival relies on a capacity for role distance, or 'surface acting', which means the performance of empathy or care divorced from genuine feelings, eventually resulting in cynicism. Hochschild recognises the acts of resistance devised by those in routine service work, such as the slowdown in smiles, rebellion over appearance and shared jokes and humour. She is however ultimately pessimistic, seeing resistance as heavily constrained by the subordinate position of staff in a sharply unequal capital–labour relationship, and the structural impossibility of employees gaining effective control over the terms of their emotional labour. The consequences of emotional labour are therefore expected to be predominantly negative, producing the 'transmutation' of feeling by commercial organisations, such that personal mood and emotions seem to belong more to the organisation than to the self.

Why should people be susceptible to the normative and discursive controls used in contemporary organisations? The answer, from a radical perspective, tends to be that, in postmodern conditions of rapid organisational and social change, people struggle to achieve, but continue to need, a secure sense of self. Insecurity is exacerbated by the organisational demands of continuous adaptability to new problems, changing project teams and responsibilities, making employees more vulnerable to 'the appeal ofcorporate identifications, and less inclined to engage in organised forms of resistance' (Alvesson and Willmott, 2004: 442). Where alternative sources of self-evaluation are eroded or excluded, identity becomes an evermore 'precarious achievement', subject to self-doubt and anxiety. In these circumstances, organisations provide a sense of belonging to a corporate community and employees are willingly seduced by such a promise (Casey, 1995).

Critique of the Effectiveness of Organisational Control through the Regulation of Identity

In this section, I examine the critique of the view that organisations can control and regulate identity. Corporate culture programmes, teamwork, coaching and the requirements of emotional labour are undoubtedly ambitious in their goals, but the extent of their use, their effectiveness and their effects on self-identity are matters of contention. Moves to regulate identity interact with the realities of employment relations, employee awareness of the structural inequalities in the relationship, and the active will of labour. The evidence that corporations have created willing automatons without minds of their own is generally lacking, and it is clear that attempts to engineer corporate identification are not received with universal enthusiasm among employees (Ackroyd and Thompson, 1999; Thompson and Findlay, 1999).

The Continuity of Bureaucratic Control

Recent critical analyses of normative and cultural control in organisations have stepped back from the more radical claim that identity is 'colonised' by the instruments of corporate culture, and they acknowledge the over-socialised account of identity on which this perspective relied. Alvesson and Willmott (2004), for example, acknowledge that the regulation of identity is contested, and that employees are not passive consumers of managerially designed identities. Discursive constructions of reality are 'constrained, as well as enabled, by material conditions, cultural traditions and relations of power' (p. 446).

Whatever the rhetoric of corporate culture, the 'material conditions' of markets and competitive performance pressures on business and public services have been instrumental in ensuring increasing management reliance on structured, direct and bureaucratic means of control over labour. Corporations with explicitly and elaborately articulated cultures also have systematically structured terms and conditions of employment that reward individual compliance and achievement, indicating 'the inherent flexibility and durability of contemporary bureaucratic organization' (Courpasson and Reid, 2004: 11). In Kunda's (1992) ethnography of Tech, he details the bureaucratic monitoring, appraisal and pay systems that reinforce normative control. Karreman and Alvesson (2004) explore the construction of social identities in a large, multinational IT/management consultancy that combines cultural/normative regulation with bureaucratic ordering systems to create what the authors describe as an 'iron cage of subjectivity'. Bureaucratic controls in the form of hierarchy, regulated career paths, performance feedback and standardised work methodologies provided a framework for shared meanings and identities within an organisation driven by an ideology of individual 'excellence' and 'delivery'. Far from culture and bureaucracy being alternative forms of control, they acted as mutually reinforcing: 'HRM practices and hierarchical structures are important for the definition of the temporary identities of individuals and reinforce their identity projects' (p. 171).

Direct performance measures, monitoring and appraisal had increased in each of the seven organisations analysed by Beynon et al. (2002), representing banking, local government, health services, media, pharmaceuticals, retail and telecommunications. Information and communication technologies, such as those used in call centres, have enabled reward systems to be tied more directly to performance monitoring and appraisal, through measures such as customer surveys, supervisor observation, recording and playback of calls. Supermarkets reinforce 'smile campaigns' by surveillance (Ogbonna, 1992) and in the airlines, the use of 'ghost fliers' to report on cabin crew performance during flights (Bolton and Boyd, 2003) indicates managers' awareness that employees' hearts and minds are likely to be elsewhere. Appraisals are used to direct the minutiae of performance, assessing factors such as demeanour, attitude and rapport, as well as quantity of work. These are very direct and structured forms of control, which taken together comprise a kind of 'assembly line in the head' (Taylor and Bain, 1998), through performance targets and demands for continuous improvement. Such direct management of work may indeed produce highly regulated behaviour and the subjective experience of intensive, if not oppressive, control, but this is by no means equivalent to identification with the organisation or believing that corporate goals are 'my goals'.

The Intensification of Work and its Effects on Labour

As is evident from the increasing refinement of bureaucratic controls, normative and cultural control strategies have typically been combined with attempts to drive down costs and intensify work. There is growing and systematic evidence that many people are experiencing greater responsibility and working for longer hours, but with little or no improvements in financial reward or promotion prospects (Beynon et al., 2002; Burchell et al., 1999; Green, 2001; Thompson, 2003; Warhurst and Thompson, 1998; White et al., 2004). In the case of routine work, as well as much of middle management and professional services, employees are well aware of the contradiction between the promises of an 'empowered' self and organisational belonging, and the actuality of intensive, closely monitored work, oriented to quantity rather than quality, and the perpetual risk of 'downsizing' and 'not belonging'. The result is a calculative and pragmatic distancing of self-identity from employer demands for engagement, energy and enthusiasm.

In the growth industries of financial, business, travel and communications services, intensive competition, cost-cutting and the development of mass markets have rationalised and intensified work, making it more exhausting. Labour is a major component of total costs, and although employers invest significantly in selection and training, poor morale and high labour turnover are endemic (Callaghan and Thompson, 2002; Taylor et al., 2003). Physical health and well-being in the airline industry have also suffered as a result of intensive and irregular shift patterns (Boyd and Bain, 1998; Boyd, 2001). In routine service jobs, such as those in supermarkets or fast-food restaurants, 'smile campaigns', competitive games and prizes and corporate sociability do not override people's awareness of monotonous, low-paid work, with few opportunities (Silver, 1987). Even in the professional sphere, more intensive assessment, audit and monitoring and appraisal systems have led to a perceived reduction in autonomy and self-regulation, with negative effects on loyalty and commitment (Beynon et al., 2002; Webb, 1999).

The Effects of Low Trust Employment Relations

Corporate culture programmes, teamwork and flexible work initiatives were meant to be accompanied by more progressive forms of organisational governance, in recognition of the increased demands of work that requires more investment of the self. Such 'high performance work systems' would in theory enable mutual gains through a partnership of capital and labour, and workforce participation in decisions about work organisation and strategy (Applebaum et al., 2001). In practice, such initiatives have been the exception rather than the rule, leaving low trust employment relations as the norm. Part of the explanation for this resides in a lack of managerial commitment to change, in the context of organisational power relations where most discretion resides with senior managers (Milkman, 1998). The endemic low trust is indicated by British Social Attitude Survey data, which show that around two-thirds of employees believe that management will always try to get the better of them, and increasing numbers of those surveyed doubt that they would have *any* say over decisions at work (Bryson and Mackay, 1998).

Limited managerial commitment needs to be understood, however, in the context of the logics of global markets and finance capital, which, as Thompson (2003) argues, prevent employers from keeping their side of the bargain. The emphasis on the financial performance of firms, in markets oriented to short-term return on investments, has led to successive waves of mergers and acquisitions, the shedding and externalisation of labour, and the centralisation of corporate control over strategy. Data from repeated Workplace Employment Relations Surveys (Millward et al., 2000) show that

> during the 1990s ... decisions on senior appointments, on union recognition and derecognition, and on the use of budgetary surpluses were all decreasingly a matter for workplace managers and increasingly decided at higher level. (p. 227)

At the same time that markets have created continuing instability in organisations, and employers have intensified work and invested less in training, career development and workplace democracy (Beynon et al., 2002), employees have been expected to identify with corporate goals and to invest more of themselves in the organisation. This is hardly conducive to identification with corporate values and goals.

It is important therefore to focus on the employment relations in which forms of cultural and normative controls are located. The growing emphasis placed by employers on identification with corporate values raises expectations that employees' input will be valued and accepted as legitimate. When expectations are contradicted by the experience of feeling less valued, the employer is seen as hypocritical. The effect is to render managerial rhetoric about partnership, loving the company and empowering the workforce susceptible to considerable scepticism. Thus when employers claim to value employees for their social and communication skills, but fail to give recognition to those skills in practice, people become disaffected, as illustrated in Williams' (2003) study of airline cabin crew. In this case, employers used market rationales to emphasise the subservience of staff to customers, and paid no attention to employee concerns about the bad behaviour of some customers. Consequently, employees felt that their contribution was not respected, and the work was experienced as exhausting and demoralising. Where worker concerns about customer abuse and harassment prompted a proactive response, through training and policies to counter bullying, aggression or harassment, then the negative effects of the work were ameliorated. The extent to which employment relations are conducted in the context of trust and respect is thus critical to the interpretation of managerial attempts to persuade employees to identify with organisation goals and to invest more of themselves in work.

Organisational Power Relations, Social Divisions and the Meanings of Emotional Labour

The employment relationship is central to the interpretation of all organisational devices to regulate identity through forms of normative or cultural control. None of these have fixed meanings, because their meaning depends on the social relations in which they are embedded (Pahl, 1988). We can, for example, make sense of the apparently contradictory findings that emotional labour can be both a source of satisfaction and a source of degradation, if we recognise that such work is carried out under relations of dominance and subordination, framed by gender, class and ethnic divisions, which make it potentially demoralising and exhausting, or satisfying and engaging.

The negative effects of emotional labour have been exemplified in a range of occupations, including checkout operators (Ogbonna and Wilkinson, 1988), nurses (James, 1989), prison officers (Rutter and Fielding, 1988) and theme park employees (van Maanen, 1991), as well as call centre operators and airline cabin crew. It is notable that in all cases, the jobs studied are situated in a division of labour where employees are subject to intensive work practices and have limited autonomy. In private services, performance is typically scripted and monitored, and managers espouse a strong version of customer sovereignty (Wharton, 1993) in a low trust employment relationship. This suggests that the organisational context in which it is embedded is crucial to its meanings.

The term 'emotional labour' draws attention to a gendered division of labour, which locates primary responsibility for caring and emotion work with women in both public and private. A cultural ideology of heterosexual femininity underlies managers' beliefs that women are 'naturally' more patient, polite, thoughtful and caring, good at playing the support role in conversation and building rapport with customers, and able to tolerate sexualised, and sometimes abusive, interaction (Hochschild, 1983; James, 1992; Smith, 1992; Taylor and Tyler, 2000). They are expected to perform 'deferential service' better than men, and in face-to-face interaction to use their bodies to appeal to a naturalised male gaze. Each of these links to women's domestic role as managers of feelings in private life, where femininity is associated with responsiveness to the needs of others and with balancing competing demands for care (James, 1989).

Employers do not regard such capacities as 'skills', asserting instead that women are 'naturally' able to please customers by virtue of their attributed femininity. A conventional association of women with sexuality is treated, in this context, not as an organisational liability, but as a commercially exploitable asset. In face-to-face customer service work, bodily presentation is sexualised, with women subject to explicit pressure to manage their appearance and to use their bodies to express their compliance with (male) customer demands (Adkins, 1995; Bolton and Boyd, 2003). Bodily compliance is routinely monitored and appraised, with supervisors checking appearance, weight, conformity to uniform, hair and make-up regulations and suggesting ways in which attentiveness to customers could be improved; while norms relating to appearance may also be reinforced by peer pressures (Taylor and Tyler, 2000; Williams, 2003). Facilitated by a one-sided management rhetoric of customer sovereignty, gendered power relations are also evident in customer reactions, since women are typically treated with less deference than men, making the requirements of apparently similar work different in practice for men and women. Airline passengers, for example, assumed that male cabin crew had greater authority and men frequently had an easier time dealing with diffi-cult passengers. Women were more likely to be assumed to be sympathetic and were more likely to receive people's complaints, troubles and to be subject to sexual harassment (Bolton and Boyd, 2003; Hochschild, 1983; Korczinski, 2003; Williams, 2003).

Although most attention has focused on the gendered experience of emotional labour, such work is also located in a division of labour strati-fied by class and racialised inequalities. There is relatively little research on 'race', ethnicity and emotional labour, but Gunaratnam and Lewis's (2001) study of welfare organisations shows the divisions among women, in work interactions between black and white welfare professionals, and in service interactions between professionals and clients. They give a psychoanalytically informed account of the complexity of emotion work in welfare services, when the often unspoken dynamics of anxiety, anger, fear, shame, guilt and defensiveness mark the interaction between racialised social categories. The failure to acknowledge and discuss such dynamics, they suggest, is immobilising in professional practice and dam-aging to both practitioners and clients. Their work is an apt reminder that emotional labour is neither one-dimensional, nor determined by function-alist organisational routines. It is also 'produced by the complexities and contradictions of multiple and intersecting categories of social differenti ation' (p. 138). Emotionally inflected work is not therefore contained by hard and fast organisational rules, because its meanings are not fixed. Racialised understandings intersect with gender, affecting its articulation and experience.

Social class, as located in occupational hierarchies, also cuts across the meanings and consequences of emotional labour. Higher status service work, in the professions for example, typically offers a higher degree of autonomy and relies on the exercise of judgement and discretion. In this context, emotional labour is frequently a source of satisfaction (Wharton, 1993), although there may also be personal costs in the form of exhaustion and 'burnout' (Harris, 2002; Wolkowitz, 2002). The extent of emotional labour in professional work is demonstrated by Harris's (2002) study of barristers, whose work is governed by long occupational socialisation in formalised ethical codes and standards. Such work entails a high degree of discretion, reflexivity and creativity and exemplifies the autonomy of the non-organisational professions. Barristers regarded their work as routinely requiring emotionally informed performance, not just formally in the court room, but less formally with the wider legal community, who were central to the continuing flow of work. They saw their effectiveness as dependent not on identification with the role, but on the maintenance of emotional detachment, which was crucial to the ability to survive physical and emotional exhaustion.

Those in routinised occupations, in low trust employment relations, lack this degree of autonomy and control, and are more likely to experience the negative aspects of emotional labour. Occupational divides within healthcare, for example, illustrate the ways in which emotional labour is subject to intersecting class, gender and racialised meanings. At the top of the hierarchy, doctors exercise most control over the terms of their labour, while nurses do the lower status work of emotional and physical clearing up after them (Davies, 2002). Within nursing, there are further class and racialised divisions. Black women are more likely to be in the least desirable, dirtiest jobs, which place them at most risk of harassment from patients (Anderson, 2000; Glenn 1996). Even when the content of work is superficially similar, as for instance in the case of domestic help in private households, its status may be differentiated according to racialised distinctions, such as those implied when white women are referred to as 'au pairs', but black women as 'maids'. In this case, the presumption that the au pair does more care work and less physical labour dignifies emotional labour, in contrast with the use of the term 'maid', which simultaneously renders invisible the emotional labour of the black woman, as well as the emotional injuries sustained (Wolkowitz, 2002). A similar process of emotional injury seems likely to be created as call centre jobs are exported to areas where labour costs are lower, and workers are expected to hide their identity by changing their accent and engaging in conversation about the equivalent of British weather or American football.

Emotional labour therefore has different meanings and consequences for self-identity, depending on its location in a class-based, gendered and racialised social hierarchy. For those in higher status occupations, long-term occupational socialisation and training in formal expertise are generally accompanied by a high degree of internalised normative control and autonomy over the performance of emotional labour, although the intensification of work threatens the satisfaction derived. Gendered and racialised categorisations intersect with occupational class, such that black women in professional occupations may be subject to demands for deference that white men or women in the same job may not encounter, making them more likely to experience harassment or abuse. In more routine occupations, the employer aims to channel and control emotional labour more directly, in an employment relationship characterised by low trust, repetitive and intensive work with limited discretion. Again this is unlikely to result in high levels of willing identification with the organisation.

Teams Create their own Subcultures and Norms

Teamwork itself is a precarious and unstable form of managerial control over identity, because work groups develop informal norms and rituals that are not inevitably aligned with those of management. The improvisatory character of social interaction means that work group norms, rituals, shared humour and so on sustain a degree of autonomy and space for group-defined action. In Motorola, for example, despite the concerted efforts of management to use teams to increase peer pressure and raise productivity, McKinlay and Taylor (1998) conclude that the process was quietly dismantled by workforce resistance and pragmatic adaptations by management. In the airline industry, cabin crew draw on a sense of professional identity to emphasise their safety, first aid and rescue skills, suggesting alternative sources of self-esteem and dignity in the job.

Surveillance and individualised performance appraisal does not prevent peer group support, resistance and alternative understandings of the organisation from those espoused by corporate media. Annoying customers, long hours and poor conditions are made more tolerable by camaraderie and humour (Bolton and Boyd, 2003), with the negative effects of aggressive and irate customers limited by the development of informal subcultures among peers (Korczinski, 2003). In call centres and airlines, 'back stage' areas (Goffman, 1959) such as lavatories or kitchen areas are used as places for shared jokes, parodies of job requirements and alternative commentaries on work (Bolton and Boyd, 2003; Taylor and Tyler, 2000). Such areas may be more symbolic than material, consisting of a smile or a gesture to a co-worker to indicate shared understanding outside the formal performance (Fineman and Sturdy, 2001). Group subcultures function despite individualised labour processes and management prescriptions that discourage workers from discussing their feelings with peers. In Korczinski's (2003) study of call centre work, for example, work teams prevented management using individual performance data to individualise competition between workers.

Collective coping sustains people by allowing them to express hurt, anger and frustration, and generates a strong sense of mutual support. The potential for significant acts of resistance to managerial prerogative should not of course be overstated: these are tactics deployed in a situation of unequal power, where there are few 'exit opportunities' in the form of alternative employment. Such informal work norms in one sense serve the purposes of management, by creating emotional support and enabling people to set their experiences in perspective with those of others. Hence they probably contribute to reduced labour turnover and higher morale. At the same time however, the peer group is a means of collective resistance to management control, acting as a counter to the most individualising, isolating aspects of the job.

Teamwork has been widely introduced, but Harley's (2001) survey concludes that it has left employees' perspectives on work unchanged. Workers have been drawn into the micro-management of production, which may be well received to the extent that this acknowledges the capacities and expertise of the workforce (Rosenthal et al., 1997), but teamwork has not led to significant improvements in workplace democracy and control over strategic decisions (Baldry et al., 1998; Danford, 1998; Milkman, 1998; Procter and Mueller, 2000; Stewart and Martinez Lucio, 1998).

The Resilience of Self-identity

The relationships between organisational instability, demanding work and self-identity thus need to be evaluated more critically. It has become almost a commonplace for postmodern analysis to assert that contemporary culture is leading to a fragmented, insecure sense of self and more pronounced existential dilemmas. In the context of organisations, this has been the basis for assertions that self-identity is vulnerable to the seductive appeal of corporate culture and values in an ultimately self-defeating attempt to find psychological security (Casey, 1995; Deetz, 1992). Without denying the anxieties and uncertainties associated with modern societies, where identity is achieved rather than ascribed (see Chapter 1), or the significance of organisational strategies to capture hearts and minds, it is nevertheless important to ask whether self-identity is as universally fragile and precarious as sometimes implied.

The same self-identity that is seen as increasingly fragmented and precarious from one point of view can also be represented as an attribute of modern forms of agency and adaptability to changing conditions, brought about through the historical development of rational-legal forms of authority and organisation, the operation of labour markets and the 'decoupling of people's life chances from status or other hereditary social relations' (Kallinikos, 2003: 604). Greater social mobility and the requirement that people constitute their identity in multiple, intersecting, but divisible ways in private and public life are conditions of modernity. Although experiences of work and organisations are likely to be central to who we become, modern social relations rely on separation between spheres of activity: bureaucracy, as argued in Chapter 1, distinguishes between the person and the office, and allocates responsibility to the person for their own actions. This imposes considerable demands on conduct and self-control, but the organisational 'role' remains separable from the person performing it, and the person differentiates between different aspects of identity, relating not just to occupation or profession, but to family and intimate relations, friends and public life. The resulting sense of identity can be seen as an unstable collage, subject to continual remaking, but it can also be seen as conferring a degree of resilience and adaptability, as well as insight into the limits of self-determination.

These assertions receive support from organisational case studies which show that employees are perfectly aware of the ambitions of corporate culture and normative controls, and hold different attitudes towards them, depending on whether or not such initiatives improve their working lives, or whether they are perceived as 'hot air'. In customer services work, for example, far from being seduced by employer claims that customer interaction is all about quality, care, rapport and empathy, employees adapt by managing the boundaries of the 'emotional effort bargain' (Callaghan and Thompson, 2002: 251) and develop a self-reliant adjustment to the 'organisational realities' of work primarily requiring stamina, patience and tolerance (Bolton and Boyd, 2003; Callaghan and Thompson, 2002; Korczinski, 2003; Taylor and Tyler, 2000; Williams, 2003). Various coping mechanisms were relied on to limit the invasion of organisational values into self-esteem. The low trust organisational context tends to result in competent performances, without personal identification with the organisation. In this way, space for resistance to, and alternative understandings of, an employer-promoted reality is maintained.

The reliance on forms of direct performance management, through the monitoring and appraisal of performance, shows the centrality of resistance to the relationship and continuing tension over the wage–effort bargain. Even in jobs with limited authority, service sector employers are dependent on the workforce to produce convincing performances, and have to balance the pressure to standardise and control interactions with the need to maintain the willing engagement of workers (Bolton and Boyd, 2003; Callaghan and Thompson, 2002; Taylor and Tyler, 2000). British Airways, for example, has recently had to offer extra payments to cabin crew to persuade them to staff long-haul flights. The suggestion to staff that they should be 'natural' and rely on their own personality when dealing with customers creates a source of resistance to management demands to comply with externally imposed routines and scripted interactions. Employees point out the contradiction that, if they were chosen for their personality, then management cannot insist that they change the way they interact (Taylor and Tyler, 2000). Employer injunctions to empathise with customers may also be a source of resistance to overly scripted or manipulative sales techniques (Korczynski et al., 2000).

Self-identity is thus not overwhelmed by organisational prescriptions. In work settings, employees often engage simultaneously on three or four different levels, with customers, superiors, subordinates and peers, each requiring different social skills and capacities (Bolton and Boyd, 2003). Some studies of emotional labour have concluded that it can be a key source of meaning (Black and Sharma, 2001), satisfaction and pleasure even in routine work (Crang, 1994; Korczinski, 2003), and does not necessarily destroy self-esteem (Frenkel et al., 1998). Actors draw on personal resources that are not dictated by commercial motives, displaying the capacity to move between roles, ranging from friend to authority figure, balancing conflicting demands and delivering polished performances. Role distance does not necessarily imply cynical performance, or the pretence of feeling. It could instead be interpreted as a properly dispassionate and reflexive understanding of the role and its requirements. The tenacity of such skilful self-presentation and emotion management is valuable to employers, but it also means that self-identity is relatively enduring and not swept away by organisational prescription.

Conclusion

Organisational attempts to align self-identities with corporate values are therefore limited by labour's recognition of the lack of genuine reciprocity and the limits of the corporate commitment to them, leaving employment relations issues of limited trust and a contested work–effort bargain in place. Individualised employee loyalty to an organisation is structurally one-sided. It is based not on reciprocal exchange and mutual respect, but on the valuation of the person according to a limited liability calculus of their use value to the corporation. The continuity of bureaucratic controls and the intensification of work leads Beynon et al. (2002) to conclude that employees, 'empowered to death' in public and private sector organisations, are conscripts rather than converts to new work regimes. In these circumstances, measures to regulate identity through corporate culture and normative control may accentuate sceptical and cynical responses among the workforce, producing more distancing of self from an organisational identity and a calculated compliance with work requirements.

Arguably, the organisations of capitalist consumer societies demand increasingly skilful 'identity work' in the form of self-restraint, flexibility and sensitivity. In the light of evidence of continuing sources of resistance to an overly exploitative work–effort bargain, it is important to recognise that such sources of reflexivity make self-identity less fragile than pessimistic analyses predict. Informal work group subcultures, as well as family and intimate relations, and the public spheres of education, culture and politics continue to create the space for alternative understandings of organisational rationalities, and opposition to the intensification of work.

In the next chapter, I will develop these themes concerned with the nature of identity in advanced capitalist societies in order to explore the ways that organisations shape individualism and pressures for continuous self-improvement in relation to both work and consumption. Critical analysis has argued that regardless of reflexivity and self-awareness, self-identity is powerfully shaped by the obligation to make choices in a competitive market for individual distinction: we can choose to be anyone or anything, trying on different identities at will, as long as we 'choose' to consume in work and outside it.

8

Organisations Are Us: Understanding Self-identity in Organised Societies

Social life, selfhood and identities are increasingly understood through the medium of organisations. Organisations are not simply 'outside us' as places of work, or consumption, or rationalised means of governing through the rule of law. They *are* us: large organisations are 'our fate for the foreseeable future' (Perrow, 2002: 228). They are the means of turning human capacities into instruments for the pursuit of diverse goals, notably in capitalist societies those concerned with wealth creation, profitability, economic growth or the protection of private property. This far, at least, modernist and postmodernist accounts agree. Charles Perrow offers a modernist analysis of the origins of US corporate capitalism, concluding that 'a weak state allowed the private accumulation of wealth and power through the medium of big organisations' (p. 226), creating an economy based on the autonomy of corporations and the wage dependency of populations. Nikolas Rose (1999) based his analysis of the shaping of a 'productive subjectivity', aligned with the productivity concerns of modern capitalism, on Foucault's postmodernist concepts of power. He concluded that organisations 'fill the space between the "private" lives of citizens and the "public" concerns of rulers' (p. 2). In each case, large-scale organisations are the means of enacting the power relations of capitalist societies in all spheres – the intimate and private as well as the public.

In this chapter I examine some of the ways in which contemporary self-identity, as something 'achieved' through projects and plans, rather than ascribed by heritage and status, is significantly shaped by organisational processes. Historically, the emergence of rational-legal organisations created the foundations of an individualised agency (see Chapter 1), which has been progressively refined and remade in 'forging a symmetry between the attempts of individuals to make life worthwhile for themselves, and the political values of consumption, profitability, efficiency and social order' (Rose, 1999: 10). This takes the arguments examined in the previous chapter to a different level of analysis. There I looked at managerial interests in devising means to align personal identity with corporate goals, in order to suggest that there is no division of interest between capital and labour. The evidence, however, showed people's awareness of the contradictions between promises of empowerment and experiences of work intensification and direct control. I argued that such awareness and resistance to identification with corporate values show the resilience of self-identities and a pragmatic adaptation to circumstances, and not the existence of 'colonised minds'.

It might seem contradictory therefore to begin this chapter by suggesting that 'organisations are us', but I hope the reader will bear with me while I explain the argument and its strengths and weaknesses. To start from this perspective is not to suggest that self-identity is 'colonised' or determined by the conspiratorial powers of governments, corporations, technologies and expertise. Although we may be made 'knowable' to government and business leaders, through concepts and measures devised by the human sciences, social statistics, organisational expertise and so on, I argue that we are also *made knowledgeable* by the same processes. Through social and collective identities devised from the circumstances of work and consumption, people continue to exercise critical judgement about the values and goals of organisations and governments, in a complex and shifting process of partial resistance, consent and compliance. Those judgements are powerfully framed by organisational rationalities: who we are is inevitably connected to the organisational processes of contemporary capitalist societies, and understanding that condition is part of conceiving alternatives.

Globalising Markets, Organisations and Individualisation

Globalising financial markets, competitive pressures on business, and the drive to expand consumer capitalism are central to the organisational dynamics of contemporary self-identity, because they are creating the conditions of individualised responsibility for social and economic well-being. The political dominance of neoliberal economics, discussed in Chapter 2, has led to the freeing up of finance capital, the retrenchment of socialised welfare provisions and the weakening of organised labour. Life chances have been made more dependent on the individualised opportunity structures presented by a competitive market system for qualifications and jobs with better incomes, which give more access to proliferating consumer choice, in more polarised and unequal societies.

In advanced capitalist societies, consumption and production are materially interdependent, because economic prosperity and employment rely significantly on income spent on shopping, entertainment, travel and so on (Gershuny, 2000). Since the 1980s, growth in disposable incomes among significant proportions of the populations of North America, Europe and the Pacific rim and higher expectations among consumers have enhanced competition for the spending (and borrowing) power of the relatively affluent. In economic terms, 'leisure' is a vital source of profit, and is subject to the same logic of market expansion and diversification as production. The proliferation of leisure products and services at all levels in the market, alongside more intensive marketing and advertising in the competition for disposable incomes, creates pressures to organise 'free time' productively, to fit in more activities, and to reassure ourselves that we are making the most of whatever disposable income we have. But these pressures may in turn make the activities of consumption feel more like work. Conversely, the corporate culture initiatives discussed in the last chapter, aimed at persuading people to identify with the organisation and to work harder, lead to the construction of work as a resource for consumption and self-improvement:

> The individual is not to be emancipated *from* work ... but to be fulfilled *in* work, now construed as an activity through which we produce, discover and experience our selves. (Rose, 1999: 103)

This idea of work and consumption as a combined means to self-growth might be expected to appeal predominantly to those with university qualifications, who have already made considerable investments in their 'social capital', but it can also be argued that the idea of self-identity as a project subject to continuous improvement through work and consumption is increasingly promoted to the entire population. Growing numbers of routinised jobs in services, for example, rely on skilled capacities for self-presentation, impression management and emotional expressiveness. Such capacities require the ability to think of one's self as a 'product' with a 'market value', where work can be construed as a resource for improving our social capital. Ridderstråle and Nordström's (2004) account of *Karaoke Capitalism*, which is intended as a guide to winning in business in 'the age of the individual', asserts that 'today more than ever human beings are brands' (p. 13). They exemplify their point mainly with reference to public figures such as Bill Clinton, who received more than $8 million in the contract for his memoirs, but they also assert that everyone has to 'cash in on their life' (p. 13), by crafting a unique, individual market identity through acts of self-expression. This is not straightforward 'domination by the powerful' so much as a structured requirement to engage in a competitive calculation about the individualised achievement of a distinctive, marketable identity.

The Organisation of a Productive Self:
a Postmodernist Analysis

Postmodernist accounts of identity, as well as modernist accounts, have swung between oversocialised and undersocialised models of the self (see Chapter 1). Nikolas Rose (1999) sets out to avoid both these extremes in his postmodernist analysis of the organisation of contemporary subjectivity. I set this out here because of its value in understanding the aspirations of governments and business leaders to shape self-identity and to constitute the person as a knowable subject, but also because I wish to comment on its limitations, which centre on the tendency to elide the language and ideology of the 'productive self' with experience. Rose's evidence is derived principally from textual sources, and not from accounts of organisational attempts to operationalise such discourses, or from discussions of people's experiences of them (Thompson and Findlay, 1999). The result is the marginalisation, or invisibility, of other sources of identity, knowledgeability and values, perversely reinforcing a nihilistic sense that subjectivity is entirely governed by power.

Nevertheless, Rose's analysis offers valuable insights into the development of new *languages* for construing, understanding and evaluating ourselves and others. At this point, Rose is at pains to point out that he is not suggesting a conspiracy by the powerful to dominate the subject, but the gradual alignment of political aspirations with personal ambitions through the constructed obligation to make our own choices and shape our own destiny. What is distinctive about the current era, Rose argues, is the progressive incorporation of the subjective capacities of populations into the government of public life, with the aim of organising the forces of society to maximise wealth, productivity, efficiency and social order. The human sciences, social statistics, education and welfare, human resource management and so on have provided the languages and expertise of subjectivity, which enable the transformation of human powers into calculable resources for the achievement of public goals. Such expertise offers particular ways of thinking and talking about feelings, hopes, ambitions and disappointments, encouraging a form of self-consciousness oriented to projects of self-improvement.

In his account of the managerial applications of the sciences of subjectivity, Rose traces the historical development of ideologies interested in harnessing the discretionary powers of labour to the goals of organisation, through the refinement of theories of human motivation. Work has increasingly been construed as a resource to be consumed: the harder we work, the more we 'profit' through self-fulfilment. By the 1960s, the rising costs of labour and industrial conflict and the drive to improve productivity stimulated debate about the need for new systems of labour motivation and discipline. The doctrines of the 'human relations' school, which emphasised social satisfaction at work, were seen as fostering social conformity, at the cost of innovation and competitiveness. The therapeutic culture, conveyed through writers such as Abraham Maslow, Carl Rogers, Viktor Frankl and Erich Fromm, emphasised ideas of individual growth, fulfilment and self-actualisation through striving to achieve and taking responsibility. These ideas were deployed by management consultants and business schools to create new theories of labour motivation, based on an image of the worker seeking self-fulfilment. It was suggested that jobs could be designed to tap into people's capacity for creativity and problem-solving, in line with organisational goals of innovation, flexibility and competitiveness. In his influential text, Douglas McGregor (1987 [1960]) criticised managers' traditional Theory X view of labour as disliking work and actively avoiding responsibility. Problems of low productivity and recalcitrance, he argued, stemmed from inadequate organisation and managers who found it easier to blame the workers rather than acting to engage their interest and abilities. He challenged managers to redesign organisations according to his proposed Theory Y, which construed people as self-directing and able to take responsibility for problems, and exercise ingenuity and creativity in their solution.

Americanised concepts of self-actualisation and personal growth crossed the Atlantic, notably through the popularity of business texts such as Peters and Waterman's *In Search of Excellence* (1982), discussed in Chapter 7. The image of the person promoted was that of an autonomous individual, willingly engaged in an enterprise of self-improvement (Gordon, 1987). This image portrayed work not as a duty but as a resource to be consumed in the making of a better self. In du Gay's (1996) study of the restructuring of work in retailing, the language of enterprise was, for example, used by managers to persuade staff that committing themselves to customer service and taking responsibility for 'their store' was a means to self-fulfilment. Sales assistants were trained in the psycho-technologies of self-growth, in a way designed to cut across divisions between work and non-work. Such techniques encouraged staff to act reflexively on interactions with customers and peers, but also to apply a philosophy of self-improvement throughout their lives. Building on Rose's analysis, du Gay (1996) concludes that:

> the 'employee', just as much as the 'sovereign consumer', is represented as an individual in search of meaning and fulfilment, one looking to 'add value' in every sphere of existence. (p. 65)

The consumer too, as we saw in Chapter 3, is constructed as making choices designed to enhance individual distinction, personal control and self-growth. From this perspective, in work, at home, in social life and in the activities of consumption, the postmodern subject is represented as engaged in a calculative project of continuous self-improvement (or 'life-long learning' as the current UK government terminology expresses it), regulated by organisation goals and 'lifestyle choices' that enhance self-esteem through individualistic achievements in competitive markets (Casey, 1995; Ezzy, 2001; Graham, 1995; Grey, 1994; Grugulis et al., 2000; Hochschild, 1997; Kunda, 1992).

An Expertise of Self-improvement?

Arguments about productive subjectivity and the calculative treatment of the self as a project for improvement are impossible to evaluate in an absolute sense. There is however a growing self-improvement industry, which is instrumental in promoting and elaborating the idea that a con-sciously stylised self is central to social and economic success in a com-petitive market for a distinctive identity. Image consultancy, life coaching, bodywork and cosmetic surgery, fashion and interior design and personal shopping services have expanded rapidly in the past decade (Black and Sharma, 2001; Fenwick, 2002). Popular TV programmes restyle self-identity through the 'soft technologies' of confessional talk and the remodelling of appearance. In Britain, the Trinny and Susannah TV show subjects volun-teers to rituals of psychological and physical 'undressing' in front of the cameras, so that an improved self, in control in public and private, can be rebuilt. Politicians and their spouses have consciously restyled behaviour, speech and demeanour, through the use of 'image consultants' and 'life coaches', in order to improve their public identity and voter popularity.

In some cases, gendered skills of empathy, household management and shopping have been transformed into market capacities centring on style and taste. Such consultants offer

> symbolic and material services in . . . the presentation of the self (image con-sultants, presentation and communication skills); care of the body/mind (stress counselling, nutrition, alternative medicine, therapies); aesthetics and design (interior design, dress design, feng shui, gardening and landscaping). (Gray, 2003: 491)

Pierre Bourdieu (1984) coined the term 'cultural intermediaries' to high-light the growth of such workers in twentieth-century France. He described this group as a new petite bourgeoisie, with indeterminate status and skills, whose work centres on the organisation, presentation and articulation of an aesthetic of cultural distinction, taste and style. To be effective, such 'need merchants' (p. 365) have to embody the lifestyle and values promoted, and hence are simultaneously the consumers and the producers of the same symbolic goods: they 'play a vanguard role in the struggles over everything concerned with the art of living' (p. 366).

Service sector organisations increasingly regard the stylised self-presentation of labour as critical to the value of the 'organisational brand' (Gabriel, 2005). The cultivation of a slim and physically toned body is seen as necessary to convey the qualities of a 'fit' and enterprising organisation (McDowell, 1997; Witz et al., 2003). Over 800 businesses in the UK alone are concerned with image consultancy through colour analysis, wardrobe audit, personal shopping, make-up, grooming and deportment (Wellington and Bryson, 2001). Corporate clients include major accountancy and management consultancy firms, such as KPMG, CapGemini and Pricewaterhouse-Coopers, all of whom employed consultants to instruct senior employees in self-presentation and impression management. Employees in the City of London regarded self-presentation as critical to work success: style, body shape, sexuality and gender performance were all integral to the job (McDowell, 1997). The body had to be elegantly attired and posture, demeanour and gestures deliberately moulded to create the desired impression of confidence, authority and expertise. People's command of the requisite language of ambition, achievement and enterprise were also significant sources of cultural and social capital, which discriminated between 'winners' and 'losers' in the organisational hierarchies of career advancement.

As part of the 'cultural industries' of mass media, design, PR and marketing (Amin and Thrift, 2003), the self-improvement industry erodes the boundaries between production and consumption: the work of design, marketing and lifestyling demands investment in self-presentation through consumption choices, and consumption choices are presented back to us as critical to the development of a distinctive self in an identity market.

Is Work Treated as a Resource for Self-improvement?

The phenomenon of the self-improvement industry is not, however, direct evidence that technologies of subjectivity are 'able to infiltrate the interstices of the human soul' (Rose, 1999: 8). It may instead offer a variety of semi-scripted ways of performing different identities, adapted to different settings, but not necessarily felt as deeply meaningful. In the workplace, there is adequate evidence, as we saw in the previous chapter, that employees are 'conscripts' rather than 'converts' (Beynon et al., 2002) to the ambitions of the organisational regulation of identity and 'productive subjectivity'.

Nevertheless, it is worth considering the argument that the techniques and ideologies of self-actualisation are highly influential in the values and aspirations of employees in general, even if the experience does not live up to expectations. Ideas of self-development through work are fairly common, and many people complain that their aspirations for improved work performance as a means to self-fulfilment are continually undermined by added burdens and intensification of work in a direct system of control that perversely prevents them from meeting the espoused goals of the organisation (Burchell et al., 1999; Gallie et al., 1998). Neither are concerns with self-improvement through work the sole preserve of those in higher level occupations. A quarter of Li et al.'s (2003) sample of working-class people aged 30–70 and over half of 20–29-year-olds made aspirational plans in relation to their work and housing, despite some sense of insecurity and financial pressures. Such attitudes correlated with greater success in the labour market, with those who made plans being more likely to have jobs and higher incomes (Anderson et al., 2002).

Such ideologies seem likely to operate most powerfully in relation to those groups who have invested heavily in the currency of self-improvement, through higher education or professional qualifications. This group may be more willing to internalise values of self-actualisation through work and career prospects. They are also likely to be in occupations where they are responsible for using the ideologies of self-improvement to motivate other employees, and thus may feel more directly identified with such values (Thompson and Findlay, 1999). Management ideologies are also a vehicle for legitimating the authority of managers themselves, giving them a direct interest in their advocacy, while professionals are implicated in the production of the requisite expertise of self-growth through education, counselling, self-therapies, organisation development techniques and so on. Above all, however, it could be argued that the ideology of self-growth is particularly influential over managers and professionals, because they are the groups most likely to benefit materially, as well as socially, through rising incomes and conspicuous consumption.

Evidence from studies of managerial and professional occupations generally confirms that people with skills and credentials in demand in a competitive labour market are likely to identify themselves with the values of self-actualisation (Halford et al., 1997; Hanlon, 1998; Whittington et al., 1994). Australian senior managers surveyed by Wajcman and Martin (2002), for example, ostensibly regarded their jobs as 'virtual consumer goods' in a market for prestige and status. Skilled software developers studied by Grugulis et al. (2000) identified the success of the organisation with personal success, working long hours to win contracts and neglecting family and other activities. They were also expected to devote their social lives to the company, and lines between work and home were blurred, as family were drawn into semi-compulsory social events. Managers and professionals studied by Hochschild (1997) and Casey (1995) were similarly encouraged to consume work as a means to self-fulfilment. Organisations deliberately played on the metaphor of company as 'family', blurring the distinction between loyalty to friends and family, and loyalty to the organisation as an extension of family. In the management and IT consultancy firm studied by Karreman and Alvesson (2004), being an employee of 'Big' was considered highly prestigious and new recruits identified themselves enthusiastically and willingly with corporate values, striving to conform by dressing in the right way, working long hours and taking their mobile phones on holiday.

Corporate rivalries and competition, team and peer pressures, and the marginalising of alternative sources of identification with occupational, trade union or professional groups intensify the pressures on employees to see investment in work as a resource for self-growth and at the centre of their lives. In some instances, it is argued, community engagement, family and friends are consequently devalued, and instead of being treated as ends in themselves, they are regarded in a calculative way as a means to the end of personal gain (Ezzy, 2001). Accountants in Grey's study (1994), for example, evaluated non-work activities, including their choice of marriage partners, in terms of their likely usefulness to career advancement. It is evident, however, from classical English literature and historical studies of bourgeois life that there is nothing new about the adoption of a calculating attitude to friendship and social ties. If anything, modern societies are distinctive for a belief in romantic love and personal intimacy as central to partnerships. Indeed, Lynn Jamieson's (1998) study of empirical research on intimate relationships indicates the relative absence of 'selfish individualism', rather than its increasing pervasiveness.

Nevertheless, those managers and professionals who see their identity as closely tied to work and organisations are likely to have limited capacity for non-work life and personal relationships. The increase in dual-career households (Crompton, 1999) may therefore result in increasing pressures to 'rationalise' home life. Hochschild (1997) concludes from her study of men and women employees of a US corporation that, for those in career occupations, work had become home and home became work: work was the source of emotional satisfaction for her informants, but the more time spent at work, the more uncomfortable home life became. The ethos of unlimited commitment to the organisation militated against people using formal provisions for leave, and informal peer pressures reinforced the sense of illegitimacy of putting family before work. Despite apparently progressive 'family friendly' paper policies, entitlements to leave were underused, particularly by those higher up the corporate ladder. Among her sample, long working hours were the norm, with the longest hours worked by those in senior jobs. In households with children, those with higher incomes opted to buy more hours of childcare rather than working less.

Consequently, home became a 'second shift', which was subject to rationalisation, through the application of techniques for the efficient use of time. The speed-up at home came with emotional costs, however, with children in particular resisting the pace, the deadlines and the irrationalities of 'efficiency routines'. Work and home were reversed: more investment in the organisation made home more like work, because the other members of the household refused to accept the efficiency regime. Conversely, work became the place where emotional warmth and caring was sought, until the corporation made a tranche of people redundant, at which point the one-sided, non-reciprocal nature of identification with the organisation was clear.

In each of these cases, the apparent internalisation of an organisational identity has to be seen in the context of competitive career hierarchies and intensive monitoring and evaluation of performance, which create powerful structural incentives to identify with the organisation and reduce the scope for alternative choices. For those at the early stage of a career, belief in the probability of future advancement was instrumental in encouraging the belief that hard work was not exploitation, but a way of proving their capacities in the competition for promotion. A 'long hours culture' in general encourages the belief that domestic commitments are in conflict with commitment to the organisation, making it unacceptable to reduce hours of work to care for dependents. Hochschild, for instance, notes the ridicule experienced particularly by men who prioritised the family and took leave to care for children. Corporate redundancies however provided a changed set of contingencies, and those at later stages of a career are likely to be more sceptical about identifying themselves too closely with an organisation. Differences between men and women managers also suggest that women remain sharply aware of the tensions between organisationally defined, individualised ambition and self-growth, and private commitment to, and attributed responsibility for, children and family, making them more critical of organisational demands (Wajcman and Martin, 2002).

Identification with an organisation, and the promise of self-growth and fulfilment through it, can be highly seductive, particularly for those in career occupations where the material and social rewards may be enormous. Even for this group, such identification is unlikely to be total. Instead, it is likely to remain situationally specific and subject to change over time, depending on people's location in an organisational hierarchy, their career trajectory, socioeconomic status, family commitments, life stage and other values and beliefs. For most people, identification is partial, shifting and pragmatic rather than total and internalised into the soul.

Subversive Responses to the
Enterprise of the Self

The postmodernist focus on text and the lack of attention to practice in organisations tend to result in an overestimation of the universality and coherence of the application of discourse. In practice, new ideas are typically applied in partial and inconsistent ways, and contradictions between discourses and organisational experiences provide ample opportunities for their critique and deconstruction. In work organisations, managerial discourses of 'empowerment' and enterprise may be subject to reinterpretation through tactics aimed at the creative capture of organisational norms for unofficial ends. The 'creative consumption' of organisational resources, through a variety of forms of pilferage, for example, is widely known about and frequently tolerated within certain limits (Ackroyd and Thompson, 1999). In retail, employees illegally consume almost the same value of goods as those taken by shoplifters. Personal use of work telephones, computers or other resources is relatively common, as is the use of work space for socialising. Retail store managers studied by du Gay (1996), for example, made creative use of their operational 'ownership' of store performance by using the store as a site for entertaining friends and family; others sought to use performance targets to ease pressures on themselves and to maximise the morale of employees. Inventive use of store training requirements could secure pay increases for staff, turning enterprise to new ends unintentionally arising out of corporate objectives. In each case, the rationalities of enterprise and self-improvement acted as constraints around which calculative adaptations were made, but employees continued to find ways to ensure some degree of control and freedom of manoeuvre.

Probably the most common form of subversion of managerial rationalities concerned with productive subjectivity is their debunking through jokes, irony and humour. As contest over the work–effort bargain has shifted to the terrain of identity, satirical forms of humour have become more important as a means of self-distancing for employees. Among other things, humour is a means of dissenting from dominant organisational rationalities and retaining a sense of perspective and 'free space' (Collinson, 1988). Ackroyd and Thompson (1999) discuss the popularity of cartoon strips such as Dilbert, the put-upon engineer who suffers each succeeding wave of management ideology with a knowing and satirical commentary. Although satire and other forms of joking may be limited as tools of subversion, they indicate the continuing creativity of self-understanding and forms of self-awareness that are resistant to discourses of self-improvement. When incentives to be 'entrepreneurial' in the interests of the organisation encounter the obstacles of bureaucracy, a lack of trust and workplace democracy, people turn their enterprising capacities to the subversion of corporate goals, through whatever means are available to them (Parker and Slaughter, 2000).

'Being Productive' in Work, Non-work and Leisure?

Humour, creative forms of self-distancing, and pragmatic adaptation to organisational norms of 'productive subjectivity' exist alongside a common perception that life in advanced capitalist societies is characterised by having too much to do and too little time to do it. This could be, as suggested by Schor's (1992) *The Overworked American*, and by Hochschild (1997), the result of longer working hours, dual-earner households and the consequent decrease in 'free time', uncommitted to paid or unpaid work. There is, however, disagreement about whether working hours in capitalist societies are increasing or declining. Schor's study used data from US labour force surveys to conclude that the 'work and spend' capitalism of the 1970s and 1980s resulted in people working longer hours and taking less vacations, regardless of occupational level. Using the same data, however, Robinson (1997) concludes that there has been a decline in hours of work for both sexes, even though this does not accord with people's own estimates of time pressures.

Longitudinal data, derived from diary studies of time use between the 1960s and the 1990s, shows a decline in total working hours for both men and women. Focusing on the core economically active ages of 20–59, Gershuny (2000) derived his analysis from 35 surveys in 20 developed countries, ranging from Bulgaria to the USA and the UK. Three main trends are evident. First, there was an average decline in total (paid and unpaid) hours of work. Second, time use in different countries had converged around a common balance of 55% paid and 45% unpaid work, and, third, there was a degree of convergence between men and women in their total hours of work. Women on average do more domestic work and less paid work than men, while the majority of men's work is paid.

There is therefore a contradiction between the *evidence* from time use diaries, which suggests declining average hours of work, and a commonly *perceived*, publicly debated sense of time pressure and busyness. Numerous factors may contribute to explaining this contradiction. Here I focus on the implications of ideologies of productive subjectivity and self-improvement for time use, and hypothesise that the perception of time pressure, despite evidence of some decrease in average hours of (paid and unpaid) work, is associated with the increasing incursion of organisational rationalities of productivity into the private sphere. In particular, to the extent that people are influenced by the idea of self-improvement as a 'life project', then they are likely to try to use their time productively, treating it as a commodity that requires economising, balancing or budgeting. Influenced by the time is money equation of consumer capitalism, the endlessly available consumption opportunities and the observed speed up of a globalising market, free time itself may be subjected to the organisational logics of efficiency and productivity. People may, for example, save time preparing food in order to make time to go to the gym or to pursue further education. The market in turn provides goods and services oriented to saving time to spend on other forms of commodified leisure.

Changes in the balance of unpaid work activities provide some evidence of the influence of an ethic of self-improvement. Women continue to do the majority of unpaid household work and their hours of unpaid work have increased, despite time-saving products and services. The time spent on routine domestic work has declined, while time spent travelling, shopping, doing odd jobs and childcare has increased (Robinson, 1997; Sullivan and Gershuny, 2000), suggesting changed priorities and attitudes towards valued activities. An increase in childcare activities may reflect increased consciousness of debates about the need to be a good parent (Sullivan and Gershuny, 2000), which in turn results in increased involvement in, for example, supervising homework or accompanying children to organised activities. Parents may also be reflecting social pressures to invest in children's social capital, through buying extracurricular activities, holidays and so on. In this way, children are subject to the same self-improvement rationales as their parents and their lives are subject to similar organisational rationalities.

Increased time spent on shopping may reflect two related forms of self-improvement 'projects', one to do with the work of self-presentation for the public sphere, and the other to do with the marketing of aspirational lifestyling in the private sphere. Organisational demands for 'stylised' employees require considerable investment of time in buying clothes, make-up, accessories, trips to the gym, hairdressers and health and beauty treatments. The stresses and strains of intensive work in turn stimulate markets for therapies to overcome its adverse effects and self-indulgences to reward periods of self-denial. In the private sphere, the home improvement ethos encourages the purchase of commodities, which translate into the increased odd jobs of laying new flooring, building flat-pack furniture, redecorating and so on. With respect to time used in travelling, the growth in private car ownership is itself aspirational, and is associated with people travelling longer distances for work, shopping and leisure activities, as well as doing all of these in any given day. The application of organisational principles of productivity to leisure is reflected in evidence that people are participating in a greater number of leisure activities, but each is done for less time (Gershuny and Jones, 1987). The notion of quality time with children and partners (which seems to be gaining currency in Europe as well as the USA) is also a reflection of the incursion of organisational logics of consumption into leisure, which becomes filled with commodified activities. The result is that free time is subject to higher levels of organisation, creating the intensification of leisure and a sense of time pressure, even though recorded work hours have not increased.

Although average work hours have declined, there is evidence of a reversal in the patterns of time use of different groups. Those with higher levels of educational attainment, which Gershuny (2000, 2005) uses as a proxy for higher social status, report an increase in their paid work time relative to those with fewer qualifications. In the past, privileged social status was associated with more leisure. Even as recently as the 1960s, higher status groups had most free time, but this has now reversed, suggesting that being busy may itself now be regarded as a sign of high status, and that the discourse of productive subjectivity and continuous improvement is therefore generally influential in the way that we think about our lives. Hochschild (1997) describes this as a process of rationalisation of the private sphere, which she attributes to the emergence of increasingly compulsive relationships to paid work, rather than to increased ambitions for the use of non-work time, but I have argued that ideologies of self-improvement and productive subjectivity, spanning both work and consumption, connect the two spheres in interlocking processes of intensification stemming from the opportunity structures of consumer capitalist societies.

Evaluating the Concept of a Productive Subjectivity

While the rationalities of productive subjectivity appear to be influential in informing values and social relations, particularly among more affluent groups, we also need to ask whether such values translate into self-identities governed by nothing more than individualised market choices, willingly bought into? Perpetual change in advanced capitalist societies, and the attribution of individualised responsibility for our lives, poses personal and moral dilemmas about how to live and what we value, and answers to such questions of identity are typically provisional and contingent: what seems important today may seem irrelevant in a year, or even in a week, because of changes in our work or private lives. Modern social theorists such as Giddens (1991) and Sennett (1998) broadly agree with Rose (1999) that the result is an existential search for meaning in a narrative of self-control, growth and autonomy. The conditions of advanced capitalism and associated systems of expertise create the obligation to achieve an identity, but they also make the problem of identity insoluble. Such a self is a perpetual work in progress, 'a pliant self, a collage of fragments unceasing in its becoming, ever open to new experience' (Sennett, 1998: 133).

This is a very different subjectivity, even from that portrayed by a modern work ethic, which emphasised duty, thrift and self-denial, but its implications are disputed. Rose (1999) concludes that, having identified ourselves with the project of individual freedom, we have no alternative values to guide our lives. Sennett (1998) pessimistically suggests that its individualism corrodes moral *character*, constituted out of 'loyalty and mutual commitment . . . or the practice of delayed gratification for the sake of a future end' (p. 10). Unlike Sennett or Rose, Giddens (1991) sees the public realm as expanding, giving more people opportunities to participate, to adapt available knowledge and skills to their own purposes, informed by their own experience, and to make informed choices about society. He recognises the pathologies of self-growth, not least the fact that the pressures of achievement in a competitive market provoke anxiety and threats to a stable sense of self-worth. Nevertheless, he regards the obligations and responsibilities of choice, and the need for adaptability, as constructive sources of freedom from traditional authoritarian modes of control, where ultimate values were dictated by religion and monarchy. From this perspective, organisations offer one means of dealing with modern uncertainties and anxieties, and their costs have to be considered in relation to the expansion of autonomy, enabling people to participate in diverse social networks, and to acquire considerable social and technical skills and knowledge. The obligation to confront existential dilemmas and to come to some accommodation in relation to them is potentially a means of gaining perspective on our circumstances and greater insight into the operations of power.

The risk of an inner-directed sense of self, aspiring to control and self-growth, is that such a demanding and anxiety-provoking responsibility is construed as an individualised problem susceptible to market solutions, such that identity is reduced to a matter of lifestyle choices framed by commodified goods and services. In these terms, 'identity' is a kind of fetish, which has the effect of obscuring the processes of its formation and reproduction, and perpetuating the organisational structures that limit insight (Knights and Willmott, 1989). Craib (1994) suggests that a preoccupation with self-construction is encouraged by the contemporary emphasis in social theory on issues of self-identity, which fuels fantasies of individual omnipotence. A belief in the possibility of limitless personal growth is, he argues, a product of a market economy, producing an infantile delusion of immortality. It is, however, a belief that encounters the realities of personal failure, disappointment and human mortality, all of which emphasise the non-materialistic values of mutual dependence, empathy, love and care, as well as producing personal fears, anger and resentment. Even those apparently advantaged in an 'enterprise of the self' are likely to encounter its limits, and the potential for disappointment and regret is significant. Hochschild highlights the 'shadow lives' of career-driven executives, who acquire consumer artefacts that symbolise their aspiration to find time to devote to partners, children and friends outside work; Sennett (1998) and Hochschild describe the disappointments of middle-aged executives made redundant by the 'corporate family'; Newman (1988) describes the loss of a secure sense of self experienced by downwardly mobile executives in the USA; and Pahl (1995) discusses the self-doubt of overtly successful men about whether their lives have been a failure. The practical accomplishments of living, disappointments and set-backs lend other meanings to the attribution of responsibility for selfhood and identity, which create a standpoint from which to gain perspective on discourses of self-growth (Craib, 1994).

It is not clear therefore that contemporary self-understandings *are* encapsulated within the frame of individualised, market-oriented self-improvement projects, or that people live devoid of other values. Intimate relationships with partners and children, awareness of class, gender and ethnic divisions, and of mortality continue to inform existential values. Adopting a modernist perspective, Taylor (1989) treats existential questions about identity as an important component of a contemporary pluralistic moral order. The requirement to make our own decisions calls into being the expectation of being held accountable to others for our actions. Being accountable requires the enactment of judgement and consideration of alternatives, as a condition of respect. Such agency and self-determination is constrained by circumstances, but it is not one-dimensional, nor does it have fixed meaning and content. It can provide a basis for resistance, critique and scepticism towards the ruling ideas of the day, as well as a basis for unrealistic aspiration and individualism.

Nor is it clear that the 'obligations of freedom' opened up by public and private organisations, and professional and organisational expertise dedicated to measuring and regulating the self, have produced governable, knowable subjects. This model effectively treats global social and economic developments as having a determinate or fixed content and singular direction, which produce individuals wedded to an aspirational and self-conscious subjectivity. The analysis of productive subjectivity offers valuable insights into the power relations of advanced capitalist societies, but at the end of the day, Rose's analysis does not avoid the pitfalls of an oversocialised model of identity. By concluding that we are obliged to act as active, willing employees, citizens and parents, *as if* we are acting on our own desires, he offers an overdetermined model of identity, where there is no possibility of developing a standpoint from which to criticise current forms of power, or even to subvert the organisational rationalities of self-improvement to other, indeterminate and alternative, socialised ends. It suggests that people's experience of the constraints and contradictions of capitalism, and the disappointments of self-growth, does not give them a basis from which to evaluate its promises, draw conclusions and challenge the claims of those in power.

Looking at the bigger picture, I have argued that the current directions of global markets and deregulated capital are informed by the political choices that govern contemporary neoliberal economic ideology and expertise. Other choices remain available, because market institutions and expertise-based systems themselves are the products of indeterminate and shifting political coalitions and are shaped by different cultural and institutional contexts to create different varieties of capitalism (Hall and Soskice, 2001; Thelen, 2004). The result is new kinds of knowledge and the questioning of political and economic orthodoxy, which transform the conditions of action. New social movements, concerned with feminism, environmental sustainability, peace and community, juxtapose expressive values against mainstream expert solutions centred on the values of materialism and individualism. Such an identity politics is actively mobilised around questions of how we live, and puts ultimate values, repressed by an emphasis on the instrumental priorities of productivity and economic growth, back on the mainstream political agenda (Giddens, 1991). The capacity of social movements to redirect neoliberal economics and market individualisation is disputed (Castells, 1997; Bauman, 1996), but questions of substantive rationality remain prominent in public debate. Women's pursuit of autonomy, expressed in the refusal of a subordinate feminine identity, and attempts to craft new relations between men and women that are not confined by modern gender ideologies have stimulated enormous social change. Such new social movements challenge the instrumentalism of modern societies, and argue for a society that prioritises care and mutual interdependence. In the current period, for example, evidence of the economic and social failures of neoliberalism is forcing the reappraisal of IMF and World Bank priorities and practices (Weisbrot et al., 2005). The science of global climate change is also provoking renewed criticism of the economics of perpetual growth, as exemplified in the work of organisations such as the New Economics Foundation (www.neweconomics.org).

Setting this perspective on agency and selfhood in an organisational context is a reminder that organisations are more than the embodiments of formal expertise and technical knowledge, which form the basis for instrumental and calculative action. They are also sites where practical values and interests are deliberated and forms of social accountability are tried out (Flyvbjerg, 2001), leading to the formation of alternative social

and collective identities. Consent to an individualised, productive subjectivity inevitably remains partial and prone to reversal.

Conclusion

This chapter has examined the contemporary organisational shaping of
self-identity, as something 'achieved' through projects and plans, rather
than ascribed by heritage and status. Globalising financial markets, competitive pressures and the drive to expand consumer capitalism are the
political-economic circumstances in which contemporary self-identities
are crafted. This flexibilised capitalism entails the intensification of *all*
economic activities, spanning work and consumption, and eroding the
boundaries between work, non-work and leisure. Both production and
consumption are likely to be experienced as interconnected through the
idea of a self-identity achieved through an individualised project of continuous improvement, which can be derived from lifelong 'investments'
in education, work, consumption choices and social life. Organisations,
as employers, producers and public service providers, are instrumental
in constructing and channelling an aspirational subjectivity, and play a
prominent part in moulding personal motivations in work, non-work and
leisure. An important illustration of this process is provided by the growing self-improvement industry in image consultancy, life coaching, bodywork, fashion and interior design. The self-improvement industry is one
aspect of the rapidly developing cultural industries of mass media, design,
PR and marketing. The rise of the cultural industries is associated with the
more diffuse boundaries between production and consumption, as much
of the work of media, design, marketing, retailing and customer service is
itself dependent on an aesthetic of self-presentation and the dramatisation
of identity. Creating a marketable work identity for the cultural industries
depends in turn on an interconnected aesthetics of consumption and lifestyle
choices, which enable the development of a distinctive self-presentation
through dress, demeanour, physical appearance and performance.

Ideologies of self-growth, continuous self-improvement and productive subjectivity are powerful and seductive influences over people's lives,
even if the experience does not live up to expectations. This is particularly
the case for those groups who are relatively advantaged by hierarchies
of occupational career, class and status distinctions, where the intensification of work and consumption is most evident. But it also extends to those
in more routinised occupations, whose work with clients and customers
requires them to convey the brand values of the organisation through their
appearance and communication. Outside work as well as inside, there is
evidence that the discourse of productive subjectivity and continuous

improvement is generally influential in the way that we think about our selves: being busy appears to be increasingly regarded as a sign of high status. I have argued that this is connected to the opportunity structures of consumer capitalist societies, whose ideologies of self-improvement span both work and consumption, connecting the two spheres in interlocking processes of intensification.

The organisational nexus of advanced consumer capitalism does not however determine consciousness, or overwhelm alternative sources of social identity and self-understandings. Even for those groups who are highly identified with the idea of a productive subjectivity, such identification is partial and situationally specific. It is likely to change over time, depending on people's life stage, career trajectory, socioeconomic status, family commitments and the other values and beliefs that arise from the associated life experiences, set-backs and disappointments. For most people, identification is partial, shifting and pragmatic rather than total and internalised into the soul.

Attempts to align people's ascribed capacities for self-fulfilment with organisational goals are therefore only ever partially attained, because that same resourcefulness attributed to the enterprise of the self is susceptible to being deployed in alternative ways. The postmodernist model proposed by Rose (1999) is flawed by the reduction of identity to the obligations of productive subjectivity, which is seen as resulting in an individualised and self-defeating search for existential meaning. In practice, subjectivity remains contested terrain (Collinson, 2003); people struggle to make themselves knowledgeable, rather than knowable, but they do not do this in isolation. Social and collective identities, crafted out of the circumstances of work and consumption, have recently been marginalised as themes for research in much contemporary organisational theory (Ackroyd and Thompson, 1999; Thompson and Findlay, 1999). This is a significant practical and conceptual loss, which does a disservice to the understanding of the complexity and indeterminacy of social relations, power and subjectivity in organisations. It excludes from view the potential for the emergence of new historical subjects, which challenge the values of individualisation and perpetual growth, and re-emphasise mutual interdependence.

Conclusion: Bringing Life Back to Organisations

In concluding the book, I want to return to the discussion about what complex organisations have done to us and for us. In doing this, I summarise the key themes of each chapter and reflect briefly on the wider implications for social life in an era of global capitalism. First, however, I present a summary of the overall argument.

A Summary of the Argument

In the Introduction, I drew on C. Wright Mills' concept of the sociological imagination to suggest that insights into the making of selves and social identities can be gained from an analysis of the connections between personal biography, social structure, history and politics. The book has examined the interconnections between selfhood, identities and organisations, in this particular period of history and political economy. Historically, large-scale bureaucratic organisations have been the levers of modernisation and have therefore been instrumental in facilitating a profound historical shift in processes of identity formation. Notably, personal and social identity has changed from something that is ascribed through birth and heritage to something that has to be achieved, through circumscribed choices and forms of market competition structured by class, gender and ethnic divisions. While contemporary organisations shape self- and social identities in every conceivable dimension, the content and expression of achieved identities is malleable and adaptable to circumstances. We are increasingly expected, and expect, to have choice over how we identify ourselves and how we act in the light of such negotiated and fluid identities. In the past hundred years, organisations have provided significant capacities and resources through new forms of knowledge and wealth creation: greater social mobility, diversity and freedom of association have enabled a degree of choice and opportunities for voluntaristic processes of identity formation. They also promote particular normative identities. Notably, in the present period, it is the distinctive circumstances of globalising financial markets and competitive pressures oriented to the extension and intensification of markets that inform the crafting of identities. In everyday life, such pressures result in the intensification of *all* economic activities, spanning work and consumption, and the erosion of the boundaries between work, non-work and leisure. Increasing the productivity of capital relies on the extension and intensification of market activities, which in turn relies on individualised self-identities oriented to continuous, competitive self-growth and productivity through more intensive work and higher levels of consumption.

Modern and postmodern social theories have often portrayed the social consequences as a loss of meaning, mutual respect and capacity for critical reflexivity. In the current era of global financial markets, the individualistic pursuit of money as an end in itself has been regarded as dominating over, and eroding, values of care and mutual dependence. Personal and social identity cannot however be read off from political-economic arrangements. A deterministic account of identity, whether expressed in the modernist theories of Weber or the postmodernist theories of Foucault, is flawed because such theories confuse organisational prescription with the diversity of practical experience, and misread the connections between macro-levels of political economy and the micro-level of everyday life and its meanings (Giddens, 1991). A focus on the intermediate level of organisations makes the diversity and richness of practical experience visible, and provides insight into the ways that people deal with the contradictions, complexities and ironies of lives framed by organisational rationalities and continue to gain knowledge and understanding of the workings of power. Empirical studies of organisations show the innovative and creative purposes that people pursue in making political and pragmatic adjustments to circumstances. In some cases, this leads to new forms of social identities, which in turn influence organisational priorities and strategies. A prominent example of this in the past hundred years is the revolution in gender relations and women's use of organisational rhetorics of equal opportunity to lay claim to a share of the public domain. A more powerful theory of the interconnections of organisations and identities therefore requires recognition of the dialectical relationship between these spheres, as personal biographies, assembled out of experiences, and new collective identities influence the goals, trajectories and practices of organisations.

These arguments are not intended to encourage us to sit back and relax; rather they are intended as encouragement to critical analysis of contemporary organisations and the conditions of life in advanced capitalist societies.

Key Themes from Chapter 1

Chapter 1 developed the main theoretical argument of the book, through an analysis of modernist and postmodernist concepts of self and identity, and an appraisal of the historical development of large-scale organisations. I concluded that agency is not so much undermined by organisations, as reinvented and reshaped according to the predominant concerns of economic life.

Oversocialised models of identity, whether modernist or postmodernist, are based on a reductionist account of human agency, on the one hand, and a neglect of the essential indeterminacy of markets, organisations and social relations, on the other. Both the radical postmodernist model of disciplinary power and Weberian theories of the inevitability of rationalisation are better understood as tendencies variably enacted in different social and economic circumstances, where power and its norms are susceptible to unstable and contradictory effects. The practices of organisations are more culturally diverse, internally fluid and contradictory than much social and organisational theory recognises, resulting in less structured and determined connections between markets, public and private organisations, identities and biographies than pessimistic analyses suggest. Rather than passively or uncritically accepting constructed identities, whether in relation to work or consumption, people reflect on and make sense of these in the light of their own circumstances and experiences.

The depressing prospect of 'imperative command' envisaged as the central feature of bureaucracy was always, and inevitably, only partially attained. Political and cultural resistance to the 'bureaucratisation of the self' means that part of the story of the transition from industrial to informational capitalism can be told as a story of the emergence of more negotiable and contested authority relations, which continue to offer the potential for more participative, democratised forms of organisation. The challenge to bureaucracy has been accompanied by a shift from concepts of the self as deferential to a superior authority to notions of the self as accountable and responsible for our own actions. The postmodern theories of Foucault have highlighted the disabling effects of an accountable self, 'governed through freedom', with a self-disciplining and self-defeating belief in an individualised responsibility for our own well-being. I have argued that such a theory of power identifies tendencies inherent in the governance of modern societies, but overinterprets their effects. Normative expectations of self-reliance and responsibility are not inevitably reduced to a self-defeating 'struggle for identity', and can (amongst many other things) be directed to a struggle for critical knowledge of the activities of governments and organisations. People's actions are undoubtedly highly constrained by circumstances, and their power to influence and control contemporary organisations, particularly private corporations, is limited. Nevertheless, the structural requirements of agency, reflexivity and self-awareness also create the conditions for critical enquiry into the social order, its benefits and its injustices. Moreover, people are not inevitably individualised and isolated by the workings of markets. New forms of collective social identities have been crafted out of a continuing critical awareness of the history of political and economic change, and out of the experienced contradictions between rhetoric and reality, ensuring that organisations are not able to 'colonise identities'.

An adequate explanation of the interrelations between organisations and identities is therefore one that recognises the dialectical relationships between the structural power of instrumental and rationalising logics of action, which are themselves the products of economic expertise, and personal, social and cultural meanings, which embed instrumental action in diverse forms of social and cultural organisation. Although contemporary social life is experienced through numerous, complex organisations, there are also multiple sources of identity in any situation, derived from our physical embodiment, our practical concerns, relationships and our experiences. The ways that these are drawn on and articulated will depend on the complex and uncertain contingencies of economic, political and cultural variation. Agency is 'situated' in all these; it derives its logics of action from them and has contradictory and uncertain effects on them, as different interests are shaped and struggle for expression. Rationalised, instrumentalised organisation is not automatic, but is the outcome of political and cultural choices, which have placed a high value on economic growth and profit-making.

The predominance of these values has not eradicated alternative concerns and other values, which contest rationalisation. A politics of identity continues to make public the connections between global deregulated finance and local troubles manifest in social division, rising inequality, conflict, anxiety and fear. It sustains organisations with alternative goals concerned with care, mutual dependence, social justice and a sustainable economics. Corporations themselves are not characterised by uniformity of values; public service and non-profit organisations debate the substantive rationality of organisational goals, values and social priorities, and the regulation of private profit through forms of public accountability continues to be a major concern, as reflected in the current interest in issues of corporate social responsibility.

Key Themes from Chapter 2

Globally deregulated, shareholder-driven capitalism, with high levels of speculative financial trading, shaped by neoliberal political economy, is not an inevitable outcome of the 'natural' laws of the market, even though it is often presented in this way. Instead, neoliberal economics is purposefully organised through political choices enacted in bodies such as the IMF, the World Bank and the WTO. Deregulated financial markets enable a short-termist, shareholder-driven capitalism that draws everyone into its reach, through the need to increase the productivity of finance capital in every transaction across the entire process of value creation. Capitalism spans the globe, organised through electronic networks of continuous, speculative, financial transactions. Finance capital is invested in all forms of activity from biotechnologies to personal services, but 'whatever is extracted as profit . . . is reverted to the meta-network of financial flows' (Castells, 2000: 503), which increasingly drive all sources of profit and loss.

Global, deregulated markets are not however the end point of capitalism, with different varieties of capitalism evolving rapidly. The dynamism and indeterminacy of capitalism is illustrated by the current shift in capital, technology and mass manufacturing capacity towards the Asia Pacific region. Uncertainty over the future directions of capitalist economic arrangements are also increased by evidence of the substantive irrationalities of deregulated finance, which have resulted in recent rises in corporate scandals, corruption and fraud, and large-scale corporate bankruptcies, illustrated here in the case of Enron. The emergence of collective identities resistant to neoliberal economics and its social costs add a further level of uncertainty, suggesting that the trajectories of political economy are critically dependent on the struggle between governments, corporations and civil society.

Key Themes from Chapter 3

Chapter 3 examined the implications of global capitalism for the organisation of consumption, the development of concern with organisational identities and branding, and the shaping of consumerist identities. I argued for a theorising of consumerism, which examines the interdependence of production and consumption arrangements through the lens of organisation. This prevents a misleading overemphasis on either the supposed voluntarism of consumption or the supposed determination of consumer identities by big business.

The drive to expand markets, according to the logics of deregulated finance and mobile capital, has resulted in the simultaneous hollowing out of global corporations and the centralisation and concentration of corporate power. This creates a significant new business need for the active construction of an organisational identity: anonymous, fragmented organisations are now less identifiable and less accessible at local level. Manufacturing, retailing and financial services are dispersed according to the logics of labour, materials and infrastructure costs; customer service may be web-based, or managed through anonymous, centralised call centres; employees of the same organisation may deal with peers on two or three different continents and have no contact with corporate executives and so on. The development of such global organisational strategies has therefore stimulated significant corporate investment in marketing, advertising and the construction of brand identities. Branding is designed to manage employee and consumer attitudes to the corporation, and to persuade employees and consumers alike to identify with it by injecting shared meanings and values into its products and services.

Rising levels of consumer spending and credit card debt suggest that consumerist values and a sense of unlimited needs and desires for goods exercise a powerful hold over the identities of people in advanced capitalist societies. Nevertheless, the complexity, variety and politicisation of actual consumption practices have often been neglected by social theories. The emergence and political activism of collective consumer identities, expressed through consumer rights, environmental and non-governmental organisations, offer significant challenges to corporate strategies. Consumerism itself is increasingly contested, as evidenced in campaigns for fair trade, on the one hand, and new EU recycling laws and landfill taxes, which will massively increase the cost of waste, on the other. The next decade therefore is likely to see increasing public concern over organisational incentives to hyperconsumption.

Key Themes from Chapter 4

In Chapter 4, I examined the connections between the marketisation of welfare and the neoliberal political economy of globalised, deregulated capital. The UK is used as an example of a state that has made significant changes in the form of welfare, from a social democratic towards a neoliberal model. The government has tried to reconcile the demands of a politics of identity with the pressures of mobile capital and financial markets through the attribution of more individualised responsibility for welfare and promises of greater choice in public services. The reorganisation of public services, according to the calculative rationality of markets, managerialism and targets, has had a significant impact on the identity of public servants, emphasising performance to target, rather than an ethic of service and loyalty. The experience of contradiction between promises of empowerment and the actuality of labour rationalisation and intensification has produced considerable scepticism and self-distancing, even among employees in professional and higher level managerial occupations. The identities of public servants are thus more complex and nuanced than is suggested by a deterministic version of postmodern analysis of the discourse of new public management.

The chapter also examined the social implications of individualising responsibility for welfare, and I argued that the government-promoted identity of consumer-citizen degrades the notion of a societal interest, and invites people's withdrawal from sharing responsibility for civil society and social cohesion. Neither has the identity of consumer-citizen satisfied the demands of social movements resistant to individualisation. Such movements continue to campaign for an alternative participative democratic agenda for reform through the pursuit of well-being, dignity and autonomy in a welfare society. The pressures on governments to move towards neoliberal welfare have to be understood in the context of the global restructuring of capital, and work and occupational hierarchies.

The mobility of capital in more competitive markets has made the financial performance of the firm, through the primary indicator of share price, the driving force of corporate restructuring. Different dimensions of the resultant changes in work and occupations are discussed in Chapters 5 and 6. Overall, the proactive deployment of corporate assets and the pursuit of cost-cutting have resulted in the intensification of work and the increased exploitation of labour, particularly at the bottom end of supply chains. In affluent countries, the restructuring of work and occupations has resulted in a degree of occupational upgrading, but has also created a more unequal relationship between capital and labour, structurally individualising the employment relationship, while simultaneously reinforcing dependence on waged work. Globally integrated production, service and sales strategies are associated with an emerging global division of labour and new patterns of social stratification. The manual work of mass manufacturing, once concentrated in Europe and North America, is increasingly being transferred to areas of cheaper labour. The wealthier countries seek to retain competitive advantage by retaining control over the strategic direction of enterprise, through investments in scientific knowledge and technical innovation. However, their position remains tenuous in a globalising economy where all varieties of capitalism are changing.

Key Themes from Chapter 5

In Chapter 5, I drew comparisons between advanced capitalist societies to show that common logics of financial rationalisation continue to be significantly influenced by different cultural institutions, values and political choices and coalitions, producing continuing differentiation between the employment and occupational structures of different countries. The result is differences in the balance of occupations, the degree of inequality, the opportunities for more skilled, meaningful work and the quality of working life. The institutions of governance in each of these societies clearly exercise important forms of control over the shape of economic life and opportunities, providing further evidence that the directions and strategic organisation of capitalism are matters of political choice.

In the USA and the UK, the commitment to an individualistic model of laissez-faire capitalism has resulted in rapid declines in manufacturing employment and the growth of service economies. In contrast, Japan and Germany have maintained production-oriented economies and pursued more gradual change. In each case, the emergence of more service-based economies is associated with forms of occupational upgrading. This has to be seen in the context of a global division of labour, however, rather than being interpreted as a new form of postindustrial society, and will not necessarily be an enduring feature of employment in advanced capitalist societies. Relative upgrading in the affluent societies is moreover accompanied by increasing national and global inequality in income, which it is argued stems from the pursuit of neoliberal economic policies, socially regressive taxation and short-termist approaches to maximising corporate profitability.

Key Themes from Chapter 6

The significance of changes in work and organisations for social and personal identities in advanced capitalist countries was the main concern of Chapter 6. A prominent contention in the literature about the future of work is that the destandardisation of labour is leading to the decline of stable work and occupational identities organised around modern divisions of class and gender (Beck, 2000; Sennett, 1998). Predictions of greater individualisation and fragmentation of experience, and the loss of a coherent sense of self, have been made, as the articulation of corporate strategies at a global level, through subcontracting and externalisation, affect routes into, and progression within, labour markets.

Organisational restructuring, in the context of mobile capital and growth in services employment, has not however presaged the end of work or dependence on waged labour. Dramatic predictions of mass casualisation of work, short-termism in employment, the end of careers and the rise of self-employment are therefore highly misleading. They have distracted attention from the very significant changes that are happening, but which relate far more to the intensification of work at all occupational levels, producing a common perception of uncertainty and insecurity, rather than structural casualisation per se. If anything, the increasing numbers drawn into employment, the rising participation of women and the movement of people of minority ethnic origin into a wider range of organisations and occupations mean that work in organisations has been made more central to identity, even as its terms have become more individualised. Such work plays a significant part in structuring life chances in capitalist economies, making it salient in processes of social division, and a key, if indeterminate, influence over social and personal identities.

As a principle of economic division, class remains very powerful, but it is underanalysed. The contours of more fragmented and divided classes are harder to discern, and less immediately obvious as sources of collective identity. We now have globally dispersed, ethnically segmented and gendered class relations, given differential expression through different cultural and social practices at organisational level. Restructuring has produced a more polarised, 'hour glass' occupational structure in advanced capitalist countries, with growth in managerial, professional and technical work as well as growth in routine and semi-skilled jobs, while middle-level jobs have declined. Despite organisational commitments to the use of career ladders to retain labour, relative upgrading of occupations has been matched by declining opportunities for upward mobility from routine jobs into career occupations, which increasingly require higher levels of education. Unless governments invest significantly in education to overcome the disadvantages experienced by young people from poorer households, this is likely to result in more entrenched class divisions for the next generation.

The gradually increasing gender and ethnic diversity of any occupational class has sometimes been treated as an indicator of a new cultural individualism, encouraged by a belief in the fluidity and voluntarism of identity in market societies. I argued that it is mistaken to assume that economic individualisation is necessarily indicative of individualism. New employment relationships have shifted the balance of power in favour of capital, resulting in more intensive work, more dissatisfaction, aggravation and perceptions of insecurity. This is most evident in the worst paid, most routine jobs, and it is in these jobs, at the bottom of the occupational hierarchy, that there is most economic convergence between men and women and between people of different ethnic backgrounds. The shared experiences of exploitative conditions of work provide a basis for new kinds of collective identity, emerging from common interests in overcoming inequalities and labour market disadvantages.

Key Themes from Chapter 7

Chapter 7 examined the implications of organisational and occupational restructuring for work identities. Employers, it was argued, have become increasingly concerned to regulate the identity of employees, as a means to increase effort in a revised wage–effort bargain. The management of employee identity has become a prominent concern, because of the centrality of employee effort and commitment to customer perceptions of product and service quality in services-oriented economies, and because of the increasing diversity and spatial dispersal of the workforce in multinational corporations, many of whom never meet. Organisations have sought to regulate identity through the devices of corporate culture and branding, team-building and the proactive deployment of emotional labour. These measures continue to be reinforced through more familiar bureaucratic controls and performance monitoring.

The effectiveness of such cultural projects to align employee identity with organisational goals has foundered on labour's recognition of the lack of genuine reciprocity on the part of the employer. Corporate commitment to the development of high trust relations with labour has been limited by the difficulty that employers have in keeping their side of the bargain, in deregulated, shareholder-driven markets (Thompson, 2003). In employment relations, the gap between management promises of empowerment and aspirations for winning hearts and minds and management practices driven by cost-cutting and ongoing rationalisation is leaving low trust and a contested work–effort bargain in place. The evidence suggests that employees comply with organisational demands, but resent the intensification of work, the continuity of bureaucratic controls and the relative worsening of conditions. In these circumstances, measures to regulate identity through corporate culture and normative control accentuate sceptical responses among the workforce, producing more distancing of self from an organisational identity. Work requirements are met through a calculative engagement with employer demands, which tends to damage, rather than enhance, the desired performance of employees.

The organisations of advanced capitalist societies are caught in the paradox that they need skilful, creative 'identity work' and knowledgeable labour, and yet apparently rely on moulding and regulating those capacities in ways that limit such skilful, knowledgeable ways of working.

Key Themes from Chapter 8

In Chapter 8, I considered the arguments that the organisation of life in neoliberal capitalism marries the demands of economic growth in fast-changing markets to the prescription of a flexible, productive and consumerist self-identity. Both public and private organisations have become increasingly interested in the regulation of identity through the constitution of a productive subjectivity. Distinctions between work and leisure have become less clear-cut, as organisations rely on the unified image of a resourceful, self-reliant individual, oriented to continuous self-growth in a market competition for a distinctive, valued identity. Work, non-work and leisure are increasingly subject to the same rationalities, drawing people into the pursuit of an 'improved self' in all spheres. Ideologies of self-growth, continuous self-improvement and productive subjectivity are seductive, even if the experience does not live up to expectations. This is particularly evident among those groups who are relatively advantaged by hierarchies of occupational career, class and status distinctions. But people in more routinised occupations, whose work with clients and customers requires them to convey the brand values of the organisation through their appearance and their enactment of a brand identity, are also drawn in. Life in advanced consumer capitalist societies is informed by aspirational values and individualised market competition, which prioritise the requirements of productive subjectivity and continuous improvement. The everyday influence of such norms is reflected in evidence that being busy in all spheres is now regarded as a sign of higher status. The opportunity structures of consumer capitalist societies emphasise values and norms of self-improvement in both work and consumption, connecting the two spheres in interlocking processes of intensification.

Pessimistic analyses of the consequences of a discourse of productive subjectivity tend to conclude that this results in the loss of alternative values to guide our lives, producing a highly calculative attitude to personal relationships and devaluing care and mutual dependency. This conclusion is not however in line with the evidence of continuing practical resistance to the intensification of work and consumption, which indicates the resilience and inventiveness of social interaction and social identities. Modern selfhood and identity is less fragile and people are more resourceful than such theories predict. Informal work group subcultures, as well as family and intimate relations, and the public spheres of education, culture and politics create spaces for alternative understandings of organisational rationalities and critical reflection on the social relations of work, non-work and leisure. In experiencing the contradictions between pressures to maximise our market value and the day-to-day limits of self-determination set by constraints of political economy and personal commitments, people realise the drawbacks of market individualism and potentially become 'accomplished human beings', able to move beyond a view of the self as either omnipotent, or as inevitably defeated by economic determinism (Craib, 1994).

The neoliberal political economy of organisations, and the associated image of self-promoting, reflexive individualism, is nevertheless connected with a number of private troubles and social pathologies. A common preoccupation with self-growth is, suggests Craib (1994), a product of a flexibilised economy, where we are encouraged to treat all relationships as operating in a competitive marketplace. This is however a competition that produces few winners. Norms of self-reliance are then likely to produce anxiety and reinforce a sense of self-blame for perceived failures, particularly for those in poorer households. Other potential bases for self-confidence, derived from caring, intimate relationships, or participation in a public domain of community and civil society, are consequently damaged. In the USA, which has pursued the most aggressive version of market liberalism, increasing inequality has been associated with a decline in social cohesion, or connectedness, in every area of social life from club and political party membership to trade union and professional associations (Putnam, 2000). The decline in social capital is associated with lower levels of personal satisfaction, higher levels of crime, lower educational achievement and poorer health.

In Conclusion

The individualisation produced by contemporary organisational practices has been argued to erode mutual dependence, respect and care (Sennett, 1998), but in fact there are social indicators of a powerful resistance among men and women to further intensification of work, materialistic values and individualism. Rising economic activity rates among women, for example, have focused attention on the dual burden carried by many employed women, especially mothers working part time who continue to experience the heaviest workloads (Sullivan and Gershuny, 2000). The solution is not, however, as some conservative commentators have suggested, a return to family values. Women's increased economic activity signals their refusal of a subordinated domestic identity, and the pragmatic adaptation of ideas about self-fulfilment to the circumstances of work in advanced capitalism. A more radical renegotiation of gender relations and the sexual division of labour is beginning, despite the imperatives of the market. Recent analyses of the UK Department for Education and Employment 2000 Work-Life Balance Survey (O'Brien and Shemilt, 2003) and interviews with working parents and human resources managers (Hatter et al., 2002) found that the aspirations of fathers for more involvement with the care of their children, particularly those in the younger groups, are high and that fathers' involvement has already increased notably. The change is particularly marked for those with children under five, who in the mid-1970s spent less than fifteen minutes per day looking after their children, but now spend approximately two hours a day doing so. The main barriers to further equalisation of caring by fathers are organisational norms of unlimited liability commitments to work.

Personal biography and private troubles are thus reintegrated into the public sphere, in the form of experience of the practical effects of business and government priorities. Such experience is channelled into the development of alternatives, notably through non-governmental and social movement organisations defending the values of a public domain beyond the market. These activities in turn generate new circumstances for corporations. Demands for change in organisational norms are however circumscribed by the terms of competition in the labour market. Daily life is framed by the corporate world and its ideologies, and a structured dependence on wage labour, producing the appearance of routine collective consent to the values of consumerism, productivism and perpetual growth. Protest may be too risky, the challenges are hard and government may seem unresponsive; thus corporate scandals, such as that surrounding Enron, produce public criticism, but no long lived, irresistible populist revolt against the excesses of corporate power.

I have been concerned nevertheless to show that the organisations we have, and their operations through markets and governments, are brought about and reconfigured through human agencies, reliant on shifting political coalitions and associated forms of specialist expertise in economics and technology. While a 'non-organisational society' is increasingly unimaginable, this does not mean that there are no choices to be made about the strategic direction and control of the resources and scientific and technological knowledge produced. In this sense, this book is an argument against a functionalist analysis of markets and organisations. I have shown, through evidence comparing the employment and occupational structures of advanced capitalist societies, the continuing diversity of organisations, depending on their goals, their economic and cultural contexts, political priorities and processes of coalition-building and negotiation between conflicting interest groups. In other words, there is nothing inevitable about the shape or scale of organisations, or the contemporary concentration of power and wealth.

There is a need therefore for tools that enable people to counter assumptions that the excesses of capitalism are simply a matter of 'the way the world works'. Organisational, financial and technological developments are arguably running ahead of the social infrastructure needed to make them publicly accountable. Contemporary organisations have been designed to maximise money-making in the name of economic growth and wealth creation, raised to its highest levels in the financial centres of the world in the global cities of London, New York and Tokyo. Neoliberal political economy has become 'part of the mental furniture of the political elite' (Marquand, 2004: 118). Historically, however, the political prioritising of economic growth and the pursuit of money-making as an end in itself are recent phenomena (Greenfeld, 2001). The existing global economic order is not an iron cage

from which there is no escape, but one deliberately organised by global institutions of economic governance, pursuing neoliberal political and economic
measures. We need to raise the level of public debate about the directions
and varieties of capitalism, and the constitution of markets, and to prob-
lematise the goals of perpetual economic growth when these render other
values susceptible to dismissal.

The institutions of global democratic governance able to pose the alternatives to deregulated markets are lacking. Indeed, Marquand (2004) suggests, 'measures to protect the public domain from further incursions by
the market domain . . . are conspicuous by their absence' (p. 117). The challenge therefore is to use the democratic accountability of governments to
create a global infrastructure with local and regional legitimacy. This would
entail states acting in coordination to set common social objectives and to
reform the laws governing corporations (Townsend and Gordon, 2002).
Corporate governance requires legally enforced standards of good practice, preventing the abuses of power evident in the exploitative treatment of
labour through global supply chains, and ensuring better public accountability. Such an infrastructure is needed in order to give weight to the
value of the public domain, which recognises a common interest in the
future security and prosperity of societies.

A public domain does not necessarily mean public ownership or centralised state provision of welfare, but is a means of legitimising human
equality through citizenship and participation, and this counterbalances
the inevitable inequalities of market competition. Its key components are
intermediate organisations such as local authorities, social movement organisations and voluntary groups, trade unions, professional associations and
educational and cultural institutions. Given a degree of autonomy from
centralised control, such organisations offer the means to pose questions
about the accountability of corporations and governments to ordinary
people, through democratic participation and control, rather than through
individualised market choices. Such a public domain provides for forms
of self-fulfilment, freedom and dignity that are not captured by the language of producing and consuming, but are brought about by a public
conscience and common interests in society. Meaningful choices are never
the ones most easily available.

Bibliography

Acker, J. (2000) 'Revisiting class: thinking from gender, race and organizations', *Social Politics*, 7: 192–214.

Ackroyd, S. (2000) 'Connecting organisations and societies: a realist analysis of structures', in S. Ackroyd and S. Fleetwood (eds) *Realist Perspectives on Management and Organisations*. London: Routledge.

Ackroyd, S. and Fleetwood (eds) (2000) *Realist Perspectives on Management and Organisations*. London: Routledge.

Ackroyd, S. and Thompson, P. (1999) *Organisational Misbehaviour*. London: Sage.

Adib, A. and Guerrier, Y. (2003) 'The interlocking of gender with nationality, race, ethnicity and class: the narratives of women in hotel work', *Gender, Work and Organization*, 10: 413–32.

Adkins, L. (1995) *Gendered Work*. Buckingham: Open University Press.

Adkins, L. (2002) *Revisions: Gender and Sexuality in Late Modernity*. Buckingham: Open University Press.

Adkins, L. and Lury, C. (1999) 'The labour of identity: performing identities, performing economies', *Economy and Society*, 28: 598–614.

Aglietta, M. (1980) *A Theory of Capitalist Regulation*. London: New Left Books.

Ailon-Souday, G. and Kunda, G. (2003) 'The local selves of global workers: the social construction of national identity in the face of organizational globalization', *Organization Studies*, 24: 1073–96.

Albrow, M. (1970) *Bureaucracy*. London: Pall Mall.

Albrow, M. (1997) *Do Organisations Have Feelings?* London: Routledge.

Alvesson, M. (2004) 'Organization: from substance to image', in M. Hatch and M. Schultz (eds) *Organizational Identity*. Oxford: Oxford University Press.

Alvesson, M. and Willmott, H. (2004) 'Identity regulation as organizational control producing the appropriate individual', in M. Hatch and M. Schultz (eds) *Organizational Identity*. Oxford: Oxford University Press.

Amin, A. and Thrift, N. (eds) (2003) *The Blackwell Cultural Economy Reader*. Malden, MA; Oxford: Blackwell.

Anderson, B. (2000) *Doing the Dirty Work: the Global Politics of Domestic Labour*. London: Zed Books.

Anderson, M., Bechhofer, F., Jamieson, L., McCrone, D., Li, Y. and Stewart, R. (2002) 'Confidence amid uncertainty: ambitions and plans in a sample of young adults', *Sociological Research Online*, 6, http://www.socresonline.org.uk/6/4/anderson.html.

Anderson, S. and Cavanagh, J. (2000) *Top 200: the Rise of Global Corporate Power*. Washington DC: Institute for Policy Studies.

Anthias, F. (2005) 'Social stratification and social inequality: models of intersectionality and identity', in F. Devine, M. Savage, J. Scott and R. Crompton (eds) *Rethinking Class: Culture, Identities and Lifestyle*. Basingstoke: Palgrave Macmillan.

Aoki, M. (1988) *Information, Incentives and Bargaining in the Japanese Economy*. Cambridge: Cambridge University Press.

Applebaum, E., Bailey, T., Berg, P. and Kalleberg, A. (2001) *Manufacturing Advantage: Why High Performance Work Systems Pay Off*. Ithaca: ILR Press.

Archer, M. (2000) *Being Human: the Problem of Agency*. Cambridge: Cambridge University Press.

Armstrong, P. (1984) 'Competition between the organisational professions and the evolution of management control strategies', in K. Thompson (ed.) *Work, Employment and Unemployment*. Milton Keynes: Open University Press.

Armstrong, P. (1986) 'Management control strategies and inter-professional competition: the cases of accountancy and personnel management', in D. Knights and H. Willmott (eds) *Managing the Labour Process*. Aldershot: Gower.

Ash, L. (2002) 'Inside China's Sweatshops', *From Our Own Correspondent*, http://news.bbc.co.uk.

ASH Scotland (2005) *The Unwelcome Guest: How Scotland Invited the Tobacco Industry to Smoke Outside*. Edinburgh: ASH Scotland.

Atkinson, A. (2002) 'Is rising income inequality inevitable? A critique of the "Transatlantic consensus" ', in P. Townsend and D. Gordon (eds) *World Poverty: New Policies to Defeat an Old Enemy*. Bristol: Policy Press.

Auer, P. and Cazes, S. (2003) *Employment Stability in an Age of Flexibility*. Geneva: International Labour Organisation.

Bagguley, P. (1995) 'Middle class radicalism revisited', in T. Butler and M. Savage (eds) *Social Change and the Middle Classes*, London: UCL Press.

Bakan, J. (2004) *The Corporation: the Pathological Pursuit of Profit and Power*. London: Constable.

Baldry, C., Bain, P. and Taylor, P. (1998) ' "Bright satanic offices": Intensification, control and team Taylorism', in P. Thompson and C. Warhurst (eds) *Workplaces of the Future*. Basingstoke: Macmillan – now Palgrave Macmillan.

Barker, J. (1993) Tightening the iron cage: concertive control in self-managing teams', *Administrative Science Quarterly*, **38**: 408–37.

Baudrillard, J. (1981) *Simulacres et Simulation*. Paris: Galileé.

Baudrillard, J. (1983) 'Simulations', in P. Foss, P. Patton and P. Beitchman (eds) *Semiotext(e)* New York: Routledge.

Baudrillard, J. (1988) *Selected Writings*, edited by M. Poster. Cambridge: Polity Press.

Bauman, Z. (1987) *Legislators and Interpreters: on Modernity, Postmodernity and Intellectuals*. Cambridge: Polity Press.

Bauman, Z. (1996) 'From pilgrim to tourist: a short history of identity', in S. Hall and P. Du Gay (eds) *Questions of Cultural Identity*. London: Sage.

Bauman, Z. (1999) *Work, Consumerism and the New Poor*. Buckingham: Open University Press.

Baxter, J. (2002),'A juggling act: a feminist poststructuralist analysis of girls' and boys' talk in the secondary classroom', *Gender and Education*, **14** (1): 5–19.

Beardsworth and Bryman, A. (1999) 'Late modernity and the dynamics of quasification: the case of the themed restaurant', *Sociological Review*, **47**: 228–57.

Beck, U. (1992) *Risk Society: Towards a New Modernity*. London: Sage.

Beck, U. (2000) *The Brave New World of Work*. Cambridge: Polity Press.

Beck, U. and Beck-Gernsheim, E. (2002) *Individualization: Institutionalized Individualism and its Social and Political Consequences*. London: Sage.

Beckett, A. (2000) 'Is Coke still it?' *Guardian*, G2, 2.10.02: pp. 2–3, http://www.guardian.co.uk/g2/story/0,3604,376008,00.html.

Bell, C. and Newby, H. (1981) 'Narcissism or reflexivity in modern sociology', *Polish Sociological Bulletin*, **1**: 5–19.

Bell, D. (1960) *The End of Ideology: on the Exhaustion of Political Ideas in the Fifties*. Glencoe, IL: Free Press.

Bell, D. (1976) *The Coming of Post-industrial Society : a Venture in Social Forecasting*. London: Heinemann.

Berger, P. and Luckmann T. (1966) *The Social Construction of Reality: a Treatise in the Sociology of Knowledge*. Garden City, NY: Doubleday.

Berthoud, R. (1998) *The Incomes of Ethnic Minorities*, ISER Report 98-1. Colchester: University of Essex, Institute for Social and Economic Research.

Berthoud, R. (1999) *Young Caribbean Men and the Labour Market: A Comparison with Other Ethnic Groups*. York: Joseph Rowntree Foundation.

Beynon, H., Grimshaw, D., Rubery, J. and Ward, K. (2002) *Managing Employment Change*. Oxford: Oxford University Press.

Black, P. and Sharma, U. (2001) 'Look good, feel better: beauty therapy as emotional labour', *Sociology*, **35**: 913–31.

Blair, T. (1998) *The Third Way*. London: Fabian Society.

Blair, T. (1998) Foreword to: *Our Competitive Future: Building the Knowledge Driven Economy*. London: Department of Trade and Industry White Paper, http://www.dti.gov.uk/comp/competitive/wh_int1.htm.

Blau, P. (1963) 'Critical remarks on Weber's theory of authority', *American Political Science Review*, **57**: 305–16.

Blythman, J. (2004) *Shopped: the Shocking Power of British Supermarkets*. London: Fourth Estate.

Bolton, S. (2005) 'Making up managers: the case of NHS nurses', *Work, Employment and Society*, **19**: 5–24.

Bolton, S. and Boyd, C. (2003) 'Trolley dolly or skilled emotion manager?', *Work, Employment and Society*, **17**: 289–308.

Booth, A., Francesconi, M. and Frank, J. (1999) *Glass Ceilings or Sticky Floors?*, University of Essex: ISER Working Papers.

Bottero, W. (2000) 'Gender and the labour market at the turn of the century: complexity, ambiguity and change', *Work, Employment and Society*, **14**: 781–91.

Bourdieu, P. (1984) *Distinction: a Social Critique of the Judgement of Taste*. London: Routledge & Kegan Paul.

Bowlby, R. (1993) *Shopping with Freud*. London: Routledge.

Boyd, C. (2001) 'HRM in the airline industry: strategies and outcomes', *Personnel Review*, **30**: 438–53.

Boyd, C. (2002) 'Customer violence and employee health and safety', *Work, Employment and Society*, **16**: 151–69.

Boyd, C. and Bain, P. (1998) ' "Once I get up there where the air is rarefied": health, safety and the working conditions of airline cabin crews', *New Technology, Work and Employment*, **13**: 16–28.

Braverman, H. (1974) *Labor and Monopoly Capital: the Degradation of Work in the Twentieth Century*. London: Monthly Review Press.

Brennan, T. (2003) *Globalization and its Terrors: Daily Life in the West*. London: Routledge.

Breugel, I. (2004) 'Seeking the critical mass: quantitative and qualitative aspects of the feminisation of management in Britain in the 1990s', in P. Stewart (ed.) *Employment, Trade Union Renewal and the Future of Work*. Basingstoke: Palgrave Macmillan.

Brewer, J. (2003) *C. Wright Mills and the Ending of Violence*. Basingstoke: Palgrave Macmillan.

Brewer, M., Goodman, A., Myck, M., Shaw, J. and Shephard, A. (2004) *Poverty and Inequality in Britain*. London: Institute for Fiscal Studies.

Bridges, W. (1995) *Jobshift: How to Prosper in a Workplace Without Jobs*. London: Nicholas Brealey.

Broadbent, J., Dietrich, M. and Laughlin, R. (1997) 'The development of principal-agent contracting and accountability relationships in the public sector: conceptual and cultural problems', *Critical Perspectives on Accounting*, **7**: 259–84.

Brubaker, R. and Cooper, F. (2000) 'Beyond identity', *Theory and Society*, **29**: 1–47.

Bryce, R. (2002) *Pipe Dreams: Greed, Ego, Jealousy and the Death of Enron*. New York: PublicAffairs.

Bryman, A. (1999) 'The Disneyization of society', *Sociological Review*, **47**: 25–47.

Brynin, M. (2002) 'Overqualification in employment', *Work, Employment and Society*, **16**: 637–54.

Bryson, A. and McKay, S. (1998) 'What about the workers?', in R. Jowell, J. Curtice, A. Park, L. Brook and K. Thomson (eds) *British Social Attitudes* (14th report): *the End of Conservative Values?* Aldershot: Ashgate.

Burchell, B., Day, D., Hudson, M., Ladipo, D., Mankelow, R., Nolan, J., Reed, H., Wichert, I. and Wilkinson, F. (1999) *Job Insecurity and Work Intensification: Flexibility and the Changing Boundaries of Work*. York: Joseph Rowntree Foundation.

Burrell, G. (1988) 'Modernism, postmodernism and organisational analysis: the contribution of Michel Foucault', *Organisation Studies*, **9**: 221–35.

Butler, J. (1991) *Gender Trouble: Feminism and the Subversion of Identity*. New York: Routledge.

Caiazza, A., Shaw, A. and Werschkul, M. (2004) *Women's Economic Status in The States: Wide Disparities by Race, Ethnicity, and Region*. Washington DC: Institute for Women's Policy Research.

Callaghan, G. and Thompson, P. (2002) 'We recruit attitude: the selection and shaping of routine call centre labour', *Journal of Management Studies*, **39**: 233–53.

Callon, M. (1998) *The Laws of the Markets*. Oxford: Blackwell.

Campbell, C. (1989) *The Romantic Ethic and the Spirit of Modern Consumerism*. London: Blackwell.

Casey, C. (1995) *Work, Self and Society after Industrialism*. London: Routledge.

Casey, C. (1996) 'Corporate transformations: designer culture, designer employees and "post-occupational solidarity"', *Organization*, **3**: 317–39.

Castells, M. (1997) *The Power of Identity*. Oxford: Blackwell.

Castells, M. (2000) *The Rise of the Network Society* (2nd edn). Oxford: Blackwell.

Cheney, G. and Christensen, L. (2004) 'Organizational identity: linkages between internal and external communication', in M. Hatch and M. Schultz (eds) *Organizational Identity: a Reader*. Oxford: Oxford University Press.

Clarke, J. and Newman, J. (1997) *The Managerial State*. London: Sage.

Clarke, J., Gewirtz, S. and McLaughlin, E. (eds) (2000) *New Managerialism, New Welfare?* London: Open University Press/Sage.

Clegg, S. (1990) *Modern Organizations: Organization Studies in the Postmodern World*. London: Sage.

Clegg, S. (2005) 'Puritans, visionaries and survivors', *Organisation Studies*, **26**: 527–45.

Clegg, S. and Dunkerley, D. (1980) *Organizations, Class and Control*. London: Routledge, Kegan & Paul.

Cockburn, C. (1991) *In the Way of Women: Men's Resistance to Sex Equality in Organizations*. Basingstoke: Macmillan – now Palgrave Macmillan.

Cohen, L. (2003) *A Consumers' Republic: the Politics of Mass Consumption in Post-war America*. New York: Alfred A. Knopf.

Collinson, D. (1988) *Barriers to Fair Selection: a Multi-Sector Study of Recruitment Practices*. London: HMSO.

Collinson, D. (2003) 'Identities and insecurities: selves at work', *Organization*, **10**: 527–47.

Connell, R. (1987) *Gender and Power: Society, the Person and Sexual Politics*. Cambridge: Polity Press.

Connell, R. (2002) *Gender*. Cambridge: Polity Press.

Conrad, C. (2003) 'Stemming the tide: corporate discourse and agenda denial in the 2002 "corporate meltdown"', *Organization*, **10**: 549–60.

Courpasson, D. and Reid, M. (2004) 'Introduction: bureaucracy in the age of enterprise', *Organization*, **11**: 5–12.

Cox, T. (2004) 'Problems with research by organizational scholars on issues of *race* and ethnicity', *Journal of Applied Behavioral Science*, **40**: 124–45.

Craib, I. (1994) *The Importance of Disappointment*. London: Routledge.

Craib, I. (1997) *Classical Social Theory*. Oxford: Oxford University Press.

Crang, P. (1994) 'It's showtime: on the workplace geographies of display in a restaurant in southeast England', *Environment and Planning D: Society and Space*, **12**: 675–704.

Creegan, C., Colgan, F., Charlesworth, R. and Robinson, G. (2003) 'Race equality policies at work: employee perceptions of the "implementation gap" in a UK local authority', *Work, Employment and Society*, **17**: 617–40.

Crompton, R. (1997) *Women and Work in Modern Britain*. Oxford: Oxford University Press.

Crompton, R. (1998) *Class and Stratification: an Introduction to Current Debates*. Cambridge: Polity Press.

Crompton, R. (1999) *Restructuring Gender Relations and Employment: the Decline of the Male Breadwinner*. Oxford: Oxford University Press.

Crompton, R. and Scott, J. (2005) 'Class analysis: beyond the cultural turn', in F. Devine, M. Savage, J. Scott and R. Crompton (eds) *Rethinking Class: Culture, Identities and Lifestyle*. Basingstoke: Palgrave Macmillan.

Crouch, C., Finegold, D. and Sako, M. (1999) *Are Skills the Answer? The Political Economy of Skill Creation in Advanced Industrial Society*. Oxford: Oxford University Press.

Dandeker, C. (1990) *Surveillance, Power and Modernity: Bureaucracy and Discipline from 1700 to the Present Day*. Cambridge: Polity Press.

Danford, A. (1998) 'Work organisation inside Japanese firms in South Wales: a break from Taylorism?', in P. Thompson and C. Warhurst (eds) *Workplaces of the Future*. Basingstoke: Macmillan – now Palgrave Macmillan.

Davidson, M. and Burke, R. (eds) (2000) *Women in Management: Current Research Issues*. London: Sage.

Davies, C. (2002) 'What about the girl next door? Gender and the politics of self-regulation', in G. Bendelow (ed.) *Gender, Health and Healing*. London: Routledge.

De Certeau, M. (1984) *The Practice of Everyday Life*. London: University of California Press.

Deacon, B., Hulse, M. and Stubbs, P. (1997) *Global Social Policy: International Organisations and the Future of Welfare*. London: Sage.

Deakin, N. (1993) *The Politics of Welfare: Continuities and Change* (rev. edn). London: Harvester Wheatsheaf.

Deakin, S. and Konzelmann, S. (2003) 'After Enron: an age of enlightenment?' *Organization*, **10**: 583–87.

Deal, T. and Kennedy, A. (1988) *Corporate Cultures: the Rites and Rituals of Corporate Life*. Harmondsworth: Penguin.

Deetz, S. (1992) 'Disciplinary power in the modern corporation', in M. Alvesson and H. Willmott (eds) *Critical Management Studies*. London: Sage.

Deetz, S. (1995) *Transforming Communication, Transforming Business: Building Responsive and Responsible Workplaces*. Cresskill, NJ: Hampton Press.

Devine, F. and Savage, M. (2005) 'The cultural turn, sociology and class analysis', in F. Devine, M. Savage, J. Scott and R. Crompton (eds) (2005) *Rethinking Class: Culture, Identities and Lifestyle*. Basingstoke: Palgrave Macmillan.

Devine, F., Savage, M., Scott, J. and Crompton, R (eds) (2005) *Rethinking Class: Culture, Identities and Lifestyle*. Basingstoke: Palgrave Macmillan.

Devine, F., Britton, J., Mellor, R. and Halfpenny, P. (2000) 'Professional work and professional careers in Manchester's business and financial sector', *Work, Employment and Society*, **14**: 521–40.

Dickens, R., Gregg, P. and Wadsworth, J. (2003) *The Labour Market Under New Labour. The State of Working Britain*. Basingstoke: Palgrave Macmillan.

Donaghy, M. and Clarke, M. (2003) 'Are offshore financial centres the product of global markets? A sociological response', *Economy and Society*, **32**: 381–409.

Du Gay, P. (1996) *Consumption and Identity at Work*. London: Sage.

Du Gay, P. (2000) *In Praise of Bureaucracy: Weber, Organization and Ethics*. London: Sage.

Du Gay, P. and Salaman, G. (1992) 'The cult(ure) of the customer', *Journal of Management Studies*, **29**: 615–33.

Durkheim, E. (1984) *The Division of Labour in Society*. Basingstoke: Macmillan.

Duvell, F. and Jordan, B. (2003) 'Immigration control and the management of economic migration in the United Kingdom: organisational culture, implementation, enforcement and identity processes in public services', *Journal of Ethnic and Migration Studies*, **29**: 299–336.

Edwards, T. (2000) *Contradictions of Consumption*. Buckingham: Open University Press.

Eldridge, J. (1994) 'Work and authority: some Weberian perspectives', in L. Ray and M. Reed (eds) *Organizing Modernity: New Weberian Perspectives on Work, Organization and Society*. London: Routledge.

Elger, T. and Smith, C. (eds) (1994) *Global Japanization? The Transnational Transformation of the Labour Process*. London: Routledge.

EOC (Equal Opportunities Commission) (2005) *Facts about Women and Men in Great Britain*. Manchester: EOC.

Erikson, R. and Goldthorpe, J. (1992) *The Constant Flux: A Study of Class Mobility in Industrial Societies*. Oxford: Clarendon Press.

Esping-Anderson, G. (1990) *The Three Worlds of Welfare Capitalism*. Cambridge: Polity Press.

ESRC (Economic and Social Research Council) (2002) *Future of Work Programme*, www.leeds.ac.uk/esrcfutureofwork.

Etzioni, A. (1961) *A Comparative Analysis of Complex Organizations: On Power, Involvement and their Correlates*. New York: Free Press of Glencoe.

Etzioni, A. (1964) *Modern Organizations*. Englewood Cliffs, NJ: Prentice Hall.

Eurostat (2005) *Labour Force Survey Results*. Luxembourg: Office for Official Publications of the European Communities.

Ewen, S. (1976) *Captains of Consciousness: Advertising and the Social Roots of Consumer Culture*. New York: McGraw-Hill.

Ezzy, D. (2001) 'A simulacrum of workplace community: individualism and engineered culture', *Sociology*, **35**: 631–50.

Faggio, G. and Nickell, S. (2003) 'The rise in activity among adult men', in R. Dickens, P. Gregg and J. Wadsworth (eds) *The Labour Market Under New Labour*. Basingstoke: Palgrave Macmillan.

Falk, P. (1997) 'The Benetton-Toscani effect: testing the limits of conventional advertising', in M. Nava, A. Blake, I. McRury and B. Richards (eds) *Buy This Book: Studies in Advertising and Consumption*. London: Routledge.

Farrell, C. (2005) 'Governance in the UK public sector: the involvement of the governing board', *Public Administration*, **83**: 89–110.

Featherstone, M. (1991) *Consumer Culture and Postmodernism*. London: Sage.

Fenwick, T. (2002) 'Transgressive desires: new enterprising selves in the new capitalism', *Work, Employent and Society*, **16**: 703–23.

Ferner, A., Almond, P., Clark, I., Colling, T., Edwards, T., Holden, L. and Muller-Camen, M. (2004) 'The dynamics of central control and subsidiary autonomy in the management of human resources: case-study evidence from US MNCs in the UK', *Organization Studies*, **25**: 363–91.

Fine, B. and Leopold, E. (1993) *The World of Consumption*. London: Routledge.

Fineman, S. (ed.) (2000) *Emotion in Organizations* (2nd edn). London: Sage.

Fineman, S. and Sturdy, A. (2001) '"Struggles" for the control of affect', in A. Sturdy, I. Grugulis and H. Willmott (eds) *Customer Service*. Basingstoke: Macmillan – now Palgrave Macmillan.

Fjellman, S. (1992) *Vinyl Leaves: Walt Disney World and America*. Boulder, CO: Westview Press.

Fligstein, N. (2001) *The Architecture of Markets*. Princeton: Princeton University Press

Fligstein, N. (2005) 'The political and economic sociology of international economic arrangements', in N. Smelser and R. Swedberg (eds) *The Handbook of Economic Sociology*. Princeton: Princeton University Press/Russell Sage Foundation.

Flynn, N. (2000) 'Managerialism and public services: some international trends', in Clarke, J., Gewirtz, S. and McLaughlin, E. (eds) *New Managerialism, New Welfare?* London: Open University Press/Sage.

Flyvbjerg, B. (1998) *Rationality and Power: Democracy in Practice*. Chicago: University of Chicago Press.

Flyvbjerg, B. (2001) *Making Social Science Matter: Why Social Inquiry Fails and How It Can Succeed Again*. Cambridge: Cambridge University Press.

Foucault, M. (1970) *The Order of Things: an Archaeology of the Human Sciences*. London: Tavistock Publications.

Foucault, M. (1972) *The Archaeology of Knowledge* London: Tavistock Publications.

Foucault, M. (1977) *Madness and Civilisation*. London: Tavistock Publications.

Foucault, M. (1979) *The History of Sexuality*, Volume 1. Harmondsworth: Penguin.

Foucault, M. (1980) *Power/Knowledge: Selected Interviews and Other Writing, 1972–1977*, ed. C. Gordon. Brighton: Harvester Press.

Foucault, M. (1982) 'The subject and power', Afterword to H. L. Dreyfus and P. Rabinow, *Michel Foucault: Beyond Structuralism and Hermeneutics*. Chicago: Chicago University Press.

Foucault, M. (1984) 'What is enlightenment?' in P. Rabinow (ed.) *The Foucault Reader*. Harmondsworth: Penguin.

Foucault, M. (1986) *The Care of the Self*. New York: Pantheon.

Foucault, M. (1987) 'The ethic of care for the self as a practice of freedom: an interview with Michel Foucault', in J. Bernauer and D. Rasmussen (eds) *The Final Foucault*. Cambridge: MIT Press.

Fox, A. (1974) *Beyond Contract: Work, Power and Trust Relations*. London: Faber.

Frank, T. (2001) *One Market Under God*. London: Secker & Warburg.

Frankfurt, H. (2004) *On Bullshit*. Princeton: Princeton University Press.

Fraser, N. (1995) 'From redistribution to recognition? Dilemmas of justice in a "post-socialist" age', *New Left Review*, **212**: 68–94.

Fraser, N. (2000) 'Rethinking recognition' *New Left Review*, **3**, May–June: 107–20.

Frenkel, S., Korczynski, M., Shire, K. and Tam, M. (1998) 'Beyond bureaucracy? Work organization in call centres', *International Journal of Human Resource Management*, 9: 957–79.

Friedman, A. (1977) *Industry and Labour: Class Struggle at Work and Monopoly Capitalism*, London: Macmillan.

Fuller, L. and Smith, V. (1991) " 'Consumers' reports": management by customers in a changing economy', *Work, Employment and Society*, 5: 1–16.

Gabriel, Y. (2005) 'Glass cages and glass palaces: images of organization in image-conscious times', *Organization*, 12: 9–27.

Gallie, D. (2000) 'The labour force', in A.H. Halsey and J. Webb (eds) *Twentieth Century British Social Trends*. Basingstoke: Macmillan – now Palgrave Macmillan.

Gallie, D., Felstead, A. and Green, F. (2004) 'Changing patterns of task discretion in Britain', *Work, Employment and Society*, 18: 243–66.

Gallie, D., White, M., Cheng, Y. and Tomlinson, M. (1998) *Restructuring the Employment Relationship*. Oxford: Clarendon Press.

Gereffi, G. (2001) 'Shifting governance structures in global commodity chains, with special reference to the internet', *American Behavioral Scientist*, 44: 1616–37.

Gereffi, G. (2005) 'The global economy: organization, governance and development', in N. Smelser and R. Swedberg (eds) *The Handbook of Economic Sociology*. Princeton. Princeton University Press/Russell Sage Foundation.

Gergen, K. (1991) *The Saturated Self*. New York: Basic Books.

Gershuny, J. (2000) *Changing Times*. Oxford: Oxford University Press.

Gershuny, J. (2005) 'Busyness as the badge of honor for the new superordinate working class', *Social Research*, 72: 287–315.

Gershuny, J. and Jones, S. (1987) 'Changing use of time: Britain 1961–1984', *Sociological Review Monographs*, 33: 9–50.

Gherardi, S. (1995) *Gender, Symbolism and Organisational Culture*. London: Sage.

Giddens, A. (1971) *Capitalism and Modern Social Theory: an Analysis of the Writings of Marx, Durkheim and Max Weber*. Cambridge: Cambridge University Press.

Giddens, A. (1982) *Sociology: a Brief but Critical Introduction*. London: Macmillan – now Palgrave Macmillan.

Giddens, A. (1991) *Modernity and Self-identity*. Cambridge: Polity Press.

Giddens, A. (1993) *The Giddens Reader* (ed. P. Cassell). Basingstoke: Macmillan – now Palgrave Macmillan.

Giddens, A. (1996) *In Defence of Sociology*. Cambridge: Polity Press.

Giddens, A. (1998) *The Third Way: the Renewal of Social Democracy*. Cambridge: Polity Press.

Gioia, D., Schultz, M. and Corley, K. (2004) 'Organizational identity, image and adaptive instability', in M. Hatch and M. Schultz (eds) *Organizational Identity: a Reader*. Oxford: Oxford University Press.

Glenn, E. (1996) 'From servitude to service work: historical divisions in the racial division of paid reproductive labour', in C. Macdonald and C. Sirianni (eds) *Working in the Service Sector*. Philadelphia: Temple University Press.

Goffman, E. (1959) *The Presentation of Self in Everyday Life*. Harmondsworth: Penguin.

Goffman, E. (1983) 'The interaction order', *American Sociological Review*, 48: 1–17.

Goldthorpe, J. (1987) *Social Mobility and Class Structure in Modern Britain*. Oxford: Clarendon Press.

Goldthorpe, J. (1995) 'The service class revisited', in T. Butler and M. Savage (eds) *Social Change and the Middle Classes*, London: UCL Press.

Goldthorpe, J. and Marshall, G. (1992) 'The promising future of class analysis', *Sociology*, 26: 381–400.

Goos, M. and Manning, A. (2003) 'McJobs and MacJobs: the growing polarisation of jobs in the UK', in R. Dickens, P. Gregg and J. Wadsworth (eds) *The Labour Market Under New Labour*. Basingstoke: Palgrave Macmillan.

Gordon, C. (1987) 'The soul of the citizen: Max Weber and Michel Foucault on rationality and government', in S. Whimster and S. Lash (eds) *Max Weber: Rationality and Modernity*. London: Allen & Unwin.

Gordon, D. (1996) *Fat and Mean: the Corporate Squeeze of Working Americans and Corporate Downsizing*. New York: Free Press.

Gordon, D. (2002) 'The international measurement of poverty and anti-poverty policies', in P. Townsend and D. Gordon (eds) *World Poverty: New Policies to Defeat an Old Enemy*. Bristol: Policy Press.

Gore, C. (2000) 'The rise and fall of the Washington Consensus as a paradigm for developing countries', *World Development*, **28**: 789–804.

Gorz, A. (1999) *Reclaiming Work: Beyond the Wage-based Society*. Cambridge: Polity Press.

Gouldner, A. (1955) *Patterns of Industrial Bureaucracy*. London: Routledge & Kegan Paul.

Gouldner, A. (1957) 'Cosmopolitans and locals: towards an analysis of latent social roles', *Administrative Science Quarterly*, **2**: 281–306.

Gouldner, A. (1960) 'The norm of reciprocity: a preliminary statement', *American Sociological Review*, **25**: 161–78.

Graham, L. (1995) *On the Line at Subaru-Isuzu: the Japanese Model and the American Worker*. Ithaca, NY: Cornell University Press.

Granovetter, M. (1985) 'Economic action and social structure: the problem of embeddedness', *American Journal of Sociology*, **91**: 481–510.

Gray, A. (2003) 'Enterprising femininity: new modes of work and subjectivity', *European Journal of Cultural Studies*, **6**: 489–506.

Gray, J. (1998) *False Dawn: the Delusions of Global Capitalism*. London: Granta.

Green, F. (2001) 'It's been a hard day's night: the concentration and intensification of work in late twentieth-century Britain', *British Journal of Industrial Relations*, **39**: 53–80.

Greenfeld, L. (2001) *The Spirit of Capitalism: Nationalism and Economic Growth*. Cambridge, MA: Harvard University Press.

Green Paper (1998) *New Ambitions for our Country: A New Contract for Welfare* (Cm 3805). London: Stationery Office.

Grey, C. (1994) 'Career as a project of the self and labour process discipline', *Sociology*, **28**: 479–97.

Grey, C. (2003) 'The real world of Enron's auditors', *Organization*, **10**: 572–76.

Grimshaw D., Beynon H., Rubery J. and Ward K. (2002) 'The restructuring of career paths in large service sector organizations: 'delayering', upskilling and polarization', *Sociological Review*, **50**: 89–116.

Grugulis, I., Dundon, T. and Wilkinson, A. (2000) 'Cultural control and the "culture manager": employment practices in a consultancy', *Work, Employment and Society*, **14**: 97–116.

Guillen, M. (2001) *The Limits of Convergence: Globalization and Organization Change in Argentina, South Korea, and Spain*. Princeton: Princeton University Press.

Gunaratnam, Y. and Lewis, G. (2001) 'Racialising emotional labour and emotionalising racialised labour: anger, fear and shame in social welfare', *Journal of Social Work Practice*, **15**: 131–48.

Halford, S. and Leonard, P. (1999) 'New identities? Managerialism, professionalism and the construction of self', in M. Exworthy and S. Halford (eds) *Professionals and the New Managerialism in the Public Sector*. Buckingham: Open University Press.

Halford, S. and Leonard, P. (2001) *Gender, Power and Organisations: an Introduction*. Basingstoke: Palgrave Macmillan.

Halford, S., Savage, M. and Witz, A. (1997) *Gender, Careers and Organisations*. Basingstoke: Macmillan – now Palgrave Macmillan.

Hall, P. and Soskice, D. (eds) (2001) *Varieties of Capitalism: the Institutional Foundations of Comparative Advantage*. Oxford/New York: Oxford University Press.

Hall, S. (1996) 'Introduction: who needs identity?', in S. Hall and P. du Gay (eds) *Questions of Cultural Identity*. London: Sage.

Hall, S. (1997) *Representation: Cultural Representations and Signifying Practices*. London: Sage.

Hall, S. and Gieben, B. (eds) (1992) *Formations of Modernity*. Cambridge: Polity Press.

Handy, C. (1994) *The Empty Raincoat*. London: Hutchinson.

Hanlon, G. (1998) 'Professionalism as enterprise: service class politics and the redefinition of professionalism', *Sociology*, **32**:43–64.

Harley, B. (2001) 'Team membership and the experience of work in Britain: an analysis of the WERS98 data', *Work, Employment and Society*, **15**: 721–42.

Harris, L. (2002) 'The emotional labour of barristers: an exploration of emotional labour by status professionals', *Journal of Management Studies*, **39**: 553–84.

Harrison, B. (1994) *Lean and Mean: the Changing Landscape of Corporate Power in the Age of Flexibility*. New York: Basic Books.

Harvey, D. (1989) *The Condition of Postmodernity: an Enquiry into the Origins of Cultural Change*. Oxford: Basil Blackwell.

Harzing, A. and Sorge, A. (2003) 'The relative impact of country of origin and universal contingencies on internationalization strategies and corporate control in multinational enterprises: worldwide and European perspectives', *Organization Studies*, **24**: 187–214.

Hatch, M. and Schultz, M. (2004) 'The dynamics of organizational identity', in M. Hatch and M. Schultz (eds) *Organizational Identity: a Reader*. Oxford: Oxford University Press.

Hatter, W., Vinter, L. and Williams, R. (2002) *Dads on Dads: Needs and Expectations at Home and at Work*. Manchester: EOC.

Hayek, F. (1967) *Studies in Philosophy, Politics and Economics*. London: Routlegde & Kegan Paul.

Healy, G., Bradley, H. and Mukherjee, N. (2004) 'Individualism and collectivism revisited: a study of black and minority ethnic women', *Industrial Relations Journal*, **35**: 451–66.

Hearn, J. and Parkin, W. (2001) *Gender, Sexuality and Violence in Organizations: the Unspoken Forces of Organization Violations*. London: Sage.

Heath, A. and Savage, M. (1995) 'Political alignments within the middle classes, 1972–89', in T. Butler and M. Savage (eds) *Social Change and the Middle Classes*, London: UCL Press.

Hebdige, D. (1981) 'Object as image: the Italian scooter cycle', *Block*, **5**: 44–64.

Held, D. (ed.) (2000) A *Globalizing World? Culture, Economics, Politics*. London: Routledge.

Held, D., McGrew, A., Goldblatt, D. and Perraton, J. (1999) *Global Transformations: Politics, Economics and Culture*. Stanford, CA: Stanford University Press.

Hennock, M. (2003) 'China's tearaway economy sparks envy', BBC News Online, http://newsvote.bbc.co.uk.

Henriques, J., Hollway, W., Urwin, C., Venn, C. and Walkerdine, V. (1998) *Changing the Subject: Psychology, Social Regulation and Subjectivity*. London: Routledge.

Herman, E. and McChesney, R. (1997) *The Global Media: The New Missionaries of Corporate Capitalism*. London: Cassell.

Hochschild, A. (1983) *The Managed Heart: Commercialization of Human Feeling*. Berkeley: University of California Press.

Hochschild, A. (1997) *The Time Bind: When Work Becomes Home and Home Becomes Work*. New York: Metropolitan Books.

Hofstede, G. (1980) *Culture's Consequences: International Differences in Work-related Values*. Beverly Hills, CA: Sage.

Hoggett, P. (1996) 'New modes of control in the public service', *Public Administration*, **74**: 9–32.

Hoggett, P. (2000) *Emotional Life and the Politics of Welfare*. Basingstoke: Macmillan – now Palgrave Macmillan.

Hood, C. (2000) *The Art of the State: Culture, Rhetoric, and Public Management*. Oxford: Oxford University Press.

Hood, C. and Scott, C. (2000) 'Regulation of government: has it increased, is it increasing, should it be diminished?', *Public Administration*, **78**: 283–304.

Hood, C., Scott, C., James, O., Jones, G. and Travers, A. (1999) *Regulation Inside Government: Waste Watchers, Quality Police and Sleaze Busters*. Oxford: Oxford University Press.

Hoque, K. and Kirkpatrick, I. (2003) 'Non-standard employment in the management and professional workforce: training, consultation and gender implications', *Work, Employment and Society*, **17**: 667–89.

Huber, E. and Stephens, J. (2005) 'Welfare states and the economy', in N. Smelser and R. Swedberg (eds) *The Handbook of Economic Sociology*. Princeton: Princeton University Press/Russell Sage Foundation.

Hughes, A. (2004) 'Retailers, knowledges and changing commodity networks: the case of the cut flower trade', in A. Amin and N. Thrift (eds) *Cultural Economy Reader*, Oxford: Blackwell.

Hutton, W. (2001) 'Why sexual equality is still a joke' *Observer*, 25.03.2001, http://observer.guardian.co.uk/comment/story/0,6903,462654,00.html.

Hutton, W. (2002) *The World We're In*. London: Little, Brown.
Hyman, P. (2005) *1 out of 10: From Downing Street Vision to Classroom Reality*. London: Vintage.
Jackson, S. (1999) *Heterosexuality in Question*. London: Sage.
James, N. (1989) 'Emotional labour: skill and work in the social regulation of feeling', *Sociological Review*, **37**: 15–42.
James, N. (1992) 'Care = organisation + physical labour + emotional labour', *Sociology of Health and Illness*, **14**: 488–509.
Jameson, F. (1988) 'Postmodernism and consumer society', in E.A. Caplin (ed.) *Postmodernism and its Discontents*. London: Verso.
Jameson, F. (1990) *Late Marxism: Adorno, or, the Persistence of the Dialectic*. London: Verso.
Jameson, F. (1991) *Postmodernism or the Cultural Logic of Late Capitalism*. London: Verso.
Jamieson, L. (1998) *Intimacy: Personal Relationships in Modern Societies*. Cambridge: Polity Press.
Jamieson, L. (2002) 'Theorising identity, nationality and citizenship', *Slovak Sociological Review*, **34**.
Jenkins, R. (1986) *Racism and Recruitment: Managers, Organisations and Equal Opportunity in the Labour Market*. Cambridge: Cambridge University Press.
Jenkins, R. (1996) *Social Identity*. London: Routledge.
Jenkins, R. (2003) 'International development institutions and national economic contexts: neo-liberalism encounters India's indigenous political traditions', *Economy and Society*, **32**: 584–610.
Jenkins, S. (2003) 'Restructuring flexibility: case studies of part-time female workers in six workplaces', *Gender, Work and Organization*, **11**: 306–33.
Jenson, J., Hagen, E. and Reddy, C (eds) (1988) *Feminization of the Labour Force: Paradoxes and Promises*. Cambridge: Polity Press.
Jewson, N. and Mason, D. (1994) ' "Race", employment and equal opportunities: towards a political economy and an agenda for the 1990s', *Sociological Review*, **42**: 591–617.
Jones, R. (2003) 'Eight million still can't get credit', *Guardian*, 8.01.03: 19, http://www.guardian.co.uk/business/story/0,3604,870332,00.html.
Juniper, T. (2003) 'Davos still in the surreal world', *Guardian*, Society, 29.01.03: 9, http://society.guardian.co.uk/societyguardian/story/0,7843,883944,00.html.
Kallinikos, J. (2003) 'Work, human agency and organizational forms: an anatomy of fragmentation', *Organization Studies*, **24**: 595–618.
Karreman, D. and Alvesson, M. (2004) 'Cages in tandem: management control, social identity, and identification in a knowledge intensive firm', *Organization*, **11**: 149–175.
Kelly, J. and Waddington, J. (1995) 'New prospects for British labour', *Organization*, **2**: 415–26.
Kenney, M. and Florida, R. (1993) *Beyond Mass Production: the Japanese System and its Transfer to the US*. Oxford: Oxford University Press.
Kerr, C., Dunlop, J., Harbison, F. and Mayers, C. (1960) *Industrialism and Industrial Man: the Problems of Labor and Management in Economic Growth*. Cambridge, MA: Harvard University Press.
Khan, S. (2003) 'Bombay calling', *Observer*, 7.12.03, http://observer.guardian.co.uk/focus/story/0,6903,1101659,00.html.
Klein, N. (2000) *No Logo*. London: Harper Collins/Flamingo.
Knights, D. (2004) 'Michel Foucault', in S. Linstead (ed.) *Organization Theory and Postmodern Thought*. London: Sage.
Knights, D. and Willmott, H. (1989) 'Power and subjectivity at work – from degradation to subjugation in social relations', *Sociology*, **23**: 535–58.
Knights, D. and Willmott, H. (eds) (1990) *Labour Process Theory*. Basingstoke: Macmillan – now Palgrave Macmillan.
Kolko, G. (1999) 'Ravaging the poor: the International Monetary Fund indicted by its own data', *International Journal of Health Services*, **29**: 51–7.
Kondo, D. (1990) *Crafting Selves*. Chicago: University of Chicago Press.
Korczynski, M. (2003) 'Communities of coping: collective emotional labour in service work', *Organization*, **10**: 55–79.

Korczynski, M., Shire, K., Frenkel, S. and Tam, M. (2000) 'Service work in consumer capitalism: customers, control and contradictions', *Work, Employment and Society*, **14**: 669–87.

Kotler, P. (1991) *Marketing Management: Analysis, Planning, Implementation and Control*. London: Prentice Hall International.

Kumar, K. (1988a) *The Rise of Modern Society*. Oxford: Blackwell.

Kumar, K. (1988b) 'From work to employment and unemployment: the English experience', in R. Pahl (ed.) *On Work*. Oxford: Blackwell.

Kumar, K. (1995) *From Post-Industrial to Post-Modern Society*. Oxford: Blackwell.

Kunda, G. (1992) *Engineering Culture: Control and Commitment in a High-Tech Corporation*. Philadelphia: Temple University Press.

Kyotani, E. (1999) 'New managerial strategies of Japanese corporations', in A. Felstead and N. Jewson (eds) *Global Trends in Flexible Labour*. Basingstoke: Macmillan – now Palgrave Macmillan.

Labour Market Trends (2003) Vol. 111. London: HMSO, http://www.statistics.gov.uk/STATBASE/Product.asp?vlnk = 550&More = Y.

Lace, S. (2005) *The Glass Consumer: Life in a Surveillance Society*. London: Policy Press.

Lang, T. (2003) *Food and Health Wars: A Modern Drama of Consumer Sovereignty*, www.consume.bbk.ac.uk, working paper no. 014.

Lasch, C. (1980) *The Culture of Narcissism: American Life in an Age of Diminishing Expectations*. London: Abacus Press.

Lash, S. and Urry, J. (1994) *Economies of Signs and Space*. Cambridge: Polity Press.

Lawrence, F. (2004) *Not on the Label*. Harmondsworth: Penguin.

Lawrence, F. and Evans, R. (2004) 'Food firms go all the way to No 10 in fight over what we eat', *Guardian*, http://www.guardian.co.uk/uk_news/story/0,3604,1224776,00.html.

Leadbetter, C. (2000) *Living on Thin Air: the New Economy*. London: Viking.

Lee, M. (1993) *Consumer Culture Reborn: the Cultural Politics of Consumption*. London: Routledge.

Leidner, R. (1993) *Fast Food, Fast Talk: Service Work and the Routinization of Everyday Life*. Berkeley: University of California Press.

Leonard, P. (2003) ' "Playing" doctors and nurses? Competing discourses of gender, power and identity in the British National Health Service', *Sociological Review*, **51**: 218–37.

Lewis, G. (2000) *'Race', Gender, Social Welfare: Encounters in a Postcolonial Society*. Cambridge: Polity Press.

Lewis, G. (2002) 'Categories of exclusion: "race", gender and the micro social in social services departments', in E. Breitenbach, A. Brown, F. Mackay and J. Webb (eds) *The Changing Politics of Gender Equality in Britain*. Basingstoke: Palgrave Macmillan.

Lewis, G. and Phoenix, A. (2004) ' "Race", ethnicity and identity', in K. Woodward (ed.) *Questioning Identity: Gender, Class, Ethnicity*. London: Routledge/Open University Press.

Leys, C. (2001) *Market Driven Politics: Neo-Liberal Democracy and the Public Interest*. London: Verso.

Li, Y. (2002) 'Falling off the ladder? Professional and managerial career trajectories and unemployment experiences', *European Sociological Review*, **18**: 253–70.

Li, Y., Bechhofer, F., Stewart, R., McCrone, D., Anderson, M. and Jamieson, L. (2003) 'A divided working class? Planning and career perception in the service and working classes', *Work, Employment and Society*, **17**: 617–36.

Linstead, S. (ed.) (2004) *Organization Theory and Postmodern Thought*. London: Sage.

Lister, R. (2003) *Citizenship: Feminist Perspectives*. (2nd edn). Basingstoke: Palgrave Macmillan.

Lukes, S. (2005) *Power: a Radical View* (2nd edn). Basingstoke: Palgrave Macmillan.

Lury, C. (1996) *Consumer Culture*. Cambridge: Polity Press.

Lury, C. (2004) 'Marking time with Nike: the illusion of the durable', in A. Amin and N. Thrift (eds) *Cultural Economy Reader*. Oxford: Blackwell.

Lury, C. and Warde, A. (1997) 'Investments in the imaginary consumer: conjectures regarding power, knowledge and advertising', in M. Nava, A. Blake, I. McRury and B. Richards (eds) *Buy This Book: Studies in Advertising and Consumption*. London: Routledge.

Lyon, D. (2001) *Surveillance Society: Monitoring Everyday Life*. Buckingham: Open University Press.

Lyotard, J. (1984) *The Postmodern Condition*. Manchester: Manchester University Press.

Macdonald, C. and Sirianni, C. (eds) (1996) *Working in the Service Sector*. Philadelphia: Temple University Press.

McDonald, R. (2004) 'Individual identity and organisational control: Empowerment and Modernisation in a Primary Care Trust', *Sociology of Health & Illness*, **26**: 925–50.

McDowell, L. (1997) *Capital Culture: Gender at Work in the City*. Oxford: Blackwell.

McDowell, L. (2002) 'Transitions to work: masculine identities, youth inequality and labour market change', *Gender, Place and Culture*, **9**: 39–59.

McGregor, D. (1987 [1960]) *The Human Side of Enterprise*. Harmondsworth: Penguin.

McGuire, G. (2002) 'Gender, race, and the shadow structure: a study of informal networks and inequality in a work organization', *Gender & Society*, **16**: 303–22.

MacInnes, J. (1998) *The End of Masculinity: the Confusion of Sexual Genesis and Sexual Difference in Modern Society*. Buckingham: Open University Press.

MacInnes, J. (2004) 'The sociology of identity: social science or social comment?', *British Journal of Sociology*, **55**: 531–43.

Mackay, H. (2000) 'The globalisation of culture?', in D. Held (ed.) *A Globalising World? Culture, Economics and Politics*. London: Routledge/Open University Press.

McKendrick, N., Brewer, J. and Plumb, J.H. (1982) *The Birth of a Consumer Society*. London: Europa.

McKinley, A. and Starkey, K. (eds) (1998) *Foucault, Management and Organisation*. London: Sage.

McKinley, A. and Taylor, P. (1998) 'Foucault and the politics of production', in A. McKinley and K. Starkey (eds) (1998) *Foucault, Management and Organisation*. London: Sage.

McNay, L. (1999) 'Gender, habitus and the field: Pierre Bordieu and the limits of reflexivity', *Theory, Culture and Society*, **16**: 95–117.

Maesschalck, J. (2004) 'The impact of new public management reforms on public servants' ethics: towards a theory', *Public Administration*, **82**: 465–89.

Marens, R. (2003) 'Two, three, many Enrons: American financial hypertrophy and the end of economic hegemony', *Organization*,**10**: 588–93.

Marquand, D. (2004) *Decline of the Public*. Cambridge: Polity Press.

Marshall, G., Rose, D., Newby, H. and Vogler, C. (1988) *Social Class in Modern Britain*. London: Unwin Hyman.

Martin, B. (2002) *In the Public Service*. London: Zed Press.

Mattelart (1991) *Advertising International: The Privatisation of Public Space*. London: Routledge.

Mead, G.H. (1934) *Mind, Self and Society*. Chicago, IL: University of Chicago Press.

Meadows, P. and Metcalf, H. (2006) *Survey of Employers Policies, Practices and Preferences Relating to Age*. DWP Research Report No 325/DTI Employment Relations Research Series No 49. London: DWP/DTI.

Merton, R.K. (1940) 'Bureaucratic structure and personality', *Social Forces*, **18**: 560–8.

Milkman, R. (1998) 'The new American workplace: high road or low road?', in P. Thompson and C. Warhurst (eds) *Workplaces of the Future*. Basingstoke: Macmillan – now Palgrave Macmillan.

Miller, D. (1987) *Material Culture and Mass Consumption*. Oxford: Blackwell.

Miller, D. (1998) *A Theory of Shopping*. Cambridge: Polity Press.

Mills, C. W. (2000 [1959]) *The Sociological Imagination*. Oxford: Oxford University Press.

Millward, N., Bryson, N. and Forth, J. (2000) *All Change at Work? British Employment Relations 1980–1998, as Portrayed by the Workplace Industrial Relations Survey Series*. London: Routledge.

Modood, T., Berthoud, R., Lakey, J., Nazroo, J., Smith, P., Virdee, S. and Beishon, S. (1997) *Ethnic Minorities in Britain: Diversity and Disadvantage*. London: PSI.

Molotch, H. (2003) *Where Stuff Comes From*. New York; London: Routledge.

Morris, L. (1994) *Dangerous Classes: the Underclass and Social Citizenship*. London: Routledge.

Moynagh, M. and Worsley, R. (2005) *Working in the Twenty-first Century*. Leeds: ESRC Future of Work Programme.

Mulgan, G. (1998) *Connexivity: Responsibility, Freedom, Business and Power in the New Century*. London: Vintage.

Munro, R. (1997) *Ideas of Difference: Social Spaces and the Labour of Division*. Oxford: Blackwell.

Nava, M. (1997) 'Framing advertising: cultural analysis and the incrimination of visual texts', in M. Nava, A. Blake, I. McRury and B. Richards (eds) *Buy This Book: Studies in Advertising and Consumption*. London: Routledge.

Nava, M. (2002) 'Consumption's potent political purchase', *The Times Higher*, December 20/27, p. 21.

Needham, C. (2003) *Citizen-Consumers: New Labour's Marketplace Democracy*. London: Catalyst Forum.

Newman, K. (1988) *Falling from Grace*. New York: Free Press.

Newman, J. (2000) 'Beyond the new public management? Modernizing public services', in J. Clarke, S. Gewirtz, and E. McLaughlin (eds) *New Managerialism, New Welfare?* London: Open University Press/Sage.

NHS Scotland (2005) *Delivering for Health*. Edinburgh: Scottish Executive.

Nolan, P. (2003) 'Reconnecting with history: the ESRC Future of Work Programme', *Work, Employment and Society*, **17**: 473–80.

Nolan, P. (2004) 'Shaping the future: the political economy of work and employment', *Industrial Relations Journal*, **35**: 378–87.

Nolan, P. and Wood, S. (2003) 'Mapping the future of work', *British Journal of Industrial Relations*, **41**: 165–74.

O'Brien, M. and Shemilt, I. (2003) *Working Fathers: Earning and Caring*. Manchester: EOC.

O'Donohoe, S. (1997) 'Leaky boundaries: intertextuality and young adults experiences of advertising', in M. Nava, A. Blake, I. McRury and B. Richards (eds) *Buy This Book: Studies in Advertising and Consumption*. London: Routledge.

OECD (Organisation for Economic Cooperation and Development) (1994) *Jobs Study: Evidence and Explanations*. Paris: OECD Publications.

OECD (Organisation for Economic Cooperation and Development) (1995) *Governance in Transition: Public Management Reform in OECD Countries*. Paris: OECD.

OECD (Organisation for Economic Cooperation and Development) (2003) *Employment Outlook*. Paris: OECD Publications.

OECD (Organisation for Economic Cooperation and Development) (2005) *Employment Outlook*. Paris: OECD Publications.

Ogbonna, E. (1992) 'Managing organizational culture: fantasy or reality?', *Human Resource Management*, **3**: 74–96.

Ogbonna, E. and Wilkinson, B. (1988) 'Corporate strategy and corporate culture: the management of change in the UK supermarket industry', *Personnel Review*, **17**: 10–14.

Ohmae, K. (1995) *The End of the Nation State: the Rise of Regional Economies*. London: HarperCollins.

Olins, W. (1989) *Corporate Identity: Making Business Strategy Visible Through Design*. Boston: Harvard Business School Press.

Olins, W. (1995) *The New Guide to Identity*. London: Gower.

Osborne, D. and Gaebler, T. (1992) *Reinventing Government: How the Entrepreneurial Spirit is Transforming the Public Sector*, Reading, MA: Addison-Wesley.

Ouchi, W. and Johnson, J. (1978) 'Types of organizational control and their relationship to emotional well-being', *Administrative Science Quarterly*, **23**: 293–317.

Oxfam (2004) *Trading Away our Rights*, www.maketradefair.com.

Pahl, R. (ed.) (1988) *On Work*. Oxford: Blackwell.

Pahl, R. (1995) *After Success*. Cambridge: Polity Press.

Pakulski, J. and Waters, M. (1996) *The Death of Class*. London: Sage.

Parker, M. (1998) 'Capitalism, subjectivity and ethics: debating labour process analysis', *Organization Studies*, **13**: 1–17.

Parker, M. (2000) *Organizational Culture and Identity*. London: Sage.

Parker, M. and Slaughter, J. (2000) *Working Smart: A Union Guide to Participation Programs and Re-engineering*. Detroit: Labour Notes.

Paterson, L. and Ianelli, C. (2004) 'Social class and social opportunity', in L. Paterson, F. Bechhofer and D. McCrone, *Living in Scotland: Social and Economic Change Since 1980*. Edinburgh University Press.

Peach, C. Rogers, A., Chance, J. and Daley, P. (2000) 'Immigration and Ethnicity' in A.H. Halsey, and J. Webb (eds) *British Social Trends: 1900–2000*. Basingstoke: Macmillan – now Palgrave Macmillan.

Perrow, C. (1979) *Complex Organizations: a Critical Essay*. (2nd edn). Glenview, IL: Scott, Foresman.

Perrow, C. (2002) *Organizing America: Wealth, Power and the Origins of Corporate Capitalism.* Princeton: Princeton University Press.

Peters, T. (1987) *Thriving on Chaos.* Basingstoke: Macmillan.

Peters, T. and Waterman, R. (1982) *In Search of Excellence: Lessons from America's Best Run Companies.* New York: Harper & Row.

Peterson, J. (1987) *American Automobile Workers, 1900–1933.* Albany: SUNY Press.

Piketty, T. and Saez, E. (2001) 'Income Inequality in the United States, 1913–1998 (series updated to 2000 available)', *NBER Working Papers 8467*, National Bureau of Economic Research.

Platt, L (2005) *The Intergenerational Social Mobility of Minority Ethnic Groups.* University of Essex: Institute for Social and Economic Research Working Papers Number 2003–24.

Pollitt, C. and Bouckaert, G. (2000) *Public Management Reform: a Comparative Analysis.* Oxford: Oxford University Press.

Pollock, A. (2004) *NHS plc: the Privatisation of our Health Care.* London: Verso.

Pollock, A., Shaoul, J., Rowland, D. and Player, S. (2001) *Public Services and the Private Sector: A Response to the IPPR,* London: Catalyst Forum.

Power, M. (1997) *The Audit Society: Rituals of Verification.* Oxford: Oxford University Press.

Procter, S. and Mueller, F. (2000) 'Teamworking in its context(s): antecedents, nature and dimensions', *Human Relations,* **53**: 1387–424.

Putnam, R. (2000) *Bowling Alone.* London: Simon & Schuster.

Ray, C. (1986) 'Corporate culture: the last frontier of control?', *Journal of Management Studies,* **23**: 287–97.

Ray, L. and Sayer, A. (1999) 'Introduction', in L. Ray and A. Sayer (eds) *Culture and Economy After the Cultural Turn.* London: Sage.

Redman, T. and Matthews, B. (1998) 'Service quality and human resource management: a review and research agenda', *Personnel Review,* **27**: 57–77.

Reed, M. (1985) *Redirections in Organisational Analysis.* London: Tavistock.

Reed, M. (2000) 'In praise of duality and dualism: rethinking agency and structure in organisational analysis', in S. Ackroyd and S. Fleetwood (eds) *Realist Perspectives on Management and Organizations.* London: Routledge.

Reinicke, W.H. (1998) *Global Public Policy: Governing Without Government?* Washington: Brookings Institution Press.

Revell, P. (2005) 'After the fall', *Guardian,* 1.11.05: 1–2.

Ridderstråle, J. and Nordström, K. (2004) *Karaoke Capitalism: Management for Mankind.* Harlow: Prentice Hall.

Rifkin, J. (1995) *The End of Work: the Decline of the Global Labour Force and the Dawn of the Post-Market Era.* New York: G.P. Putnam.

Ritzer, G. (1995) *Expressing America: a Critique of the Global Credit Card Society.* Thousand Oaks, CA: Pine Forge Press.

Ritzer, G. (1996) *The McDonaldization of Society: an Investigation into the Changing Character of Contemporary Social Life* (rev. edn). Thousand Oaks, CA: Pine Forge Press.

Ritzer, G. (1999) *Enchanting a Disenchanted World.* Thousand Oaks, CA: Pine Forge Press.

Ritzer, G. (2002) 'Revolutionizing the world of consumption: a review essay on three popular books', *Journal of Consumer Culture,* **2**: 103–18.

Ritzer, G. (2003) 'Rethinking globalization: glocalization/grobalization and something/nothing', *Sociological Theory,* **21**: 193–209.

Ritzer, G. (2004) *The Globalization of Nothing.* Thousand Oaks, CA: Pine Forge Press.

Robinson, H. (2003) 'Gender and labour market performance in the recovery', in R. Dickens, P. Gregg and J. Wadsworth (eds) *The Labour Market Under New Labour.* Basingstoke: Palgrave Macmillan.

Robinson, J. (1997) *Time for Life: the Surprising Ways Americans Use Their Time.* Pennslyvania: Penn State University Press.

Rose, N. (1999) *Governing the Soul: the Shaping of the Private Self.* London: Routledge.

Rosenberg, S. and Lapidus, J. (1999) 'Contingent and non-standard work in the United States: towards a more poorly compensated, insecure workforce', in A. Felstead and N. Jewson (eds) *Global Trends in Flexible Labour.* Basingstoke: Macmillan – now Palgrave Macmillan.

Rosenthal, P., Hill, S. and Peccei, R. (1997) 'Checking out service: evaluating excellence, HRM and TQM in retailing', *Work, Employment and Society*, **11**: 481–504.

Rutter, D. and Fielding, P. (1988) 'Sources of occupational stress: an examination of British prison officers', *Work and Stress*, **21**: 292–9.

Sachdev, S. (2004) *Paying The Cost?: Ppps and the Public Service Workforce*. London: Catalyst Forum.

Sainsbury, D. (ed.) (1999) *Gender and Welfare State Regimes*. Oxford: Oxford University Press.

Sayer, A (1996) *Contractualisation, Work and the Anxious Classes*, Paper presented to the Swedish Council for Work Life Research Conference, 'Work Quo Vadis', University of Karlstad.

Schlosser, E. (2001) *Fast Food Nation: the Dark Side of the All-American Meal*. Boston: Houghton Mifflin.

Schor, J. (1992) *The Overworked American: the Unexpected Decline of Leisure*. New York: Basic Books.

Scott, J. (1997) *Corporate Business and Capitalist Classes*. Oxford: OUP.

Sennett, R. (1980) *Authority*. Boston: Faber.

Sennett, R. (1998) *The Corrosion of Character*. New York: WW Norton.

Sewell, B. and Wilkinson, B. (1992) 'Someone to watch over me: surveillance, discipline and the just in time labour process', *Sociology*, **26**: 271–89.

Shiller, R. (2000) *Irrational Exuberance*. Princeton NJ: Princeton University Press.

Siltanen, J. (1994) *Locating Gender: Occupational Segregation, Wages and Domestic Responsibilities*. London: UCL Press.

Silver, J. (1987) 'The ideology of excellence: management and neo-conservatism', *Studies in Political Economy*, **24**: 105–29.

Skeggs, B. (1997) *Formations of Class and Gender: Becoming Respectable*. London: Sage.

Smart, B. (1999) 'Resisting McDonaldization: theory, process and critique', in B. Smart (ed.) *Resisting McDonaldization*. London: Sage.

Smeaton, D. (2003) 'Self-employed workers: calling the shots or hesitant independents? A consideration of the trends', *Work, Employment and Society*, **17**: 379–92.

Smelser, N. and Swedberg, R. (2005) 'Introducing economic sociology', in N. Smelser and R. Swedberg (eds) *The Handbook of Economic Sociology*. Princeton: Princeton University Press/Russell Sage Foundation.

Smircich, L. (1983) 'Concepts of culture and organisational analysis', *Administrative Science Quarterly*, **28**: 339–58.

Smith, P. (1992) *The Emotional Labour of Nursing*. Basingstoke: Macmillan – Palgrave Macmillan.

Smith, S. and Wilkinson, B. (1995) 'No doors, no office, no secrets. We are our own policemen. Capitalism without conflict', in S. Linstead, R. Grafton Small and P. Jeffcutt (eds) *Understanding Management*. London: Sage.

Social Focus in Brief (2002) *Ethnicity* (ed. Amanda White). London: Office for National Statistics.

Social Focus on Ethnicity (2002) http://www.statistics.gov.uk.

Social Trends (2001) No. 31. London: HMSO.

Social Trends (2005) No. 35. London: HMSO.

Stewart, P. and Martinez Lucio, M. (1998) 'Renewal and tradition in the new politics of production', in P. Thompson and C. Warhurst (eds) *Workplaces of the Future*. Basingstoke: Macmillan – now Palgrave Macmillan.

Stiglitz, J. (2002) *Globalization and its Discontents*. London: Allen Lane.

Streeck, W. (2001) 'Introduction: explorations into the origins of non-liberal capitalism in Germany and Japan', in W. Streeck and K. Yamamura (eds) *The Origins of Non-liberal Capitalism: Germany and Japan*. Ithaca, NY: Cornell University Press.

Sturdy, A. (1998) 'Customer care in a consumer society', *Organization*, **5**: 27–53.

Sulkunen, P., Holmwood, J., Radner, H. and Schulze, G. (eds) (1997) *Constructing the New Consumer Society*. Basingstoke: Macmillan – now Palgrave Macmillan.

Sullivan, O. and Gershuny, J. (2000) *Cross-national Changes in Time Use: Some Sociological (Hi)stories Re-examined*. Colchester: University of Essex.

Swedberg, R. (2005) 'Markets in society', in N. Smelser and R. Swedberg (eds) *The Handbook of Economic Sociology*. Princeton: Princeton University Press/Russell Sage Foundation.

Taylor, C. (1989) *Sources of the Self*. Cambridge: Cambridge University Press.
Taylor, C. (1992) *Ethics of Authenticity*. Cambridge, MA: Harvard University Press.
Taylor, P and Bain, P. (1998) 'An assembly line in the head: work and employee relations in the call centre', *Journal of Industrial Relations*, **30**: 101–17.
Taylor, P., Baldry, C., Bain, P. and Ellis, V. (2003) ' "A unique working environment": health, sickness and absence in UK call centres', *Work, Employment and Society*, **17**: 435–58.
Taylor, P., Hyman, J., Mulvey, G. and Bain, P. (2002) 'Work organisation, control and the experience of work in call centres', *Work, Employment and Society*, **16**: 133–50.
Taylor, R. (2001) 'Blair outlines strategy for schools reform', *Guardian* 12.2.02 www.education.guardian.co.uk.
Taylor, R. (2002) *Britain's World of Work: Myths and Realities*. Leeds: ESRC/Leeds University Future of Work Programme Paper 3.
Taylor, R. (2003) *Diversity in Britain's Labour Market*. Leeds: ESRC/Leeds University Future of Work Programme Paper 4.
Taylor, S. and Tyler, M. (2000) 'Emotional labour and sexual difference in the airline industry', *Work, Employment and Society*, **14**: 77–95.
Thelen, K. (2004) *How Institutions Evolve: The Political Economy of Skills in Germany, Britain, the United States and Japan*. Cambridge: Cambridge University Press.
Thomas, R. and Davies, A. (2005) 'Theorizing the micro-politics of resistance: new public management and managerial identities in the UK public services', *Organization Studies*, **26**(5): 683–706.
Thompson, E.P. (1967) 'Time, work-discipline and industrial capitalism', *Past and Present*, **38**: 56–97.
Thompson, G. (2000) 'Economic globalization', in D. Held (ed.) *A Globalizing World? Culture, Economics, Politics*. London: Routledge.
Thompson, P. (2003) 'Disconnected capitalism: or why employers can't keep their side of the bargain', *Work, Employment and Society*, **17**: 359–78.
Thompson, P. and Findlay, P. (1999) 'Changing the people: social engineering in the contemporary workplace', in L. Ray and A. Sayer (eds) *Culture and Economy After the Cultural Turn*. London: Sage.
Thompson, P. and McHugh, D. (2002) *Work Organisations: A Critical Introduction* (3rd edn). Basingstoke: Palgrave Macmillan.
Thompson, P. and Warhurst, C. (eds) (1998) *Workplaces of the Future*. Basingstoke: Macmillan – now Palgrave Macmillan.
Townley, B. (1993) *Reframing Human Resource Management*. London: Sage.
Townley, B., Cooper, D. and Oakes, L. (2003) 'Performance measures and the rationalization of organizations', *Organization Studies*, **24**: 1045–71.
Townsend, P. (2002) 'Poverty, social exclusion and social polarisation: the need to construct an international welfare state', in P. Townsend and D. Gordon (eds) *World Poverty: New Policies to Defeat an Old Enemy*. Bristol: Policy Press.
Townsend, P. and Gordon, D. (eds) (2002) *World Poverty: New Policies to Defeat an Old Enemy*. Bristol: Policy Press.
Toynbee, P. (2003) *Hard Work: Life in Low Pay Britain*. London: Bloomsbury.
Uglow, J. (2002) *The Lunar Men: the Friends Who Made the Future*. London: Faber.
UN (2005) *Human Development Report*. www.undp.org/hdr2005.
UNCTAD (2002) *World Investment Report: TNCs and Export Competitiveness*. New York: UNCTAD.
Van Maanen, J. (1991) 'The smile factory: work at Disneyland', in P. Frost, L. Moore, M. Luis, C. Lundberg and J. Martin (eds) *Reframing Organizational Culture*. Thousand Oaks, CA: Sage.
Veblen, T. (1899) *The Theory of the Leisure Class: an Economic Study of Institutions*. London: Macmillan.
Vidal, J. (1997) *McLibel*. Basingstoke: Macmillan – now Palgrave Macmillan.
Vidal, J. (1999) 'The shopper strikes back: how consumer power got big business on the run', *Guardian*, G2, 7.06.99, pp.2–3.
Von Hippel, E. (2005) *Democratizing Innovation*, Cambridge, MA: MIT Press.

Wajcman, J. (1998) *Managing Like a Man*. Cambridge: Polity Press.

Wajcman, J. and Martin, B. (2002) 'Narratives of identity in modern management: the corrosion of gender difference?' *Sociology*, **36**: 985–1002.

Warhurst, C. and Thompson, P. (1998) 'Hands, hearts and minds: changing work and workers at the end of the century', in P. Thompson and C. Warhurst (eds) *Workplaces of the Future*. Basingstoke: Macmillan – now Palgrave Macmillan.

Watkins, K. (2002) *Rigged Rules and Double Standards: Trade, Globalisation and the Fight Against Poverty*. Oxford: Oxfam.

Webb, J. (1999) 'Work and the new public service class?', *Sociology*, **33**: 747–66.

Webb, J. (2001) 'Gender, work and transitions in the local state', *Work, Employment and Society*, **15**: 825–44.

Webb, J. and Cleary, D. (1994) *Organisational Change and the Management of Expertise*, London: Routledge.

Weber, M. (1947) *The Theory of Social and Economic Organization*, trans A.M. Henderson and Talcott Parsons; edited with an introduction by Talcott Parsons. Glencoe, IL: Free Press; London: Collier-Macmillan.

Weber, M. (1968) *Economy and Society: an Outline of Interpretive Sociology*, ed. G. Roth and C. Wittich. New York: Bedminster Press.

Webster, F. and Robbins, K. (1993) 'I'll be watching you: comment on Sewell and Wilkinson', *Sociology*, **27**: 243–52.

Weisbrot, M., Baker, D. and Rosnick, D. (2005) *The Scorecard on Development: 25 Years of Diminished Progress*. Washington DC: Centre for Economic Policy and Research.

Wellington, C. and Bryson, J. (2001) 'At face value? Image consultancy, emotional labour and professional work', *Sociology*, **35**: 933–46.

Werther, W. (2003) 'Enron: the forgotten middle', *Organization*, **10**: 568–71.

West, J. (2002) 'Limits to globalization: organisational homogeneity and diversity in the semiconductor industry', *Industrial and Corporate Change*, **11**: 159–88.

West, K. (2004) 'Exodus of call centre jobs could be "catastrophe"', *The Herald*, February 25.

Wharton, A. (1993) 'The affective consequences of service work; managing emotions on the job', *Work and Occupations*, **20**: 205–32.

Wheen, F. (2004) *How Mumbo-Jumbo Conquered the World: A Short History of Modern Delusions*. London: Fourth Estate.

White, M., Hill, S., Mills, C. and Smeaton, D. (2004) *Managing to Change?* Basingstoke: Palgrave Macmillan.

Whittington, R., McNulty, T. and Whipp, R. (1994) 'Market-driven change in professional services: problems and processes', *Journal of Management Studies*, **31**: 829–45.

Williams, C. (2003) 'Sky service: the demands of emotional labour in the airline industry', *Gender, Work and Organization*, **10**: 513–50.

Williams, F. (1989) *Social Policy: a Critical Introduction*. Cambridge: Polity Press.

Williams, F. (1999) 'Good-enough principles for welfare', *Journal of Social Policy*, **28**: 667–87.

Williams, R. (2000) *Making Identity Matter: Identity, Society and Social Interaction*. Durham: Sociology Press.

Willis, P. (1978) *Learning to Labour*. Aldershot: Gower.

Willmott, H. (1993) 'Strength is ignorance, slavery is freedom: managing culture in modern organisations', *Journal of Management Studies*, **30**: 515–52.

Witz, A., Warhurst, C. and Nickson, D. (2003) 'The labour of aesthetics and the aesthetics of organization', *Organization*, **10**: 33–54.

Wolkowitz, C. (2002) 'The social relations of body work', *Work, Employment and Society*, **16**: 497–510.

Womack, J., Jones, D. and Roos, D. (1990) *The Machine that Changed the World*. New York: Macmillan – now Palgrave Macmillan.

Women's Environment and Development Organisation (2002), http://www.wedo.org/.

Woolhandler, S., Campbell, T. and Himmelstein, D. (2003) 'Costs of healthcare administration in the US and Canada', *New England Journal of Medicine*, **349**: 768–75.

World Development Movement (2002) *States of Unrest: Resistance to IMF and World Bank Policies in Poor Countries*. London: WDM, www.wdm.org.uk.

Wrong, D. (1961) 'The oversocialised concept of man in modern sociology', *American Sociological Review*, **26**: 183–93.

Yeandle, S. (1999) 'Gender contracts, welfare systems and non-standard working: diversity and change in Denmark, France, Germany, Italy and the UK', in A. Felstead and N. Jewson (eds) *Global Trends in Flexible Labour*. Basingstoke: Macmillan – now Palgrave Macmillan.

Young, K. (1996) 'Reinventing local government? some evidence assessed', *Public Administration*, **74**: 347–67.

Zuboff, S. and Maxim, J. (2003) *The Support Economy: Why Corporations are Failing Individuals and the Next Episode of Capitalism*. New York: Viking Penguin.

Index

A

accountability   6, 83–4
achieved identity   19–20, 193
Acker, J.   143
administration costs   83
advanced capitalism   13, 199–200
  convergence around a common
    occupational structure   106–9
  upgrading of occupational
    structures   109–10
  work and occupational change
    97–112
advertising   56, 57–9, 60, 61, 67, 69
  evaluative research   61
  spending on   59
African-Caribbeans   142
agency   2, 3, 9, 194–5
  dialectical relationship between
    identity, organisation and
    31–3
  empirical studies of organisations
    26–9
  historical development of self as
    agent   19–20
  identity, consumerism and   64–8
  and structure   5–7, 17–19
  Weber, rationalisation and   20–3
agency labour   131
Ailon-Souday, G.   154
airlines   159, 163, 165, 169
alienative involvement   27–8
Alvesson, M.   158, 162, 162–3
Amin, A.   68
Apple   53, 60
appraisals   163
Archer, M.   9
Argentina   42
Arthur Andersen   48, 49

ascribed identity   19–20
audit   84

B

'back stage' areas   169
Bangladeshis   142
banking   111, 139
Barker, J.   157, 161
barristers   167–8
Baudrillard, J.   65–6
Bauman, Z.   66, 69, 92
Beck, U.   128, 129
Benetton   59
Berkeley, Bishop   20
biopower   25, 29
black political identity   18
Blair, T.   91
Blau, P.   27
body, presentation of   166–7
Bourdieu, P.   68
brands/branding   11, 54, 57–8, 151
  and organisational identity   59–60
Braverman, H.   28
Brent Spar oil platform   59
Bretton Woods Conference   36, 41
British Airways   171
Brubaker, R.   17
Bryce, R.   49
bureaucracy   5, 22–3, 27–8, 42–3,
    170–1, 195
  continuity of bureaucratic control
    162–3
  welfare states and professional
    81–2
Business Week   111

C

calculative involvement   27–8
call centres   113, 158–9

Campbell, C. 55
Cancun negotiations 43–4
capital mobility 39–40, 112–13
capitalism 21, 205–6
  manipulation of consumers 64–5
car manufacturing 55–6
career hierarchies 130
career restructuring 138–9
Caribbean immigrants 141
Casey, C. 157, 160
Castells, M. 2, 37, 97, 128, 129
casualisation of work 114–17, 124,
    125, 133
  challenging myths of 129–32
children and childcare 140, 182–3,
    186, 204
China 45, 52, 118
  manufacturing 102, 113
Chinese cockle-pickers 115
choice 91–2
Christian democratic welfare states
    76
civil society organisations 79
class 67–8
  organisational power relations
    and emotional labour 167–8
  organisational restructuring and
    class divisions 133–6, 143–4,
    146–7, 201
Clegg, S. 30, 32, 60
Clinton, B. 176
coaching 159
Coca-Cola 60
Cohen, L. 56, 71
Cold War 37
collectivism 147–8
  collective consumer identities
    70–2
colonisation of identity 160–1
commitment 153, 182–3
commodity chains 45–7
competition 152–3
complaints commissioners 84
conceptual framework 12, 15–35,
    194–6

Conseco 49
consumer citizenship 13, 74–94,
    198–9
consumer credit 55, 57
consumer markets 54–7
consumer movements 13, 70–2
consumers' republic 56–7
consumerism 33, 64–8
Consumers Association (UK) 71
consumption 3–4, 12–13, 53–73,
    178–9, 197–8
  creative consumption 184
  indivisibility of production and
    68–70, 176
continuity
  bureaucratic control 162–3
  in employment 129
continuous improvement 87–8
contracts 128–9, 130–2
  diversity in 131–2
  new for public service 89–91
  temporary employment 114–17,
    125, 130–1
control 13, 151–73, 201–2
Cook, T. and Son 56
Cooper, F. 17
corporate culture 154–7, 160, 162–3,
    171
corporate scandals 48–50, 205
corporate strategies 44–7
Corporate Watch 72
corporatist welfare states 76
corruption 48–50, 83–4
'cosmopolitans' 27
Craib, I. 188, 189
creative consumption 184
credit, consumer 55, 57
critical analysis 1–2, 3
critical organisation studies 8
critical realist perspective 8
critical theory 65
cultural identity 29–30
  social divisions and processes of
    144–7
cultural intermediaries 179–80

culture 9
  consumption and 65, 66–7
  corporate 154–7, 160, 162–3, 171
  culture change and public
    management 85–8
  teams and subcultures 169–70
customer service work 158–60, 161,
  171

D
Deetz, S. 25
dependency culture 78
deregulation of markets 39–40, 57,
  152–3, 196–7
derivatives 48
deskilling 28–9
disability rights groups 79
disciplinary power 24–5, 29
Disney World 64, 159
distinctiveness of modern
  organisations 4–5
diversity 154
  in employment contracts 131–2
division of labour 21
  global 13, 45, 112–17, 117–18, 200
  sexual 77, 137–8, 140
domestic help 168
domestic responsibilities 140
Du Gay, P. 62, 63, 67, 178
Durkheim, E. 20–1
Duvell, F. 87

E
East Asian enterprise 30
economic activity rates 79, 131–2,
  137, 138, 150, 204
economic exchange 76–7
economic individualisation 147–8
education 86, 91
  secondary school head 84
effort, employee 153
electronic point of sale (EPOS)
  technology 63
embedded account of organisations
  31–3

emotional labour 158–60, 161
  organisational power relations,
    social divisions and 165–72
employee identity 13, 151–73, 201–2
employment contracts *see* contracts
employment relations 89–91, 133
  low trust 164–5
empowerment 85–8
  vs rationalisation 88–91
Enron 48–50
entrepreneurialism 85–8
Esping-Anderson, G. 75
ethnicity 77
  ethnic divisions and
    organisational restructuring
    133–6, 140–2, 146–7, 200–1
  organisational power relations and
    emotional labour 167, 168
Etzioni, A. 27–8
European Union (EU) 43–4
Ewen, S. 56
'excellent' organisations 156
expressive consumer 67–8
Ezzy, D. 26

F
family 140, 182–3, 186, 204
Fastow, A. 49
feminisation of work 136–7
financial industry irrationalities
  47–50
financial markets, global *see* global
  financial markets
Fjellman, S. 65, 70
flexibilisation of labour 114–17,
  124, 125, 130–2, 133
Flextronics 46
food 53–4
Forbes 60
Ford Motor Company 55, 56
foreign direct investment (FDI) 38–9
formal (instrumental) rationality
  21–3
Foucault, M. 7–8, 9, 24–5, 29
fraud 48–50, 83–4

Friends of the Earth 72
friendships 182
functionalism 1–2
Future Foundation 70

G
Gaebler, T. 82
gender 16
 and childcare 204
 organisational power relations
 and emotional labour 166–7,
 168
 organisational restructuring and
 gender divisions 133–40,
 146–7, 200–1
General Agreement on Tariffs and
 Trade (GATT) 43
General Motors 1, 55, 56
generalised other 16
Gergen, K. 66
Germany 126, 132, 150
 casualisation of labour 114–17,
 124, 125
 women's economic activity 137,
 138, 150
 work and occupational change
 97–112, 117–18, 121, 123, 124,
 200
Gershuny, J. 185
Giddens, A. 4, 11, 69, 146–7, 187–8
Global Crossing 49
global division of labour 13, 45,
 112–17, 117–18, 200
global financial markets 39–51,
 112–13, 196–7
 corporate strategies and identities
 44–7
 organisations and
 individualisation 175–6
 politics of identity and 50–1
global infrastructure 206
global markets
 financial *see* global financial
 markets
 inevitability of 37–8

and need for organisational
 identities 57–9
organising deregulated global
 markets 40–4
globalisation 12, 36–52, 112, 196–7,
 205–6
globalist perspective 37–8
Goffman, E. 33
Gouldner, A. 27
governance 206
Gray, J. 38
Greece 116, 125
Greenpeace 59, 72
Gunaratnam, Y. 167

H
Hall, S. 18
Harris, L. 167–8
healthcare 83, 87–8, 89, 168
Healy, G. 148
Hephaestus Corporation 157, 160
Hochschild, A. 159–60, 161, 182–3
Hoggett, P. 88
home life 182–3
Home Office 86–7
Honda Motor Corporation 46
horizontal gender segregation 137–8
human relations school 178
humour 184
Hutton, W. 138
hybridity 18
hyperreality 65–6

I
'I' 16
'ideal type' bureaucracy 22, 23, 28
identification 157–8
identity
 achieved 19–20, 193
 agency, consumerism and 64–8
 analytic distinction between self
 and 10–11
 ascribed 19–20
 collective consumer identities
 70–2

colonisation of 160–1
of consumer citizenship 91–2
cultural 29–30, 144–7
deterministic accounts 26, 194
dialectical relationship between
    agency, organisation and
    identity 31–3
new identity project for public
    servants 84–8
organisational *see* organisational
    identity
postmodernist treatment 17–19
self-identity *see* self-identity
social *see* social identity
identity politics 5, 33, 190
and global financial markets
    50–1
and welfare states 77–80
image 58–9
image consultancy 179–80
immigration 86–7, 141–2
income inequality 50–1
    gender gap 139
    global division of labour 117–18
    social polarisation and upgraded
        occupational structure
        111–12
India 52, 113, 118
individualisation 204
    globalising markets, organisations
        and 175–6
    of work 126–7, 128–9
individualism 147–8
information society 37, 129
insecurity, employment 114, 133
instrumental (formal) rationality
    21–3
intensification of work 90, 133, 144
    and employee identity 163–4
interaction order 33
intermediate organisations 206
International Monetary Fund (IMF)
    36, 40–4, 50–1, 138, 190
ISE Communications 157
Italy 138, 150

J
Japan 43–4, 126, 132, 150
    casualisation of labour 114–17,
        124, 125
    women's economic activity 137,
        138, 150
    work and occupational change
        97–112, 117–18, 122, 124,
        200
Japanese corporations 154–5
job satisfaction 133
job tenure 129
Jordan, B. 87

K
Karreman, D. 162–3
Keynes, J.M. 41
Klein, N. 59
knowing consumer 67–8
knowledge 7–8, 24–5
knowledge-based occupational
    structure 102–6, 122–4
knowledge content of work 96
    upgrading of 110–11
knowledge creation 96
Kraft 59
Kunda, G. 154, 160, 162

L
laissez-faire market capitalism
    41–3, 52
language 16
Lasch, C. 65
Lash, S. 56
Latin America 42
Lay, K. 48–9
leisure 176, 185–7
Lewis, G. 167
liberal welfare states 76, 77
life coaches 179–80
lifestyling 62, 62–4
Linux system 71
local government 89
'locals' 27
long hours' culture 182–3

low trust employment relations 164–5

Lyotard, J. 24

M

Make Poverty History 50

management 130, 143, 144
  gender ideology and 137
  managers and self-improvement 181–2
  occupational structure 102–10, 122–4
  women in 138, 139

managerialism 80–91, 93

manual jobs 134
  occupational structure 102–10, 122–4

manufacturing
  decline of employment in 96, 98–101
  global reorganisation 101–2

market research 61–2

market segmentation 62, 62–4

marketing 56, 57–9, 60, 61–2, 69

markets
  consumer markets 54–7
  global *see* global markets
  organisational regulation of identity 152–3, 164–5
  public service reorganisation 80–4

Marquand, D. 82

Marshall, G. 134

Marx, K. 20–1

Marxist theory 64–5, 134–5

Mattelart, A. 61

McDonald, R. 87–8

McDonalds 71

McGregor, D. 178

MacInnes, J. 17, 137

McKechnie, S. 71

McKinsey Consultancy 81, 155

'me' 16

Mead, G.H. 16

men's economic activity rates 131–2

mergers 44–5, 47, 153–4

Merrill Lynch 48

Merton, R.K. 27

middle class, emerging 55

migrant labour 115, 141–2

Mills, C.W. 4, 6

Millward, N. 116

mock bureaucracy 27

modernist perspective 8, 9, 18–19, 20–3, 26

moral involvement 27–8

motherhood 140

motivation 177–9

Motorola 169

Murdoch, R. 46

N

narcissism 65

National Health Service (NHS) 83, 87–8, 89

neoliberalism 57, 190, 205–6
  and globalisation 36, 40–4, 50–1, 196–7
  and welfare 75–6, 77–80, 81

network organisations 45–7

New Economics Foundation 190

New Labour 80

new public management 80–91, 93

New Puritans 70

New Zealand 76

News International 46

Nike 59, 60

non-governmental organisations (NGOs) 50–1, 205

non-manual work 152

Nordic countries 75

Nordström, K. 176

norms 169–70

nurses 89

O

occupational change 13, 97–112, 128–9, 199–200

occupational structures
  convergence around a common occupational structure 106–9, 122–4

knowledge-based 102–6, 122–4
social divisions and 137–40, 142,
    143–4, 146
upgrading of 109–10, 111–12
organisational goals 157–8
organisational identity 10–11, 57–64
global finance and 44–7
industry in 60–2
and lifestyling 62–4
organisational restucturing 13,
    126–50, 200–1
Osborne, D. 82
oversocialised concept of
    organisations 29–30

P
Pakistanis 142
panopticon 24
part-time work 114, 115, 124, 132, 150
pay, reductions in 90
performance, customer service
    work as 159–60
performance management 171
performance measurement 82,
    88–9, 163
performance monitoring 163
permanent employment contracts
    130–1, 131
Perrow, C. 174
personal biography 16
personal data 62
personal failure 188–9
Peters, T. 30, 155–6
Philip Morris Corporation 59
pleasure 55
Polaroid 60
police 86
Pollock, A. 83
postindustrialism 96–7
rise in services and 101–2
postmodernism 7–10, 23–5, 26, 195
consumerism 65–7
identity and subjectivity 17–19
organisation of a productive self
    177–9

poverty 51
'in-work' 112
Power, M. 84
power 6–7, 7–8, 18, 24–5, 66, 195
empirical studies of 29
organisational power relations,
    social divisions and emotional
    labour 165–72
productive subjectivity 189–90
private sector, and public services
    79, 82–3
producer services 99
production 3–4
indivisibility of consumption and
    68–70, 176
production economy 106
production networks 45–7
productive subjectivity 13–14,
    174–92, 202–4
evaluation of concept 187–91
organisation of 177–9
in work, non-work and leisure
    185–7
professional bureaucracy 81–2
professionals 130, 143, 144
occupational structure 102–10,
    122–4
and self-improvement 181–2
promotion 56, 69
public domain 14, 74, 206
public private partnerships (PPPs)
    82–3
public relations (PR) 60, 62
public services 153
reorganisation 13, 74–94, 198–9
public trust 49–50, 72
punishment-centred bureaucracy
    27

R
race *see* ethnicity
rail travel 56
rationalisation 20–3, 195
and consumer citizenship 91–2
of corporate structures 44–7

rationalisation – *continued*
  empirical studies of organisations
    26–9
  vs empowerment for public
    servants 88–91
  irrationalities of rationalised
    economies 47–50
rationality 21–3, 23–4
  global institutions and 40–4
  substantive *see* substantive
    rationality
realism 8
reflexive self-awareness 146–7
regulation
  employee identity 151–73,
    201–2
  public service organisations 83–4
relativism 8
representative bureaucracy 27
resilience of self-identity 170–2
resistance 28–9
  collective consumer identities and
    politics of 70–2
  in customer service work 161
  to globalisation 50–1
  teams and 169–70
restructuring, organisational 13,
    126–50, 200–1
Ridderstråle, J. 176
Rifkin, J. 128
Ritzer, G. 57, 58, 64
role distance 172
Romantic ethic 55
Rose, N. 66, 174–175, 176, 177,
    187–8, 189–90
routine work 143, 144, 163–4

S
Saatchi and Saatchi 61
Schor, J. 185
self 195
  analytic distinction between
    identity and 10–11
  historical development of self as
    agent 19–20

postmodernist treatment of
    17–19
  sociological perspective on 15–16
self-employment 129, 131
self-fulfilment 177–8
self-identity 193–4
  productive subjectivity 13–14,
    174–92, 202–4
  resilience of 170–2
self-improvement 13–14, 174–92,
    202–4
  industry for 179–80
  work as a resource for 180–3
self-reliance 86–8
Sennett, R. 26, 127, 128, 187–8
service economy 106
services 130, 164
  rise in 96, 98–102, 119–22
sexual division of labour 77, 137–8,
    140
Shell 59, 72
shopping 64, 67, 186
short-term contracts 114–17, 125,
    130–1
sign values 65
Skilling, J. 49
Smith, A. 20
social democratic welfare states
    75, 78
  and social identity 76–7
social divisions
  class *see* class
  ethnicity *see* ethnicity
  gender *see* gender
  organisational power relations
    and emotional labour
    165–72
  organisational restructuring and
    13, 126–8, 133–48, 149, 200–1
  and processes of cultural and
    social identity 144–7
social exchange 76–7
social identity 16–17, 193–4
  social democratic welfare states
    and 76–7

social divisions and processes of 144–7
social movements 5, 33, 50–1, 79, 190, 205
   consumer movements 13, 70–2
social polarisation 111–12, 143
social smiles 160
social work 86
sociological perspective
   on organisations 3–4
   on the self and social identities 15–17
software development 113
South Asian immigrants 141
Spain 116, 125, 137, 138, 150
special purpose entities 49
spectacle 63–4, 67
speculation 40
status 135–6, 187
Stiglitz, J. 41, 42, 43
strategies, corporate 44–7
structure and agency 5–7, 17–19
Subaru-Isuzu plant 158
subcontracting 45–6, 83–4
subcultures 169–70
substantive rationality 21–2
   substantive irrationality 27, 47–50
subversion 184–5
supermarkets 113–14
supply chains 44–7, 113–14
surveillance 25
symbolism 58–9, 63–4

T
target-setting 82
taxation 78
teamwork 157–8, 160–1
   subcultures and norms 169–70
Tech 160, 162
technical workers 143, 144
   occupational structure 102–10, 122–4
temporary employment contracts 114–17, 125, 130–1

Tesco 60
theme parks 64, 67, 69–70
themed entertainment 63–4, 67
Theory X and Theory Y 178
therapeutic culture 178
Third Way 80
Thrift, N. 68
time, use of 185–7
tobacco 72
total institutions 25
tourism 56, 63
Toynbee, P. 90–1
trade restrictions 43
   see also World Trade Organization (WTO)
trade unions 148
traditionalist perspective 38–9
transformationalist perspective 39–40
transnational corporations (TNCs) 38
trust
   low trust employment relations 164–5
   public trust in corporations 49–50, 72

U
United Airlines 49
United Kingdom (UK) 59, 126, 132
   casualisation of labour 114–17, 124, 125
   public service reorganisation 80, 86–7, 93
   social divisions 141–2, 144
   welfare state 76–7
   women's economic activity 132, 137, 138, 150
   work and occupational change 97–112, 117–18, 119, 122, 124, 200
United Nations (UN) 51
United States (USA) 4, 43–4, 59, 75, 126, 132, 204
   casualisation of labour 114–17, 124, 125

United States (USA) – *continued*
  consumerism and economic policy
    56–7
  social divisions   141, 143
  women's economic activity   132,
    137, 138, 150
  work and occupational change
    97–112, 117–18, 120, 123, 124,
    200
unpaid work   186
upgrading
  knowledge content of work
    110–11
  occupational structures   109–10,
    111–12
Urry, J.   56
Uruguay negotiations   43

V
Veblen, T.   68
vertical gender segregation   137–8
vertical integration   44, 46, 47
Virgin Group   60
visual spectacle   63–4

W
wage labour   20
Wal-Mart   1
Walt Disney Corporation   64, 159
Washington Consensus   41–3
Waterman, R.   30, 155–6
Weber, M.   5, 20–3, 24, 41, 135
Wedgwood, J.   55
welfare   13, 74–94, 198–9
welfare benefits, reduction in   78
welfare states   74–80
  dual crises of   77–80
  see also public services
White, M.   130, 131
Williams, C.   165
Williams, R.   19
Willis, P.   66

Willmott, H.   158, 162
Witz, A.   159
women   79, 136–40
  economic activity rates   131–2,
    137, 138, 150, 204
  part-time work   132, 150
  see also gender
work   20
  casualisation   114–17, 124, 125,
    133
  challenging myths of casualisation
    and short-termism   129–32
  control, identity and   13, 151–73,
    201–2
  intensification of   90, 133, 144,
    163–4
  and occupational change   13,
    97–112, 128–9, 199–200
  organisational restructuring and
    social divisions   13, 126–50,
    200–1
  organisations and global division
    of labour   13, 95–125,
    199–200
  productive self in non-work,
    leisure and work   185–7
  public service reorganisation and
    consumer citizenship   13,
    74–94, 198–9
  as a resource for self-improvement
    180–3
Work Permits UK   87
workforce partnership   89–91
working-class identity   134
Working Families Tax Credit   80
working hours   182–3, 185
World Bank   36, 40–4, 50–1,
  138, 190
World Economic Forum   72
World Trade Organization (WTO)
  36, 43–4, 50–1
WorldCom   49